Eye-Witness D-Day

Eye-Witness D-Day

The Story of the Battle by Those Who Were There

Edited by
JON E. LEWIS

ROBINSON
London

Robinson Publishing Ltd
7, Kensington Church Court
London W8 4SP

First published by Robinson Publishing Ltd 1994

Cover illustration shows A Troop, 41 Commando RM, shortly after
landing on Sword beach, near Lion-sur-Mer, 6 June 1944.
(Photo: Royal Marines Museum)

A copy of the British Library Cataloguing in Publication Data for this
title is available from the British Library.

ISBN 1-85487-267-2

Typeset in 11/12pt Baskerville by Hewer Text, Edinburgh
Printed by HarperCollins Manufacturing, Glasgow

10 9 8 7 6 5 4 3 2 1

CONTENTS

FOREWORD

Field Marshal Lord Carver GCB, CBE, DSO, MC

In this book Jon E. Lewis has brought together a remarkable collection from varied sources of first-hand accounts of the landings in Normandy in June 1944: the preparatory events, the landings themselves, and the fighting that followed. They paint a vivid picture of what it was like for many different men – soldiers, sailors and airmen, American, British, Canadian and German – and for some French civilians: the uncertainty and anxieties of waiting and of the Channel crossing; the confusion, hazards and heroism of action in the airborne landings and on the beaches themselves; the difficulties of fighting in the villages, orchards and fields of the Normandy *bocage*; the shock of wounds and death.

For many of the participants, the emotions these aroused were accentuated by the fact that it was the first time that they had experienced battle. In addition to worry about what lay ahead and concern about the particular part they had to play – would they land in the right place, would they recognize the landmarks, would their vehicle start, their weapon work, their radio set function? – they faced the anxiety that every fighting man knows about how he will cope, when he first comes under fire. Will he live up to the standards to which he has been trained and which everybody, especially those he leads or serves with, expects of him?

But there were many experienced soldiers, sailors and airmen there also – on both sides. There were those, like myself, who had been in action in the Middle East, and perhaps Italy also, for four years with hardly a break: the previous six months spent re-equipping and training in England was the longest period I had been out of action since 1940. We were longing to get on with the job and finish off the war as soon as possible. We had taken part in the landings at Salerno in September 1943 and thought we knew what to expect.

These contemporary accounts, some stark, some simple, some – those of the professional war correspondents – sophisticated, remind us what a tough battle it was and what a high price was paid for victory. It was no walk-over, even though the Allies enjoyed a great superiority of material resources. If the landings had failed to secure an adequate lodgement area ashore, the whole history of the Second World War would have been radically different. The pages which follow pay tribute to those who made it possible.

Michael Carver
FM

INTRODUCTION

It was going to be, said Admiral Sir Bertram Ramsay to a group of his captains gathered before him, 'the greatest amphibious operation of all time'. He apologized for the superlatives, but believed that this time they were necessary. Three days later, on 6 June 1944, the Allied invasion of Normandy – of which Ramsay was naval commander – took place. The Allied armada involved over 5,000 craft, and had by the end of 'the longest day' landed 156,000 men, and breached Hitler's much vaunted defensive wall. Ramsay had not exaggerated.

Yet, dramatic and historic though the events of D-Day were, they were but the opening shots of a much larger – and equally remarkable – battle, the battle for Normandy. A legend has grown up in the years since the war to the effect that the invasion was a matter of one glorious day in June, followed by a triumphal march on Paris. The reality was conspicuously different. It took the Allies ten weeks of bloody, painful fighting to get out of Normandy. At times the infantry casualty rate rivalled that of the Western Front in World War I. Only the lucky got out of Normandy alive.

The reason for the peculiar bloodiness of Normandy was simple; in the words of one Allied soldier, 'the Germans were bastard hard to beat.' The Germans had fifty-nine divisions in France, many of them of second-rate quality and composed of 'volunteer' foreign

(Russian, Polish, Mongolian and so forth) troops. However, even these divisions proved stubborn – denying the Allies most of their inland objectives on 6 June itself – and there were enough crack divisions like 352 Infantry, Panzer Lehr and, especially, the 12 SS Panzer to make things very difficult indeed. The Allied chiefs were all too aware of the formidability of the German Army, and that it was likely only to be beaten in the most propitious circumstances. That is, when the Germans were outnumbered, out-gunned, out-planed, out-guessed and out of luck. These circumstances were some considerable time in the making.

The Allied invasion, later to be codenamed Overlord, first stirred into life in late 1941 with the entry of the United States into the war, and was followed by a huge build-up of American forces in Britain from 1942 onwards. The original plan, as conceived by General Sir Frederick Morgan, Chief of Staff to the Supreme Allied Commander (COSSAC), foresaw a first-day landing by three divisions. Eventually, this was revised by the Supreme Commander, Eisenhower, and the Field Commander, Montgomery, to five divisions on a broader front. To ensure that adequate supplies reached the Allied divisions after they landed, two prefabricated artificial harbours, or 'Mulberries', were built to be towed to Normandy on the big day. An underwater pipeline, PLUTO, was devised to hasten the supply of fuel to the invasion army. To overcome the German beach obstacles a strange population of tanks, nicknamed 'funnies', was created by Major-General Percy Hobart, among them an amphibious tank, the DD, and the mine-clearing flail tank. The men who would fight the invasion were trained for months. Even years. The preparations were meticulous.

It was, of course, impossible to conceal from the Germans that an invasion would happen, as the Germans knew it must. The trick was to keep the Germans guessing as to when and exactly where in France it would happen.

In Spring 1944 the Allies began a brilliantly successful subterfuge, Operation Fortitude, which festooned the ports and aerodromes of south-east England with dummy landing craft and gliders. Heavy hints were dropped before German ears about Patton's 'First US Army Group' and its readiness to cross the Straits of Dover. More and more the Germans, especially the Wehrmacht's Commander-in-Chief in the West, Von Rundstedt, began to believe that the Pas de Calais would be the invasion site. In fact the Allies' chosen landing place was the bay of the Seine, the fifty-mile sweep of Normandy coast from Cape d'Antifer to the Point of Barfleur. If the German High Command had settled its internal bickering and its prejudices it would have realized that this was the only possible place for a mass landing. Most of the land behind the beaches in Seine bay is flat, the tides are mild and the approaches free of natural obstacles.

The Allies selected five main assault beaches. The Americans had the two most westerly, Utah and Omaha, the British Sword, Juno and Gold. The initial assault would be carried out by the British 3rd Division on Sword, the Canadian 3rd Division on Juno, the British 50th Division on Gold, the 4th US Division on Utah and the 1st US Division on Omaha. The left flank of the British assault was to be protected by the British 6th Airborne Division; the right flank of the American assault by its 82nd and 101st Airborne Divisions. The invasion would be prefaced by extensive bombing of roads, railways and German positions, the chaos added to by the attentions of the Resistance and a small group of SAS. Minesweepers would clear gaps in the German minefields which ran up the middle of the English Channel. The date for the invasion, the day when all the cards would come together in the right combination, was set by Eisenhower for 5 June 1944.

There was, though, a joker in the pack: the weather. The invasion required a calm sea. The weather stood fair for France until just three days before the off, when a high-pressure area above the Azores began to disintegrate. Eisenhower's meteorologist, Group-Captain Stagg, advised a postponement. But when could they go? The outcome of the Allies' mightiest operation came to rest on Stagg's judgement. He forecast a window in the bad weather for Tuesday, 6 June. This left Eisenhower the choice to go on the 6th or wait three weeks until the tidal requirements

were again favourable – but by which time the morale of keyed-up
troops would have likely sunk. Ike went for the 6th. Luck was with
him. The German weather experts divined 6 June as far too bad a
day to launch an invasion. Consequently, the Germans dropped
their guard. Some senior officers, like Rommel, even took leave. By
coincidence, the 6th was the start date for a Wehrmacht war game,
attended by senior German officers from Normandy. When the
Allies came ashore on the morning of 6 June much of the head of
the German army was missing. Eisenhower, had he known it,
could probably not have picked a better day.

   This book is the story of that fateful day, the preparations which
led up to it, and the ten weeks of fighting in Normandy which
followed it, told by the men and women who were there, who
witnessed it at first hand. It is compiled from interviews with scores
of veterans, from diaries, memoirs, and letters. Occasionally I have
sacrificed exact chronology in the interests of communicating
better the experience of Normandy, for above all this is a book
about how the invasion looked and felt to those who were there. It
is often brutally honest, far removed from the comfortable roman-
tic version of D-Day and the battle for Normandy. (For example,
there are accounts here of crimes committed against German
POWs by Allied soldiers.)

   It would be disingenuous of me to claim that I have simply
relayed the words of veterans and eye-witnesses into book form, for
no act of writing and editing is neutral. Inevitably, one chooses
some incidents and feelings above others, not least because of
constrictions of space. I could have put a shiny gloss of chauvinism
on this book, but chose against it. I was not a participant in 1944. I
was not even born then. I belong to a generation made cynical by
Vietnam. Myths have a habit of becoming exposed and there is
little point in perpetuating them. Truth in war history, as in most
things, is usually the best policy. And, anyway, the achievement of
Allied soldiery in Normandy was very considerable. Indeed, it is
especially so when one fully realizes the moral and physical
dilemmas the Tommies and the 'dog-faces' had to endure. To
survive Normandy took not only luck, but fine feats of arms,

stamina and guts. The men who fought in Normandy in 1944 were a special breed. I doubt if any generation since could have done better.

I am indebted to those veterans who so kindly wrote up their memories, lent diaries and original material, or were interviewed for this book. Although they are now fifty years older, their recollections of 1944 are crystal sharp. Where they are quoted in the text, I have given their age and rank as of June 1944. I am also grateful for the advice and help of the staff of the Imperial War Museum, the D-Day Museum at Arromanches, the Normandy Veterans Association, the British Library, Alex Stitt, Jan Chamier, Eryl Humphrey Jones, Nick Robinson, Eric Lewis, Joan Stempel, Ros and Bill Francis, Kathleen and Bill Ashman, Richard Cureton, Fiona Sewell, Mrs D.A. Collier, J.W. and P.M. Foulds, Joan Rolfe, D. Jenkins, M. and Madame Scelles, Peter Dinnis, Ring Deutscher Soldatenverbande. I owe a particular thanks to Michêle Lowe and Joyce Lewis for translation and interview work above and beyond the call of duty. My greatest thanks though goes to Penny Stempel, without whose skill in research, interviewing and translation this book would simply not have been done.

Jon E. Lewis

The Prelude

Cabourg Normandy

1944. If wars are fought by young men, they are planned for by men with age and its assumed attribute, wisdom. As England and Western Europe shivered in the snow of the New Year, the leaders of the Allied invasion of France, already selected in the last days of 1943, began taking up their appointments. Montgomery arrived in England on 2 January. Eisenhower, the Supreme Allied Commander, landed on 15 January, holding his first full meeting of staff and commanders at Norfolk House, London, six days later.

Captain H.C. Butcher, aide to Eisenhower
Diary, London, Friday 21 January 1944
The new Supreme Commander, moving into his job with an Anglo-American staff already created by General Morgan, is busily engaged in meetings.

The meeting held with Admiral Ramsay, General Montgomery, and Air Marshal Leigh-Mallory today may prove to be one of the most important of the war. Ike wanted the strength of the assault increased from three to five divisions and the area of the attack widened. He also wanted to employ two airborne divisions on the Cotentin (Cherbourg) Peninsula and not to use one against Caen. Leigh-

Mallory felt that it would be wrong to use the airborne on the Cotentin Peninsula and that losses will be seventy-five to eighty per cent. Ike believes it should be done to cut the 'neck' of the peninsula, and so does Monty. They will still use one airborne near Caen to seize bridges over the Orne and Dives, but will not try to take the city itself from the air. With all these changes, the need for postponing the assault for a month is apparent.

Three days before, the designated commander of the US First Army in the invasion, in England since the previous autumn, was confirmed in his appointment by 'Ike'. The news came in an unofficial fashion.

General Omar Bradley, US First Army Group
The news that I was to command this Army Group came to me suddenly and indirectly: I read it in a morning paper. On January 18 as I turned through the lobby of the Dorchester Hotel bound for breakfast at the mess across the street, I stopped to pick up a copy of the four-page *Daily Express*.

The clerk at the counter grinned. 'This won't be news to you, sir,' he said and pointed to a story in which Eisenhower had announced that '51-year-old Lieut.-General Omar Nelson Bradley, who led the US Second Corps in Tunisia and the invasion of Sicily, is to be the American Army's "General Montgomery" in the western invasion of Europe.'

But it was. For this was the first inkling I had that my Army Group command was to be more than a temporary one. Eisenhower had just arrived in England and I had not yet talked with him. In his press conference the day before, the first on his return, Eisenhower had been asked who would command the American ground forces on the invasion. 'General Bradley is the senior United States ground commander,' was his reply.

For the moment that statement was not clear, for it did not

indicate whether Eisenhower meant First Army on the assault or the Army Group as an opposite number to Monty. It was not until later that Eisenhower said he meant the Army Group.

It was not only on the Allied side that the commanders were taking their positions for the invasion that all knew would come, sooner or later. Though Field Marshal Geyr von Rundstedt was the Wehrmacht Supreme Commander West, Hitler had directly charged Erwin Rommel with the task of thwarting the Allied invasion of his *Festung Europa*. Rommel, with an energy that amazed his staff, set about building up the defences on the coast of France. He found himself, though, hampered in the job. He unburdened himself in his letters to his wife, Lucie-Maria.

Field Marshal Erwin Rommel, Army Group B
19 January 1944
Returned to-day from my long trip. I saw a lot and was very satisfied with the progress that has been made. I think for certain that we'll win the defensive battle in the West, provided only that a little more time remains for preparation. Guenther's going off tomorrow with a suit-case. He's to bring back my brown civilian suit and lightweight coat with hat, etc. I want to be able to go out without a Marshal's baton for once . . .
. . . Situation in the East: apparently stabilized.
. . . In the South: severe fighting and more heavy attacks to be met.
. . . In the West: I believe we'll be able to beat off the assault.

26 January 1944
The job's being very frustrating. Time and again one comes up against bureaucratic and ossified individuals who resist everything new and progressive. But we'll manage it all the

same. My two hounds had to be separated, after the older one had well nigh killed the younger with affection.

Inevitably the Allies planned and plotted their Operation Overlord in conditions of great secrecy. They were especially zealous to guard the knowledge of the time and the place of the landing. Despite this, on two occasions secrecy was breached.

Captain H.C. Butcher, aide to Eisenhower
Diary, Widewing, Thursday 23 March 1944
Possibility that essential facts of Overlord, including D-Day as originally set, may have been 'compromised' has stirred the high-level officials of SHAEF and the War Department. The G-2s are excited, particularly in Washington.

A few days ago Ike received a personal message from General Clayton Bissell, the new War Department G-2, saying that a package containing important documents concerning Overlord had been intercepted in Chicago. It had been sent from our Ordnance Division, G-4, and erroneously addressed to a private residence in a section of Chicago heavily populated by Germans. The package was poorly wrapped and, according to General Bissell, a casual perusal of the papers was made by four unauthorized persons in the headquarters of the Army's 6th Service Command in Chicago, in addition to at least ten persons in the Chicago post office.

It now appears that the package was addressed by an American soldier who is of German extraction. He states that his sister, who lives at the Chicago address, has been seriously ill and thinks he simply erred in writing the address on the package because his mind was preoccupied with thoughts of home. Thus he wrote on the package his sister's home address rather than the proper address in the War Department in Washington. The clumsy handling would indicate that no professional spy was involved, but, nevertheless, important facts, including strength, places, equipment, and tentative target date, have been disclosed to unauthorized persons – just another worry for the Supreme Commander.

Lieutenant-General Frederick Morgan, Chief of Staff to the Supreme Allied Commander [COSSAC]

What was probably the most acute internal conflict was that which took place between the so-called movement staffs of the Navy and Army branches of COSSAC. The duties of these two sub-divisions of a combined staff are of course bound of their very nature to overlap, and it is almost inevitable that friction should be set up. Over long years the general line of demarcation between Army and Navy has been set as High Water Mark at Ordinary Spring Tides. But this last war has played ducks and drakes with many land and sea marks, amongst them 'HWMOST'. Largely owing to the great work of the Combined Operations staffs, it no longer rouses comment to find soldiers attired in lammies manning ships at sea or sailors dressed in khaki battledress driving trucks in the heart of a continent. But this didn't come about overnight. When, as was the case with the COSSAC Staff, the whole affair virtually hinged upon rates of movement of men, vehicles and material from shore to sea and from sea to shore again, there was present every sort of opportunity, not only for inter-service rivalry but for inter-service jealousy and ultimately inter-service conflict. At one moment a point was reached at which the soldier glared at the sailor saying, 'This much has got to be done at this place in this time,' or words to that effect. The sailor replied with equal or greater emphasis, 'This cannot be done,' or its verbal equivalent. For a few hours it seemed as though unbreakable deadlock was reached. Figures, which as the axiom says cannot lie (though as our American staff repeatedly pointed out, liars can figure), were overhauled and recalculated *ad nauseam* with ever the same result. 'One shall have them,' said the Army. 'They shall not pass,' said the Navy. And relief came in what one would like to say was the typical COSSAC way. One of the soldier boys, though dead beat to the point of exasperation with hours and days of argument, called up his last reserves of humour, sat up all one night and produced a notable document all by himself. This took the form of a complete plan down to the last detail of an imaginary operation which the author christened 'Overboard'. Whereas our real project for the great invasion, operation 'Overlord', was classified in the terminology of the time as American Secret, British Most Secret, the plan for operation 'Overboard' bore the proud heading, American Stupid, British Most Stupid. There followed an extremely witty skit on the whole of our activities, and the subsequent laughter completely cleared the air and brought about the reconciliation so earnestly sought after.

But even this little outburst of humour had its serious side and, in fact, brought us within an ace of disaster. Our security experts were quick to see that in spite of its lightness of touch and apparently nonsensical content, the plan set forth for this hypothetical operation 'Overboard' bore of necessity many marked resemblances to the original, the aping of which was the secret of its fun. We had, therefore, to ensure as far as we could that distribution of the plan for operation 'Overboard' was severely restricted. Apart from personal complimentary copies sent to the Commander-in-Chief, Home Forces, the Chief of Combined Operations and to the Prime Minister's Chief of Staff, it was enacted that the whole affair should be kept strictly within the walls of Norfolk House. This unfortunately was not done, and a copy somehow made its way across the Atlantic. It certainly was tough that such a gem should be born to waste its sweetness on the confined spaces of COSSAC Headquarters, as the poet might have said but didn't quite. Anyway, if one had not had much experience of the necessity for absolute security, Washington DC was a whale of a way from Berlin, and what could it really matter?

But our luck held. Some weeks went by and the whole episode had been overlaid in the mind by many more pressing events before I received a note from General Gordon Macready of the British Army Staff in Washington in which he told me he had just been visited by a representative of *The Pointer*, the weekly publication by the Corps of Cadets, West Point, who considered himself fortunate to have obtained a copy of the paper produced in London entitled 'Plan for Operation "Overboard"'. This seemed eminently worthy of publication even in this august periodical but, seeing as the material was produced in England, it was thought only right that before publication, official sanction should be sought from the British authorities. Without knowing too much of what was afoot at the time in England, these same British authorities were quick to perceive a distinct aroma of rat. Hence the friendly note to me and thus it was not only that *The Pointer* was deprived of a notable contribution but what might have proved a serious leak of priceless information was effectively stopped.

But as well as maintaining secrecy about their own designs, the Allies needed information about the sites in Occupied France which were proposed for the invasion. Those who gathered such information took incredible risks.

General Omar Bradley, US First Army Group
Before recommending that the assault be made against the Calvados coast of Normandy, Morgan's planners had scrutinized the shore line of Europe from the Netherlands to Biarritz. From their intelligence archives the British had culled volumes of patient research on subsoils, bridges, moorings, wharfage, rivers, and the thousands of intricate details that went into this appraisal of the Overlord plan.

Characteristic of the enterprise the British applied to this intelligence task was the answer they brought in reply to our inquiry on the subsoil of Omaha Beach. In examining one of the prospective beach exits, we feared that a stream running through the draw might have left a deposit of silt under the sand and shingle. If so, our trucks might easily bog down at that unloading point.

'How much dope can you get on the subsoil there?' I asked Dickson when G-3 brought the problem to me.

Several days later a lean and reticent British naval lieutenant came to our briefing at Bryanston Square. From his pocket he pulled a thick glass tube. He walked over to the map on the wall.

'The night before last', he explained dryly, 'we visited Omaha Beach to drill a core in the shingle at this point near the draw. You can see by the core there is no evidence of silt. The shingle is firmly bedded upon rock. There is little danger of your trucks bogging down.'

To get this information the lieutenant had taken a submarine through the mine fields off the coast of France. There he paddled ashore one evening in a rubber boat directly under the muzzles of the Germans' big, casemated guns.

The men – the GIs, Tommies, matelots and flyers – who would put Overlord into effect, who would translate its words and lines into bullets and blood, were a diverse group. They came from Nebraska, from Glasgow from Swansea, from the Bronx, from Kentucky, from Calgary, and from small villages in England's West Country. Perhaps all they had in common was their age, for few of them were past their mid-twenties. Some had volunteered to join the armed services in a passionate desire to beat Nazism, some succumbed to pressure of the times and their peers and reluctantly 'volunteered', some were regulars and a surprising number joined up for the adventure. And many, unsurprisingly enough, were drafted.

Lance-Bombardier Stanley Morgan, RA, 112th Heavy AA Regiment, aged 26

I was a militia boy, you see, and should have gone for six months military training being over twenty-one, but the war came. I was working on a farm and everybody said, 'Oh, you'll get out [of being conscripted].' But farming wasn't a reserved occupation then. I had to go in. I did six and a half years.

John Houston, US 101st Airborne Division

We were all volunteers who had come into the paratroops because we wanted to help put an end to Hitler's evil government as fast as possible. I remember reading about the treatment of the Jews in Poland one day in the fall of 1942 and going to the recruiting station the next day.

Marine Stanley Blacker, RM, 606th Flotilla LCM, aged 19

I would have been conscripted anyway had I not volunteered, and by volunteering I could go into what I wanted to go into, which was the Royal Marines.

Corporal Ted Morris, 225 Para Field Ambulance, 6th Airborne Division, aged 24

I never did well in school. I was a lazy bugger, and just didn't settle in – I had this urge to get out and about. Now everybody of my age from around here [Towyn] joined the Air Force, which was glamorous and there wasn't any work anyway. But about 1935 they fetched out a propaganda film, *OHMS* – 'On His Majesty's Service'. John Mills starred in it and it was all about a rookie in the Army. And I'm convinced that that film and the fact I wasn't getting anywhere at school made me join the Army. This was in 1936.

Nevin F. Price, USAAF 397th Bomb Group, aged 19

I would have been drafted anyway, so I thought I might as well volunteer and get the branch of service I wanted. I didn't.

Alfred Leonard, Merchant Navy, aged 16

I wanted to join the Merchant Navy. Lots of my friends were already in it. I was chuffed to death when I got in, but I can't imagine what my parents really thought. I pressurized them to sign me in.

Leading Aircraftman Gordon Jones, Combined Operations, aged 22

Things were intensely patriotic. There were about fifteen of us – all good friends – and they had all gone into the war. I was literally the only one left and was sick and tired and fed up of being in a reserved occupation – an aircraft cost clerk, put there by a doting uncle. I was an only child and my mother obviously said to him, 'Oh my God, I'm worried about Gordon with the war!' Understandably! Anyway I stuck it for some months and then got the bus one lunchtime and went down to the RAF recruiting office in Bristol. I passed Grade 1 for aircrew. This was probably a Monday or a Tuesday and I thought I'd be in by the next week. I had to wait a year, and by then there had been many volunteers for aircrew and my eyesight was deemed below standard. So I met this Squadron Leader who said, 'Gordon, we have some rather bad news for you – you've failed your eyesight test and unfortunately we can't accept you for aircrew. As you've volunteered from a reserved occupation you have the option to go back to civvy street, but I'm sure you don't want to do that.' He gave me a cigarette and called me Gordon, so he really hit it off with me. I looked at a list of trades he gave me – armourer, policeman, pigeon keeper – and asked what armourer entailed. And that was it. I became an armourer.

To be in uniform or in the Merchant Marine, however, was no guarantee of 'seeing action' on D-Day, or any other day. To be there on 6 June 1944 was a matter of luck, good or bad. For most men under arms life in World War II was a steady routine of polish, parades and exercises, a matter of enduring the boredom that forms 95 per cent of all war. Fewer than a quarter of the British Army, Churchill lamented, would ever 'hear a bullet whistle.' Some deliberately joined units most likely to go into combat; others simply found themselves in units earmarked for Overlord, a fate over which they had no say; and some took every precaution to ensure they were not in Normandy in June 1944, but still found themselves there.

W. Emlyn 'Taffy' Jones, Commando Signal Troop, 1st Special Service Brigade, aged 23

I got fed up with doing nothing. At one time I was in tanks as a wireless operator and all you were doing was going on exercise. Then another one. I thought, 'There's a bloody war going on out there, what the hell am I doing?' Then you'd get a chap who would join you, in a new intake, and of course he'd have the Africa Star – he'd done *something*. I could see the war passing me by. So I went and joined this new unit. I didn't know it was the Commandos then.

Sergeant H.M. Kellar, Devonshire Regiment

We were called to a special parade and addressed by the Company Sergeant-Major. He read out a message from General Montgomery requesting volunteers for his 21st Army group. I was bored stiff as usual, so I stuck my hand up and I was on my way in a few days and joined the 2nd Battalion of the Devons.

Donald Thomas, 53rd Airlanding Light Regiment RA, 6th Airborne Division

I was in the Anti-Tank Regiment until 1942. Our Colonel volunteered for all of us to join the 6th Airborne.

Seaman C.J. Wells, *Empire Crossbow*, Merchant Navy, aged 20

My brother had been on the Murmansk run, Merchant Navy, and he told me not to hand over my ID card when I went up to the Shipping Federation offices because they stamp a great big V for Volunteer in it – you haven't been asked, but you've volunteered for the invasion. So I got up to the Glasgow Shipping Federation offices and they asked for my card behind the counter, which was like a Post Office counter, but I said, 'No I don't want no V in my card, I'm not volunteering for the invasion.' So I got on this *Empire Crossbow* at Glasgow and went down to Southampton. A few days before the invasion the Special Branch came aboard for a security check on all of us. I went in front of this officer with my papers, and the officer said, 'I see you haven't got a V in your card.' I said, 'No, and I aint no bloody volunteer either.' He said, 'It's like this laddie' – a Scotsman he was – 'you've been through all the security checks and you are going. But you won't get the pound a week extra danger money, a couple of bars of chocolate, the cigarettes and a couple of cans of beer if you don't have a V.' I said, 'If it's like that put a V on there.' That's how I volunteered for the invasion.

The men who went to the far shore on 6 June and in the weeks that followed were supremely trained. Many had been in training since 1942, long before the invasion details had been agreed by the political and military heads of the Allied camp. In 1944, however, the training was stepped up; and then up again. Troops and sailors practised landings on beaches in Devon, Pembrokeshire, Scotland – anywhere in Britain that resembled the coast of France they would hit on the sixth. As the invasion would be the biggest seaborne assault of all time most training required an essential ingredient – water.

Lance-Bombardier Stanley Morgan, RA

If there was a hole or gravel pit in the South of England
with water in it, we went through it in our waterproofed
vehicles.

Leading Aircraftman Gordon Jones, Combined Operations

We used to run and march eight miles to Erlin, get into
landing craft and go out in the bay, then run down these
ramps, charge ashore, back on the boats, day after day. And
then do vehicle landings in Jeeps which we had to waterproof
ourselves. There were huge drums of Harbutt's plasticine
and we used to get handfuls of this stuff, which was very
malleable, like putty, and put it all around the distributors
and all the electrical points under the bonnet. An exhaust
came straight up from the engine vertically and another pipe
went up vertically which was the air intake for the carbur-
ettor. The Jeeps were loaded on board the landing craft and
we drove them off. You were in about five feet of water. Your
head and shoulders were above the water but you were
driving this thing like a bodiless driver. You'd see busts going
through the water towards land.

Sergeant H.M. Kellar, Devonshire Regiment

There [Loch Fynne] we met up with the *Glenroy* and spent a
week on board, practising boarding our landing craft. Each
landing craft carried a platoon of infantry, about thirty men.
We would land on the beaches of the loch and return to the
Glenroy. This was what we termed a cushy number, nothing
very strenuous and good food aboard ship, plus the daily
rum ration we were allowed, the same as the crew. The
thought inevitably crossed my mind that we were being
fattened for the kill.

Major F.D. Goode, 2nd Battalion, Gloucestershire Regiment

In March [1944] the battalion moved to Inverary to train for the assault of the beaches. We practised getting in and out of the landing craft which was manned by enthusiastic marines. One of them, we were told, had been too enthusiastic and steering his assault craft across the loch in semi-darkness he hit a buoy. Thinking it was the beach he ordered 'Down doors' – and some ten fully equipped infantry dashed into the loch and vanished for ever.

Colonel H.S. Gillies, King's Own Scottish Borderers
Moray Firth, 1 January 1944

I threw myself into the uninviting swell and struggled ashore, followed by my company. During the next three days of the exercise my clothes froze on me, but it illustrates our then high state of physical fitness that I did not even get a cold.

Among those given the most extensive and safety-conscious training were the tank crews who might land General Percy Hobart's amphibious DD tanks in Normandy – in case the tanks floundered and sank like stones.

Trooper Peter Davies, 1st East Riding Yeomanry, aged 21

We had to go through a lot of swimming exercises, and everyone had to learn to swim. I couldn't as it happened. We trained in open-air baths in the middle of winter, dressed in denims which were soaking wet. We were in and out of open-air swimming pools for about a month. We also had to learn to swim underwater, and to do that we used the Davis escape apparatus that submariners use to bring you back to the surface. We tested it by having weights on us, as divers do, and we had to go down iron steps into a tank of water and walk along the bottom wearing this escape apparatus, which consisted of an airline fastened to your chest, with a nose-clip and goggles. We did this for about two days. This period culminated in us being trained by the Navy for a couple of days in a huge concrete tank about 30 feet deep, into which they had placed the hull and turret of an old tank. It was without tracks, just sitting on the bottom. We had to go down there and sit in the positions as we normally would in a fighting tank. And then they flooded the concrete tank to a depth of about 20 feet, through 20-inch pipes. Within seconds the water was rising. We had ten seconds to get the escape equipment on, then wait until the hull and turret were full and get out. We had two failures. The first time one of our crew shot out immediately before the tank was full, so we had to wait for the concrete tank to be drained again, sitting there in wet clothes. On the second time I got hit on the side of the head by one of the lads getting out. They spotted it and the test was immediately stopped again. So we had three goes at that.

The training had its desired effect. The men of June 1944 were at the peak of their physical preparedness. The comments of this commando can stand for many.

W. Emlyn 'Taffy' Jones, Commando Signal Troop, 1st Special Service Brigade

I stood in a pub in London, bought a pint and looked around and thought to myself, 'I could clear this lot out of here if I wanted to.' It wasn't that I wanted to, but I felt so fit, so full of confidence, that I could handle anything.

But a question mark hung over the combat and mental readiness of the thousands of US infantry – few of whom had any experience of war for real – pouring into Britain at the rate of tens of thousands a month in the build-up to Overlord. Accompanying General Eisenhower to the US training ground at Slapton Sands in Devon, his aide confided his worries to his diary.

Captain H.C. Butcher, aide to Eisenhower
Diary, 4 April 1944
I am concerned over the absence of toughness and alertness of young American officers whom I saw on this trip. They are as green as growing corn. How will they act in battle and how will they look in three months time?

And it was at Slapton Sands that the Americans suffered their greatest training tragedy. A force of nine German E-boats intercepted the American landing craft, sinking them in a duck-shoot. On the harbourside when the Americans returned was a young British sailor.

William Seymour, RN
A large American craft came into Poole; it was quite a mess. Six hundred of them [Americans] had been killed, and some of them were on this ship. I saw a number of bodies being carried to shore. It put us off a bit. Until then we hadn't really worried about war.

Not all of the training for the assault on Fortress Europe involved water. Huge areas of farmland were given over to infantry and tank exercises, so the 'dog-faces' and the Tommies could undertake realistic training for the battles which would come in Normandy after they got off the beaches and into the countryside. Farmers whose land was requisitioned for these exercises were seldom pleased, particularly if the Occupiers happened to be American.

Anonymous woman farmer, Berkshire

The troops would arrive in luxury coaches in the morning,
leaving them to block the lane all day, walk down the hill to
the battle area (apparently American soldiers don't march)
and begin the battle. Unfortunately they seldom warned me
that they were coming, so sometimes we were at work,
ploughing, drilling, threshing and so on in their area, and
had to abandon work and beat a hasty retreat to avoid the
bullets and shells, all of which was very annoying and
disorganizing . . . I don't know how many of their people
got shot, it was a miracle they never shot any of us . . . I once
saw them using a flame-thrower, a ghastly weapon, and they
completely burned up a little spinney with it.

It was not just farmers whose disliked the 'Yanks'. One opinion
poll found them more unpopular among the British public than
Mussolini. As far as the British were concerned, the Americans
'were oversexed, overpaid, and over here.' For their part the
Americans thought the 'Limeys' aloof – at least initially – but
tended to admire their 'pluck'.

Anonymous GI, 1st Infantry Division

You always had the feeling that the Brits were looking down
their nose at you. It didn't matter how low-born they were
themselves. They obviously thought every Yank was a hick,
a country cousin with no breeding. Someone actually used
that word with me once, 'breeding'. They weren't exactly
friendly, the men especially, but it improved after a while,
when we'd rubbed shoulders a bit.

There was one section of the Great British Public which liked the
Americans without reserve. Kids found their easy manners, their
relative affluence, and their stylishness near-magnetic.

John Keegan, schoolboy

How different they looked from our own jumble-sale-quality champions, beautifully clothed in smooth khaki as fine in cut and quality as a British officer's ... and armed with glistening, modern, automatic weapons. Thompson sub-machine guns, Winchester carbines, Garand self-loading rifles. More striking still were the number, size and elegance of the vehicles in which they paraded about the countryside in stately convoy. The British Army's transport was a sad collection of underpowered makeshifts, whose dun paint flaked from their tin-pot bodywork. The Americans travelled in magnificent olive-green, pressed-steel, four-wheel-drive juggernauts, decked with what car salesmen would call optional extras of a sort never seen on their domestic equivalents – deep-treaded spare tyres, winches, towing cables, fire extinguishers. There were towering GMC six-by-sixes, compact and powerful Dodge four-by-fours, and, pilot fishing the rest or buzzing nimbly about the lanes on independent errands like the beach buggies of an era still thirty years ahead, tiny and entrancing Jeeps, caparisoned with whiplash aerials and sketchy canvas hoods which drummed with the rhythm of a cowboy's saddlebags rising and falling to the canter of his horse across the prairie.

John G. Coleman, schoolboy

At that time I was about 12 years old and recall the massive presence of American troops camped on the Penllwyn at Pontllanfraith. We used to rush home from school at Libanus, have our tea and rush straight up to the American or 'Yankee Camp', as we called it, with my mother's wicker shopping basket. The reason for the shopping basket was, the Yanks loved our fish and chips and we would take their orders and go down to Burris's Fish Shop, get a basketful and run like hell back to the camp, which was about a mile away. When we returned to the camp and distributed the fish and chips, we would be paid with Lucky Strike or Camel cigarettes. After we had had our puff, we would rub our fingers in the grease on the bottom of the basket, lick it off our fingers to hide the smell of smoke on our breath.

Across the English Channel Erwin Rommel and his men were also preparing for, even looking forward to, the forthcoming conflagration.

Letter to his wife, Field Marshal Erwin Rommel
27 April 1944
It looks as though the British and Americans are going to do us the favour of keeping away for a bit. This will be of immense value for our coastal defences, for we are now growing stronger every day – at least on the ground, though the same is not true for the air. But even that will change to our advantage again some time.

My little dog is touchingly affectionate and loves sweet things. He sleeps in my room now, underneath my luggage stand. He's going to be inoculated soon against distemper. Went riding again yesterday, but I'm feeling my joints pretty badly to-day.

Still no signs of the British and Americans . . . Every day, every week . . . we get stronger . . . I am looking forward to the battle with confidence.

Gefreiter Werner Kortenhaus, 21st Panzer Division, aged 19
In April 1944 we were still stationed in Brittany but were then moved to the area of Caen at the end of the month. I believe that this was at the order of Rommel himself. In the weeks that followed we actually occupied ourselves less with military training, but more with manual work because we had to dig holes in which to bury our tanks, so that only the gun barrel was above the earth. It was very strenuous

physical work for young people, and when we had finished that, there were still the lorries and munition stores to dig in. And added to all this was also the fact that the large flat plains where we were were expected to be a site for enemy air landings, so we stuck lots of trees – chopped down trees – vertically into the earth. We called these 'Rommel asparagus', because it was Rommel who had ordered them. The point of them was that nobody could land on the flat plains without accident. We did all this as well as our usual army work.

Then, in May, the load became even greater because our guard duties were very, very much stepped up. Every day we had to run patrols. At the end of the month the weather was very hot – and we expected the invasion then, we were prepared for it – the only question was whether it would come in our sector or somewhere else.

Our tanks were very well prepared; that was one thing we did not have to worry about. We had spent months and months previously getting them ready. We knew our tanks, we had full command of them. The technical side of things was something which interested us young men. We were, though, not able to carry out many exercises because we always had to be frugal with petrol and also with ammunition. On shooting exercises perhaps only one or two shots would be fired. For the real thing, though, we were fully equipped, with about 100 shells for each panzer. Our big problem was rationing of food, and the quality of the food, something a lot of people complained about. Often we had potatoes which were so bad we had to throw them away. Sometimes we bought some provisions, such as eggs and butter, from the French. The French were a bit aloof, a bit isolated, but we were very, very concerned that nothing untoward should happen. If something like a theft occurred, the offender would be very, very heavily punished and locked up.

Yet, even with the workload and the poor provisions,

morale was actually quite good in our unit. Because we had spent so many months together and had celebrated together – Christmas and birthdays – we became a good team. I know I and most of my friends did not give a thought to political things, though we were already a bit sceptical about how the war would pan out for Germany. After all, we had already had Stalingrad and El Alamein, so weren't totally confident about the situation as a whole, but we assumed we would be able to push back a sea landing. Indeed, we took it for granted. You know, people are amazed by this but we young panzer men were *burning* at the thought we were perhaps going to be involved in some action. Of course, we had no idea what that would mean. No idea at all.

In Britain in late April military leave was cancelled and the Allied troops who would cross the channel were slowly moved into huge assembly camps along the south coast, which were guarded by grimfaced 'Snowdrops' (American MPs – military police) and 'Red Caps' (British MPs). Large signs dotted the perimeter of these camps, warning: DO NOT LOITER. CIVILIANS MUST NOT TALK TO MILITARY PERSONNEL. The country began to resemble a vast military encampment. The movement of the men involved – fourteen British divisions, twenty American divisions, three Canadian, one Polish, one French division and thousands of commandos and support units – choked the narrow roads with trucks, tanks, field guns and Jeeps (accidents were common). In the ports the build-up of craft was no less impressive.

Lance-Corporal R.M. Wingfield, Queen's Royal Regiment

When we returned from Embarkation Leave, they were sharpening bayonets.

'Guess who?' leered the Armourer Sergeant.

. . . We stood rigidly to attention before our kit. A sergeant stepped forward.

'The Company Commander will now inspect you and your kit for the last time before you go overseas. He is a man of vast experience. He will ask each of you a question of vital importance to see if you are really ready for battle. You *must* know the answer to that question. It may save your life one day.'

The Major looked at my kit and walked all the way round me. He now stood before me. I stared, frozen-faced, at his Adam's apple. It moved.

'How many needles in that housewife [sewing kit] of yours?'

. . . The train pulled slowly out of Halesworth Station. Our old Platoon Sergeant, grim-faced, saluted.

'Gawd!' said someone. 'He'll be presenting arms in honour of the dead next!'

As the train gathered speed past the end of the platform, we saw a sentry at the 'Present'.

We felt ill.

Captain Philip Burkinshaw, 12th Yorkshire Parachute Battalion

It was about this time that my father, mindful of the fact that the 2nd Front must be imminent and expecting that my division would be in the van of any attack, had procured for me at considerable expense a canvas covered breastplate, the strength of which he proceeded to test with the most powerful and penetrating weapons in his armoury of pistols and revolvers! He was an avid collector of all kinds of small arms from the early Colts onwards.

Having satisfied himself that it would withstand almost anything the enemy could bring to bear on it, he handed it over to me when I was home on a short leave in April 1944 and advised that once in action I should never leave it off. Suffice it for me to say that had I followed his advice and been inclined to emulate Don Quixote, I would, accoutred as

I already was with over half a hundredweight of equipment, guns, grenades and ammunition, never have risen from the Normandy soil!

George Collard, 1st RM Armoured Support Regiment, aged 23

In April we moved from Corsham to Lord Mountbatten's Estate near Romsey in Hampshire. The move was by road, and the Royal Marine tanks must have looked a little odd with ration boxes and five naval hammocks lashed up behind the turret.

Going through Devizes, near the Moonraker public house, was a high wall belonging to a large house. Our tank, driven by a three-badge Royal Artillery man, left the road and promptly crashed through the wall. When passing through in later years I've often tried to check where it was repaired.

Trooper Peter Davies, 1st East Riding Yeomanry

Tanks, lorries and everything was lined up on the roads of every town and village that we went into down on the South Coast. Streets, roads – all filled both sides with military vehicles.

Sub-Lieutenant Alun Williams, RNVR

About six weeks before D-Day I moved to Dartmouth to take charge of the minesweeping base there, and I found the transformation staggering. The width of the Dart appeared to have been halved by LST after LST moored alongside one another, manned by US Navy personnel. My abiding recollection is that endless records of Glenn Miller and his band were played over the public address equipment of such ships, presumably to boost the morale of the homesick American troops.

Bombardier Richard 'Dickie' Thomas, RA

We were put into a field – marched into a field, I should say –
which was completely surrounded by barbed wire, to make
sure we didn't get out. We didn't have the foggiest idea what
was going on. It was a good 8 foot of barbed wire.

Alan Melville, RAF war correspondent

Our assembly camp was in Hampshire, near a little village
called Hambledon. One day I want to go back to it and see
it as it really is: I imagine a very pleasant place. But by
May it had been completely engulfed by preparations for
the invasion. Three-ton lorries, trucks, tanks and Jeeps
lined its meandering main street and every house had
three or four vehicles attached to it by camouflage nets,
like barnacles on the side of a ship. The roads were a mass
of signs directing military traffic to the many camps and
headquarters in the district, and military policemen were at
every crossroad. The dear old English village bobby had
wisely decided that the whole thing was beyond him, and
had thrown in the sponge. The nature of the countryside
was ideal for concealing huge quantities of men and
supplies: rolling hills covered with glorious woods. I can't
remember a lovelier spring: the lilac and laburnum were so
heavily blossomed that they were bent almost double; the
fruit trees, even though they had been caught by a late
frost, still made a wonderful show. But, however hard one
concentrated on the setting, it was impossible to get away
from what was being hatched in it. If you looked long
enough at the laburnum, you realized that an amphibious
Jeep was tucked away behind its yellow bunches of bloom;
if you wanted to admire the tulips in somebody's garden,
you had to wedge your way between a couple of tanks in
order to lean up against the garden fence. The King came
down one day to inspect troops: several thousands of them
were drawn up in a great green well formed by a dip in the

hills. When the first part of the inspection was over, the men of the Armoured Brigades concerned in it were allowed to fall out until the rest of the ceremony had finished. I had been watching the King walk along the long lines of Lord Lovat's special brand of Commandos, and hadn't noticed the others falling out. I thought at first, on looking back at the hillside, that it was completely covered in rhododendrons. Then I realized that it was completely covered with men. There was a solid mass of them, only distinguishable as human beings when the sun glinted on some buttons or on someone wearing glasses. It was like that all over the south of England in the days before the balloon went up: the rhododendrons were as plentiful as ever, but they were crowded out by men in uniform.

Life in the assembly camps was a round of training, equipment preparation (including more waterproofing of vehicles), briefings, reviews by dignitaries and a desperate battle against boredom. The men also learnt for the first time that their destination was France.

Lance-Corporal R.M. Wingfield, Queen's Royal Regiment

The first thing which met our eyes was a large board giving details of the ever-open NAAFI and the continuous film show. This should have put us on our guard, but our suspicions were finally confirmed when . . . we marched to our quarters. There, beneath the trees, were neat two-man tents, each with two American Army cots – and sheets.

'Lofty' stared, then roared:

'I'll bet we're not here long. The condemned man ate a hearty bloody breakfast!'

He was right.

P.H.B. Pritchard, No. 6 Commando, 1st Special Brigade

We were eight to a tent and slept on canvas folding beds with US Army issue woollen blankets which impressed us with their quality, as did everything the US issued. Each group of four tents had a urinal bucket for night use. These were emptied by a US private wearing gloves, who used to grumble, 'When I left the States I thought I was going to be a soldier, but here I am emptying p—s buckets. I guess the folks back home will call me chicket s—t!' So we nicknamed him that!

· · · ·

At nights we were shown the latest films from America and the food was generally very good and plentiful. Our other spare moments were spent in reading US-Army-issued novels by Steinbeck or Hemingway and other such authors. Also for those so inclined there were the inevitable, and endless, games of 'two up' (Australian swy) which was extremely popular in No. 6 Commando generally. I did not indulge and neither did my chum Gunner Puttick (Royal Artillery); we just read the books and had our hair cut by Corporal Draper ('Ginger'), using a comb and a pair of nail scissors.

· · · ·

We paraded on a road by lining each side in single file. H.M. [His Majesty], I seem to remember, walked between our ranks, and spoke with several soldiers (not me unfortunately). In the same park various tanks and other vehicles all of special design, i.e. Flails, Crocodile, AVREs, [Armoured Vehicle Royal Engineers, a modified Churchill tank] etc., were parked under trees. I understand that these were also for inspection by H.M. To be inspected by the King was regarded as a great honour, which indeed it was.

Driver John Osborne, 101 Company General Transport Amphibious

In mid-May groups from each unit were lined up in a country lane and who should come along accompanied by a number of top brass but King George VI. As he passed us, all he said was, 'So these are the men who drive the DUKWs!' Even so, it was quite something to have been inspected by the King.

T. Tateson, Green Howards

I was most impressed though by the Yanks' washing-up facilities, which we shared. In the British Army in those days a single bin full of lukewarm grey water was all we had to dip our mess tins in, in a rather hopeless effort to clean them. The Yanks had a row of three bins of hot water to be used in sequence, so that the third one remained practically clear and clean. A simple and common-sense refinement, but one which made all the difference and seemed to us a luxury.

Alan Melville, RAF war correspondent

Two big marquees had been put up in the garden and joined together to make one enormous briefing tent. Round the walls of the tent were maps: large-scale maps of the beach sectors on which we were going to land. They were accurate in every detail except one: the place-names had been altered. You found with a slight jolt to your geography that, for example, Madrid was a village only a few kilometres west of Vienna. To supplement the maps, there were a large number of aerial photographs – the best and most detailed I have ever seen. Every feature of the beaches and the hinterland leading from them was made absolutely clear by those photographs: the obstacles which the enemy had put up on the beaches, the sand dunes, the roads leading inland, the houses and buildings beyond. There was a little port or seaside town to the left of our own sector; it looked an attractive little place, with nice houses and big gardens stretching down to the sands. The sort of place where people who could afford it would take a house for the summer and let the children run loose on the sands. As well as the maps and photographs, there were large, gaily-painted diagrams showing how our forces would deploy on landing, and the exact position of each transit area, command post, supply and ammunition dump, and so on. Plus a blackboard for such extra diagrams as were needed in the briefing. Even if we hadn't been told a thing about what was going to happen, there would have been no excuse after studying all that evidence for not knowing exactly what our own strip of the beach maintenance area looked like.

Alan Moorehead, Australian war correspondent

I found my place in one of the tents and set up my camp bed. There was nothing to do, so I lay down on the bed and stared through the open flap of the tent at a field where the soldiers were playing football. On the opposite bed a young naval officer was trying on his harness. There was a rucksack full of explosives, a trenching tool, pistol, ammunition, a butcher's knife, gas-cape, helmet, a small sack that looked as though it contained hand grenades, a tin of rations. He strapped all this gear on himself and began making alterations so as to distribute the weight more evenly. Then he practised slipping the bundles on and off until he found he could do it in the space of thirty seconds or so. I tried to think what his job was. To wade ashore and plant explosives on the sea-wall? He was a boy of twenty-one or twenty-two, and he went about this buckling and unbuckling of his kit quite oblivious of his surroundings. Presently he too lay down on his bed and began watching the footballers outside.

'It looks as though we are going to have good weather.'
'Yes.'
He did not want to talk. After an hour I got up and began

walking round the camp. Some of the soldiers were lying on the grass near the recreation tent. They were talking and listening to a radio loudspeaker hanging from one of the trees. A disembodied dialogue was coming out of the marquee marked Camp Cinema, and occasionally there was a burst of laughter from the audience inside. At the paymaster's tent I asked how much money I could change.

'Ten pounds if you like.'

'Into what currency?'

'Francs.'

So it was going to be France then; that was definite. The same flimsy notes with their pastel shades, the bundles of wheat and the buxom women in the corner, Banque de France. Five years ago, when I shut up my home in Paris, I had changed the last of those notes at the Gare de l'Est, and these were the first I had seen since then, and they were the first clear passport for my return. But it was not going to be the same. I stood outside the tent looking at the notes and expecting a nostalgia for the things that had made France a better country to live in than anywhere else on earth. But it was no good. The mind projected itself forward as far as the embarkation, as far as the landing. Then there was a blank, a kind of wall over which the mind would not travel.

In the mess tent the food was very bad. We sat at rickety trestle tables, eating slices of cold bully beef and cold white cabbage. Then there were army biscuits, margarine, a mug of tea. A few made some attempt to talk, but most of the officers sat eating silently, and brushing the flies away from their plates. Every few minutes a loudspeaker outside the tent began calling numbers. These were the numbers of units which were to prepare themselves to go down to their ships and invasion barges. As the numbers were called the men at the table cocked their heads slightly to listen. One or two men got up and left the tent. The rest went on eating the cold cabbage.

I went back to the tent and got down on the bed

again. There was nothing to do. My driver had packed the jeep. The kit was stowed on board, chains, petrol cans, blankets. The engine had been plastered with waterproofing glue so that the vehicle could travel through water. A long flexible hose ran up from the exhaust and was tied to the top of the windscreen. He too, the driver, showed that he was feeling the strain of waiting. Everybody felt it. Over all the camp, over a hundred other such camps, over all the Army at that moment there was this same dead weight, this same oppressive feeling that the delay might continue indefinitely, growing more and more unbearable as the days went by. The invasion was already like an over-rehearsed play.

Alan Hart, RCS, aged 19
Diary, June 1944
On the day after – Bank Holiday Monday – we were issued with 100-franc notes. So we at least knew that the town of 'Poland', the port of 'Oslo' and the stretch of coast we were to touch down on was France.

Stars and Stripes newspaper, [pre-invasion issue]
Don't be surprised if a Frenchman steps up and kisses you. That doesn't mean he's queer. It means he's French and darn glad to see you.

Lieutenant C.T. Cross, 2nd Battalion Oxford and Bucks Light Infantry
For quite a long and very tedious time before the thing [D-Day] began we were cooped up tightly in a tented camp opposite an operational aerodrome near Oxford. It was incredibly hot while we were there (Whitsun) but they stretched a point and allowed us out of camp to go across to the RAF mess and have a bath. ENSA sent a show down one afternoon – held in plain air – quite amusing. And

occasionally we packed a few sweaty men very tightly into a tent and showed them a film. But it was a trying time and a lot of money changed hands at cards. Meanwhile, the officers and NCOs were very busy hearing the story of what we were going to do, memorizing maps, studying models, air photograph intelligence reports and that sort of thing. All done near nude in a Nissen hut, whose doors and windows had to be kept shut!

Trooper Peter Davies, First East Riding Yeomanry

It took two or three months to prepare the tanks before D-Day. It was quite a job. We had to seal every part of the hatches where the driver and gunner get in, and where the guns come out. They had to be sealed and covered in rubberized canvas and stuck with Bostic glue. The turret flaps and turret ring had to be sealed, and the exhaust at the back was covered with a metal box affair which carried it four or five feet up into the air so that it was way above the waterline. The engines were tested as well. Exactly three weeks before D-Day we had to weld additional armour – plates about an inch thick – onto the sides of the Shermans where the ammunition sponsors were. I never forget the day the welding was done because it happened to be my twenty-first birthday and I had the greatest prank played against me. I had forgotten it was my birthday and we were working like blacks in a wood north of Portsmouth. I fell asleep lying on top of the tank in the brilliant sunshine. I suddenly realized that it had gone quiet. Everybody had gone. It was lunchtime. I tried to get off the tank and I thought I was paralysed: my legs wouldn't move. I couldn't make out what was wrong for about five minutes – what had happened was that they had welded the steel heels of my boots to the tank, and everybody had vamoosed. I had to get out of my boots, take a hammer and chisel from the tool box and cut my boots off the top of the tank. I put them on and trotted through the woods to where the mess hut was. I got in there and a tremendous cheer went up, and they sang 'Happy Birthday'. I really thought I'd been paralysed. It was a great trick.

. . . .

Most fellows were elated but impatient and wanted to get on with it, get on with the job we were supposed to do. Basically, 'Let's get it over.' One or two fellows married with children, whose wives were perhaps not that far away, wanted to sneak off home. Only a couple I know of attempted to get out of the camp, because they were fenced in by barbed-wire entanglements and the perimeter was patrolled by military police and civilian police. There wasn't much chance of getting out.

Leading Aircraftman Gordon Jones, Combined Operations

The drinking was confined to NAAFI beer, which was quite pleasant but it didn't get you anywhere. There was housey-housey and also guys would play cards. The funny thing was that after only an hour or so of having been given this French money, some of the guys were walking around with their battle dress bulging with thousands of notes and other guys were saying 'Can you give us a couple of notes for a beer?' They were completely skint.

Lance-Bombardier Stanley Morgan, RA

We were told that the Germans weren't very clean, so a lot of people had their hair cut short, in case they were getting amongst louse.

Donald S. Vaughan, 5th Assault Regiment, 79th Armoured Division, aged 19

In the holding camp we had four or five chaps blown up. They were dismantling a torpedo, a Bowes torpedo, which was a 3-

inch cast-iron pipe full of gelignite. Gelignite, after a certain time, starts to deteriorate, it sweats. So they were taking it out to refill it. Something went wrong and they were killed.

Captain Douglas G. Aitken, Medical Officer, 24th Lancers

[In May 1944 he was given the 'strange job' of organizing the loading of a landing ship tank.] I struggle with innumerable forms in duplicate trying to discover whom we have brought, who ought to be there – both our own and other units – and what and which vehicle has arrived or ought to be there. This takes me every spare moment of my time and I have my meals brought to me rather than go in next door to get them. We have chaotic conferences every morning and afternoon. They want us to go to the boat in one order. I want to go in reverse stowage order, and they promise eventually this will be done. I spend more hectic hours working out which vehicle will have to be landed first and therefore which order they will go in the boat. But the job is eventually finished and the rest depends on the organization official.

Donald Burgett, US 101st Airborne Division

The next few days were spent in briefing tents studying aerial photographs, maps and three-dimensional scale models of Normandy. Each paratrooper had to learn the whole operation by heart, know his own and every other outfit's mission to the most minute detail and be able to draw a map of the whole area from memory. We even knew that the German commandant of St Come-du-Mont owned a white horse and was going with a French schoolteacher who lived on a side street just two buildings away from a German gun emplacement. Troops wearing different German uniforms and carrying enemy weapons roamed constantly through the marshalling area to familiarize us with what the enemy looked like and what weapons they carried.

Flight Lieutenant J.G. Hayden, RAF, aged 22

A lot of time was spent studying a model of the run-in to the dropping area. The model was built in a room which was kept secret, and the navigators and bomb-aimers were taken in at certain times to study it carefully. Then you had to close your eyes, and someone would ask questions: 'What comes after the bridge X?' or 'Whereabouts is Y? Just to make sure that you had the run-in definitely in your mind, so you'd be very, very sure to be on the right place on the night.

As the big day approached some units became sombre, even shaky in their morale.

Staff Sergeant Henry Giles, US 291st Combat Engineer Battalion

Diary

The whole outfit now has a very bad case of the invasion shakes. Very little talk about anything but assault landings, what it will be like, what the casualties will be etc. Any way you look at it, it's not going to be any piece of cake. After the alert this morning, I caught myself several times looking around and wondering for the hundredth time how the hell I got here and what the hell I'm doing here – me, Henry Giles, an old farm boy from Caldwell Ridge, Knifley, Kentucky! For the first time in years a uniform doesn't seem to fit me. A little too tight.

Even the troops of the experienced US 1st Infantry Division, 'The Big Red One', were gloomy.

Corporal Sam Fuller, US 1st Infantry Division

They [the men of the division] had had their fill of combat and they had rightfully assumed . . . that somebody else should carry the ball this time . . . They would stand no chance of walking off that beach. Their luck would not stretch that far.

This pre-invasion tension was not confined to the GIs of America. There were British regiments in a near-rebellious state, considering that they had already 'done their bit.' In others the tension boiled over into fights and riots.

Major F.D. Goode, Gloucestershire Regiment

A regiment which shall be nameless had been the previous occupants of the camp and they were so bloody-minded at having to do another landing that they booby-trapped some of the area with live grenades. Removing them was good training and no one was hurt but we did have one unfortunate who was playing in his tent with a loaded rifle and accidentally shot himself in the heart. I arrived a minute after to find blood spurting literally six feet and no hope. We notified his next of kin after the landing that he had been killed in action; it seemed kinder.

Sergeant William B. Smith, Intelligence Corps, aged 36

One evening there was a riot in the camp in which a good deal of damage was done, especially broken windows. This caused some concern and nobody seemed to know exactly how it started. The next day it was announced that henceforth each night a sergeant was to be detailed to close the bars at 10.00 p.m. On inspecting the roster, I found to my horror that I was the sergeant detailed for the first night. I was not looking forward to the job, as a good many of the troops concerned were from the 7th Armoured Division [the Desert Rats] who had been brought to England from North Africa and, as the division responsible largely for the only British victory up to that time, had a very high opinion of themselves, and were not inclined to be ordered about by anybody, let alone those who themselves had never been in action. As it happened I managed things without much opposition, and for the next few days discipline prevailed.

Until the 3rd of June the date of D-Day – which was initially
intended to be the 5th of June – was known only by the most senior
planners and military commanders. On the third the men themselves were let in on the secret of 'when'. The change of mood was
tangible.

Alan Moorehead, Australian war correspondent

It was absurd to try and rationalize the thing that had to
happen in a day or two. Yet (one argued) it was a
monstrous contradiction of reason. You cannot present
fear and death and risk in this cold way, with all this
calculation. You can accept these things vicariously in a
theatre. You accept them when you are angry. But cold
cabbage. A lot of numbers shouted on a loudspeaker. A
tent with a number on it. A number even on *you*. What sort
of preparation was this? And to let it go on hour after hour.
To try and tabulate a thing that was essentially a matter of
passion and excitement. It simply drove the mind into a
fixed apathy. It made you reluctant to walk, to talk, to eat,
to sleep. There was no taste in anything any longer. Not
even in drinks, and there were no drinks in the camp
anyway. Just waiting, waiting until your number turned
up. And meanwhile no loose talk. What you had to do,
your job, your place in the machine, was everything, but
you must not talk about it. You were not even told where
you were going. You were given no idea of your place in
the plan. You had no method of assessing the black space
ahead. You had to be suspicious even of the other soldiers
in the camp. Everything had to be secret. You were driven
back into yourself to the point where you lacked even a
normal companionship with the others, who after all were
in exactly the same situation. It was not fear that oppressed
you, but loneliness. A sense of implacable helplessness. You
were without identity, a number projected in unrelated
space among a million other numbers.

On June 3rd these were the ideas that made this camp the most cheerless place that had come my way since the war began. And all around, in the mess, and along the earthen tracks, one could read the same ideas in the heavy sullen faces of the soldiers going by. No wonder another twenty men had deserted in the night.

That evening the soldiers were told the plan and what they had to do. The change was electric. The suspense was snapped. A wave of relief succeeded it. Now that the future was known and prescribed everything would be easier. We were to embark the following afternoon. We would sail during the night. H-Hour was the following morning. An immense aerial and naval bombardment would precede the landing. Ten thousand tons of bombs would fall along the coast on which we had to land. The naval guns would silence the shore batteries. The brigade had been given a small strip of beach on which to land, a strip marked on the map as 'King Beach'. Other brigades would be landing to the right and left of us. Airborne divisions would be arriving by glider and parachute to clear the way inland.

All this was an immense reassurance. As the men stood in their ranks listening to the colonel you could feel the confidence growing. Here at last was something practical and definite, something to which one could adjust oneself.

We were not yet told exactly where we would land, but maps with false names were issued. They showed every German position down to the last gun. Here a machine-gun nest. Here a minefield. Here a pill-box and a fortified wall. The defences did not appear nearly so formidable now that one knew the extent of them. Each company was given its objective, the distance it had to go, the obstacles in its way. And all the time continuous air cover, a continuous barrage of guns from the sea. Dinner was almost cheerful that night.

Private Robert Macduff, Wiltshire Regiment, aged 20 [born 6 June]

Then all hell broke loose. D-Day was to be 5 June. In came to the Signals Office a group of lads with a tiny piece of my birthday cake, and informed me that the cake had been cut up and well passed around. They handed me my tiny piece with the remark that where I was going I wouldn't have time to eat any more.

Donald Burgett, US 101st Airborne Division

On June 3rd they issued each of us with an escape kit, consisting of a small compass, an unmarked map, and seven dollars in French money. We were also issued a metal cricket apiece, one click being the challenge to anyone we met in combat and two the password to keep from getting one's head blown off. The verbal challenge for all airborne was 'Flash', the password 'Thunder', and if a man wasn't sure of who challenged him he could ask for the countersign 'Welcome'. The way to challenge a man is to draw a bead on him, wait until he is not more than fifteen or twenty feet away, then whisper, just loud enough for him to hear, the challenge word, 'Flash'. If he doesn't answer with the password or two clicks of the cricket, pull the trigger.

That night we sat sharpening knives, cleaning weapons and sorting through the personal things we figured we could or would need after the heavy fighting was over, like soap, shaving equipment and cartons of cigarettes. Phillips, Liddle, Benson, several other troopers and I were in the tent next to company headquarters with Captain Danes, Speedy West, the Teeter twins and some officers. It was raining that night, and all the canvas and blankets were wet, but we didn't mind, for most of us slept with our clothes on now, just removing our boots. After the usual joking and horseplay, things quieted down in the tent and we went to sleep.

Captain H.C. Butcher, aide to Eisenhower

Diary, Shaef Advance (near Portsmouth), Saturday 3 June 1944

Ever since I have been with Ike, I have carefully followed his admonition never to arrange for a showing of a moving picture for him if use of the film deprives soldiers of entertainment. In North Africa, films were hard to get, particularly new ones, and there were many evenings when the General could have seen a film but all were in use for the GIs. Our new office caravan is 'wired for sound' and I arranged for a movie last night. I try these days to find something light and humorous, never anything on the war. Special Services had no film at Portsmouth but were bringing one down from main headquarters at Bushy Park. As there had been no arrangement for movies for soldiers at the forward headquarters, Special Services suggested 8 o'clock, which fitted in with Ike's personal schedule. The projector, screen, and operator were driven to the camp during the day and because, as I later learned, the projector was being sent for the General, a later show was laid on for the GIs. However, Ike had some unexpected callers and we entered the caravan about 8.30, just as the GI operator was packing up the projector and the screen. He told the General – whom I had not bothered with the details then – he had another show, one for the GIs of the camp, and he would be too late if he ran the film for the General.

With this, the General was in instantaneous and complete agreement, but turned on me and gave me a good cussing out for arranging a film for him at a time which would cause GIs to see the later show and be kept up late. I knew then he really had the pre-D-Day jitters.

As Ike let the GIs in the Portsmouth camp watch movies, many of their fellows and other Allied troops were already being moved out of the assembly areas to the south coast ports where they would embark for the Great Crusade. (Indeed, some had embarked on to their LCTs, LCIs and a host of other abbreviated craft which would carry them across the Channel as early as 31 May.) The troops moved to their marshalling areas and embarkation points in huge, slow convoys.

John G. Coleman, schoolboy

Then we realized something was up when we were stopped going to the camp, and all the surrounding area was patrolled by armed soldiers who came from Canada, Australia, and some of our own soldiers as well. They did their patrol in an area of about 3 miles, so all the playing woods and fields were completely out of bounds.

This coincided with the heavy build-up of armoured vehicles on the Forge Lane road at Bassaleg down to the Tredegar House.

Then suddenly they were gone without warning and everything was dead.

Major D. Flowers, Argyll and Sutherland Highlanders

Our destination was Southampton, eighty-seven miles away by direct route, but well over a hundred miles by the way we were required to take to conform with the traffic arrangements which spread like a cat's cradle over the whole of southern England. According to the book this far exceeded the maximum mileage waterproofed vehicles were supposed to cover, but in fact they all stood the strain well except the three-ton lorries, which boiled constantly, and the 146th Battery's 'slave-chargers' which completely disintegrated.

The first event was a disappointment. So much was supposed to happen at the RCRP, in our case situated just outside Winchester, that when the advance party drew up importantly it was a shock to find nothing but a caravan beside the road containing one private who had never heard of the Regiment, and whose sole immediate ambition was to complete his shaving. We were deeply distressed, and in our state of excitement and nerves we imagined some awful disaster which would preclude our ever going abroad at all. We were not comforted by the arrival of an officer who assured us that officially we did not exist, but that he would try to fit us in somewhere. We lay on the grass half asleep after our long drive while he chattered on the telephone.

Just as Tom Geddes was setting out on his motor-cycle to stop the convoy somewhere by the roadside, so that they would not pile up at the RCRP, news came through that accommodation had been found for us in Camp 19. Thus by three o'clock in the afternoon we had got to the marshalling area on Southampton Common, the drivers remaining with their vehicles while the remainder were firmly imprisoned within barbed wire. Everyone who had been in the main column was suffering from eye strain, varying from a minimum slight soreness to Lieutenant Pothecary, who lost his sight completely and for some time had to be led about. This disturbing and painful ailment was brought about partly by the dust, and partly by the diesel fumes thrown up by M10s travelling head to tail, for the roads approaching all south coast ports carried so much traffic that normal road discipline was abandoned and the order was 'close up and get on.'

Bombadier Harry Hartill, RA, aged 24

The only place we recognized that day was Stonehenge and we spent the night in Bulford Army Camp on Salisbury Plain. Rumours were rife. We knew we were going to an embarkation port but our destination was a secret, and we seemed to be retracing our route as if to confuse enemy observations. I recognized Denham Film Studios just before we bedded down for the night at the roadside just outside London. Next morning we were off again, this time through the city of London. I felt like Montgomery himself as I drove over London Bridge at the wheel of the Bren gun carrier. We arrived at what I later found out was Tilbury docks.

Captain Douglas G. Aitken, Medical Officer, 29th Lancers

In the towns where we have long halts and more tea, the people take a little more interest, but security police keep everyone segregated and there is no mixing. The girls look much more attractive when we know we won't see any for a long time to come. Three attractive ones pass on bicycles on their way to tennis – they look very cool and very English. I occasionally find myself thinking foolish thoughts about not coming back or being away for a hell of a long time.

Mary J. Thomson, Tilbury, aged 11

There were troops – mostly American and Canadian – all around [Tilbury], living in tents – bell tents and all sorts of tents, anything they could sleep in – covering every square inch of grass. By this stage we were confined to home, we weren't allowed out. But the troops needed to get washed up, so some of them came knocking at the door and asked if we could spare a bucket of water, very politely. 'Yes certainly', we said, a bit surprised. Then we discovered that there were lots of boys outside who wanted to get washed and shaved, so we invited them in. They said they couldn't come in, but would be very grateful for the water. We filled up all the buckets and baths we could find and handed them out, and there were men washing on the lawn, on the path and on the drive. They also used our outside toilet at the back of the house, because it didn't come into the house. When they finished they were very grateful and left us with lots of chewing gum. My mother even had a pair of nylons, which were beyond price. A really nice pair of stockings.

Alan Melville, RAF war correspondent

We received our last instructions and our emergency rations – bully, chocolate, chewing gum, two 24-hour packs and the natty little cooker for boiling hot water which was alleged to transform the chunk of rather sad wood-pulp issued to us into a luscious plateful of porridge with sugar and cream thrown in. Hermione was manoeuvred into position between two DUKWs and we were off. We weren't, of course – but there is always a feeling of 'This is it!' when you leave the marshalling area. Actually, our convoy meandered through villages and country roads and then sat down for seven hours on the outskirts of Portsmouth. People didn't pay much attention to us on the way; they were fairly blasé about convoys by that time. But Portsmouth had sensed that this wasn't just another exercise, and the population turned out *en masse*. There were no bands and no flags: it was a very different farewell to the last war; but there was great friendliness. We had been given strict instructions that, for security reasons, we were not to 'fraternize' with the local inhabitants. But it is impossible not to fraternize with people who insist on bringing you out cups of tea every hour, who shower their sugar ration on you, who ask you into their homes for a wash and brush up. Anyway, no Army Council Instruction has ever succeeded in stopping the British soldier from fraternizing with the children – especially if you're driving a 'duck' with a life-size painting of Donald on its side.

Alan Moorehead, Australian war correspondent

At three o'clock we were standing in a line on the path leading up to the gate. The young naval officer came by festooned with his explosives and rather surprisingly took up a position behind me. As each new group of troops turned up they exchanged wisecracks with the others already arrived. 'Blimey, 'ere's the Arsenal.' . . . ''Ome for the 'olidays.' . . . 'Wot's that, Arthur?' 'Them's me water-wings, dearie.' Even after waiting another hour there was still optimism in the ranks. Then we marched out through the gate and got on to the vehicles. An officer was running down the line making sure everyone was on board. He blew a whistle and we started off. Five miles an hour. Down Acacia Avenue. Round the park into High Street; a mile-long column of ducks and three-ton lorries, of Jeeps and tanks and bulldozers. On the sidewalk one or two people waved vaguely. An old man stopped and mumbled, 'Good luck.' But for the most part the people stared silently and made no sign. They knew we were going. There had been rehearsals before but they were not deceived. There was something in the way the soldiers carried themselves that said all too clearly 'This is it. This is the invasion.' And yet they were cheerful still. It was a relief to be out of the camp and moving freely in the streets again. Every now and again the column halted. Then we crept on slowly again towards the hards.

Two hours went by and the soldiers began to grow bored. They seized on anything for amusement. When a girl came by on a bicycle she was cheered with salacious enthusiasm from one end of the column to the other. An athlete dressed in a pink suit began to pace round the cricket field. The soldiers watched him with relish for a minute. Then, 'Hyah, Pinkie.' 'Careful, dearie.' Derisive shouting followed him round the ground. Towards the end of the column a soldier who was trained as a sniper took down his rifle with its telescopic sights and fixed them upon two lovers who were embracing at the farther end of the park. His friends gathered round him while he gave them a lewd commentary on what he saw. The soldiers were becoming very bored. It grew dark and the cricket match ended. Every hour or so a tea-waggon came round and the men ran towards it with their enamel mugs. One after another the lights in the houses were blacked out and the soldiers, left alone in the empty street, lapsed into complete listlessness and tiredness. Rumours kept passing back and forth from vehicle to vehicle. 'Our ship has fouled its anchor.' 'There has been a collision in the harbour.' Or more spectacularly, 'We have already made a landing on the Channel Islands.'

Towards ten o'clock the officers began running down the

column shouting for the drivers to start. We began to edge forward slowly and presently came out on the dark promenade along the sea. There were many ships, both those moving in the sound and those which had brought their bows up on to the hard and had opened their gates to receive the vehicles. We were marked down for the Landing Ship Tank 816. A clamour of light and noise was coming out of its open bows. One after another the vehicles crept down the ramp and on to the great lift that took them to the upper deck. The sailors kept shouting to one another as they lashed down the trucks on the upper deck. All night the thump of army boots against the metal deck went on.

Alan Melville, RAF war correspondent

We lay at anchor for three days while our part of the invasion fleet mustered. It was difficult to realize that this *was* only part of the fleet. Whenever you came out on deck the scene had changed and new arrivals had crept into anchorage until the whole great stretch of water was a mass of grey ships. They were constantly manoeuvring: long lines of landing craft getting into their flotilla positions and moving slowly nearer the open sea, MTBs fussing round us, launches and packet boats scuttling between ships, sign-flashing all day and night. We added our own modest quota on the evening of the second day, when an immaculate RASC launch with its full crew came alongside and to my horror four more pigeons were hauled up on deck with a polite note from the Wing-Commander saying that we'd better be on the safe side, and that he hoped we were remembering to give Blood, Toil, Sweat, and Tears their water every evening.

Driver John Osborne, 101 Company General Transport Amphibious

The next few days in the Solent were rather boring and were spent in the main playing cards. Our bunks were in the sides of the LSTs and it was rather stuffy and claustrophobic down there. Up on the foredeck towards the bows, a cable ran from a winch through an eye in the bow, then to a steel raft called a rhino on which were two ambulance DUKWs belonging to 633 Company. Four of us used the cable as a ridge-pole and made tents with our ground sheets. No one moved us so we stayed there until D-Day.

Major F.D. Goode, Gloucestershire Regiment

We were issued with Mae Wests [lifebelts] and told to wear them at all times at sea. In fact, they made a very good pillow as the quarters were very cramped and one had to lie in a canvas berth with about two feet between the one above. Had we sunk there could not have been many survivors, so closely were we packed below . . . we were also issued with a pair of waterproof waders which came up to our waists and which were meant to enable us to arrive dry on the beaches: in the event they were a damn nuisance and quite useless.

The weather for D-Day had long been a preoccupation of the Allied chiefs. The assault needed a reasonable sea to disembark the troops and good visibility for the Allied aircrews who would give fighter cover and bomb the German defence installations. As June progressed the weather became increasingly bad, causing Eisenhower to make some tough decisions. No sooner had the men of D-Day been told the date for the invasion than it was postponed. The postponement inevitably increased the strain on the men waiting aboard the overcrowded ships and in the damp tents of the Airborne divisions.

Trooper Peter Davies, 1st East Riding Yeomanry

The storm when it brewed up was a real snorter of a storm. A number of barrage balloons suspended from the ships broke off and flew off God knows where. Some of the lads had been sick on the third even, some on the fourth, but on the fifth they really started to get seasick. Of course the boat was going like mad from side to side. Even though the tanks were holding the LST down it was still rocking violently at times.

General Omar Bradley, US First Army Group
At midnight I turned in and fell asleep. It was almost six when I was awakened on Sunday, June 4. The weather in Plymouth harbor was soupy and wet; visibility was down and I shivered as I dressed. Kean came in with a copy of the Admiralty radio to Kirk.

'Postponed?' I asked.

'Twenty-four hours.'

Captain H.C. Butcher, aide to Eisenhower
Diary, Shaef Advance (near Portsmouth), Sunday morning, 4 June 1944
D-Day was postponed by Ike for at least twenty-four hours last night. Weather looks very bad for air support, but suited Navy, as wind was from southwest and not expected to be so strong by morning, when the attacks were to have begun shortly after good light.

A large portion of the 4000 ships already were at sea, from landing craft to battleships. They were notified shortly after the 4 a.m. meeting this morning. Each task force was previously instructed what to do in just this possibility.

Donald Burgett, US 101st Airborne Division
We lay there talking and joking with each other, wondering what combat would really be like, when suddenly the talk in the next tent came into focus and we heard the Captain ask Speedy to play 'San Antonio Rose' on his guitar. The music sounded good, and we listened as we went about our small

chores, but the request was repeated each time the song ended. Finally someone yelled at the Captain and asked if he wouldn't like to hear something else. He replied that he was from San Antonio and the plane he was riding in was also named that and he wanted to listen to that particular song until it was time to go.

The rain kept falling harder and harder through an increasing wind until it was coming down in torrential sheets and we thought for sure the whole operation would be called off. Suddenly a runner poked his head through the tent opening and said, 'This is it, let's go.'

We hit the outside on the double, and in columns of two started slogging our way toward the waiting planes. The ground was hard packed and grassless, and with the rain, the surface became slippery and slimy. Men kept sliding around until we got to the runways on the airfield; then it was easy walking, but still a long way to go. We found our assigned places at last, and looking and feeling like a bunch of half-drowned rats, we started to get ready. I was trying to get the wet parachute harness fastened while water ran into my eyes, off my nose and down my neck, every step bringing a squishy sound from my boots. All the extra equipment we had to carry didn't make the job any easier. Jeeps were running around the field on various errands looking like shadowy ghosts through the downpour of rain. One pulled up, spraying us with grit-filled water from under its wheels, and the driver said the operation was postponed until further notice. Some of us just stood there not knowing whether to feel relieved or mad, because we knew that we would have to go through the same thing again either tomorrow or the next day at the latest. Back in the tents most of us lay on the cots and slept the best way we could in the chill dampness of night, under single blankets from the packs we had made up to carry into combat with us.

Alan Moorehead, Australian war correspondent

Up to this point the morale had been steady. Everyone's
spirits had risen as we had come on board, although this act
of embarking had been the final irrevocable break with
England. But now with this renewed delay there was time
to think again. And this at a moment when one had no desire
to think or to write letters or engage on any distraction from
the inevitable thing ahead.

816 was an American ship which had already made three
assault landings: North Africa, Sicily and Salerno. On this
their fourth landing the sailors showed no excitement or
emotion. Their attitude was summed up by, 'Another dirty
job.' The captain had sailed for twenty years. The crew had
seen the sea for the first time at New York a year or two
before. The captain himself had taken the wheel since he had
no wheelman as they left New York. He himself had trained
his officers on the voyage to Europe, during the actual
assaults. He was gloomy. 'This will be a bad one.' It was
perhaps more superstition than gloom. For eight or ten hours
through the day inconsequent American swing music poured
out of the ship's loudspeakers. The American sailors liked to
work to the music. They went about, loose-limbed, chewing
gum, not mixing much with the soldiers. A negro sat in the
stern peeling potatoes endlessly.

At least one American officer though, did take advantage of the
postponement to write a final letter home.

Captain John Dulligan, US 1st Infantry Division

I love these men. They sleep all over the ship, on the decks,
in, on top, and underneath the vehicles. They smoke, play
cards, wrestle around and indulge in general horse-play.
They gather around in groups and talk mostly about girls,
home and experiences (with and without girls) . . . They are
good soldiers, the best in the world . . . Before the invasion of

North Africa, I was nervous and a little scared. During the Sicilian invasion I was so busy that the fear passed while I was working . . . This time we will hit a beach in France and from there on, only God knows the answer . . . I want you to know I love you with all my heart . . . and I pray that God will see fit to spare me to you and Ann and Pat.

At SHAEF HQ, at 9.45 p.m. on 4 June, after polling his deputy commanders and the weather forecasters of Group-Captain Stagg, Ike decided that the invasion should go ahead for the sixth.

General Dwight Eisenhower, Supreme Allied Commander

I'm quite positive we must give the order. I don't like it, but there it is . . . I don't see how we can possibly do anything else.

The die was cast.

To The Far Shore

---

5 June 1944

D-Day minus 1

In the pre-dawn darkness of the morning of 5 June, the day before D-Day, Eisenhower held another brief meeting of his weather forecasters and confirmed the decision of the previous evening. Among the first to know was his naval aide.

Captain H.C. Butcher, aide to Eisenhower
Diary, Shaef Advance (near Portsmouth), Monday 5 June 1944
D-Day is now almost irrevocably set for tomorrow morning, about 6.40, the time varying with tides at different beaches, the idea being to strike before high tide submerges obstacles which have to be cleared away . . .

The actual decision was confirmed and made final this morning at 4.15 after all the weather dope had been assembled. During yesterday the weather looked as if we might have to postpone for at least two days, until Thursday, with possibility of two weeks. Pockets of 'lows' existed all the way from western Canada across the United States and the Atlantic, and were coming our way. What was needed was a benevolent 'high' to counteract or divert at least one of the parading lows. During the night, that actually occurred. During the day, Force U, the US task force which started from Falmouth at the western end of the Channel at 6 a.m. Sunday, had become scattered, owing to the galelike wind sweeping southern England and the Channel. But Admiral Kirk had heard some encouraging news that the scattering was not as bad as feared. It was enough improved by the early-morning session to warrant the gamble, which only Ike could take, and he did, but with the chance of decent weather in his favor for possibly only two days. After that we hope to be ashore, and while weather will still be vitally important, we will have gotten over the historic hump.

Throughout the morning the invasion 'On' signal was flashed and passed to embarkation camps and the cramped, rain-lashed ships. The postponement had frayed everybody's nerves, and for most the invasion order was a relief, an end to the waiting. From sealed envelopes and packages were pulled maps and orders. Now, for the first time, the men and junior officers were fully informed about their exact landing place and the job that would be expected of them. At least one British soldier rushed to his diary breathlessly to record the news.

Corporal G.E. Hughes, 1st Battalion, Royal Hampshire Regiment
Diary, 5 June
D-Day tomorrow. Everybody quite excited. We land at Arromanches near Bayeux.

For one British Marine waiting ashore the news was delivered with a fearsome religious accompaniment.

Marine Stanley Blacker, RM
Our commanding officer said, 'This is it chaps,' and we were ordered to kneel in the road in three ranks. Then the local vicar appeared like magic, prayed and said 'Please God give them courage to face the enemy.' There was no saliva in my mouth. I thought I was sailing to my death.

Marine Blacker was to go to France in one of the smallest invasion craft, an LCM only 50 feet in length and completely open to the elements. Aside from its small crew it carried one lorry and four soldiers. Elsewhere, for the last but umpteenth time equipment was checked, and the men made ready. In the aft wardroom of USS *Carroll*, the deputy commander of the US 29th Division gathered his advanced headquarters staff for some final words of advice.

Brigadier-General Norman 'Dutch' Cota, US 29th Infantry Division, aged 51

This is different from any other exercise that you've had so far. The little discrepancies that we tried to correct on Slapton Sands are going to be magnified and are going to give way to incidents that you at first may view as chaotic. The air and naval bombardments are reassuring. But you're going to find confusion. The landing craft aren't going in on schedule, and people are going to be landed in the wrong place. Some won't be landed at all. The enemy will try, and will have some success, in preventing our gaining 'lodgement'. But we must improvise, carry on, not lose our heads.

Throughout the Allied invasion forces senior officers gave similar 'pep talks', but Cota's words would have a particular resonance because the 29th Division was bound for Omaha beach, the bloodiest of the Allied landings. In mid-afternoon the last of the seaborne forces, including the commandos of Lord Lovat's 1st Special Service Brigade, were given their orders and driven from their marshalling points close to the ports. Awaiting them was the Allied armada, a sight which many still rank as the most 'tremendous' of their lives.

W. Emlyn 'Taffy' Jones, 1st Special Service Brigade

We sped away in trucks – destination 'Rising Sun' Warsash, where our landing craft were waiting. Cries of 'Good luck' and ladies blowing kisses. They knowing full well what was about to happen. The scene that greeted us when we arrived was fantastic; lines upon lines of craft of various sizes and overhead a ceiling of literally hundreds of barrage balloons, so awe-inspiring. Well, this was the last of terra firma and before boarding our landing craft, for some unknown reason, I kissed the ground – perhaps a comical gesture to ease the tension.

In the late afternoon, in weather which was windy but with dashes of sun, the first of the 5,000 Allied ships weighed anchor and began leaving their south coast ports, doing so amid cheers and the sound of bagpipes (if they were British) and swing music (if they were American; the Andrews Sisters' 'The Boogie Woogie Bugle Boy of Company B' was much played that day). Outside port, the ships made for the assembly point off the Isle of Wight, dividing there into huge convoys, miles wide, bound for five beaches in Normandy.

W. Emlyn 'Taffy' Jones, 1st Special Service Brigade

There was a stiffish breeze but a clear night. Sailing down the Solent through an array of ships and craft that were at anchor was tremendously impressive. As we passed by the crews stood on deck and gave us a remarkable send-off with their cheering and waving, it made one feel so proud, and above all this glorious noise we could hear the pipes, the bagpipes of Bill Millin, our commando piper.

Lieutenant H.T. Bone, 2nd East Yorkshire Regiment

The Bar was closed and everyone got themselves ready for action stations. On both sides of the ship could be seen other slower convoys moving out past the Boom, one after another, all so familiar to us, yet this time just a little more exciting. There were shouts from the local people we worked with, a wail of bagpipes, multi-coloured signal flags, new paint and our divisional sign on every vessel. It was a memorable sight. Later that night just before we sailed I collected from everybody all their written orders and all other secret bumf and descended with them into the bowels of the ship where I burned them in the boiler, ascending afterwards in a lather of sweat.

Able Seaman J.H. Cooling, RN, aboard HMS *Scorpion*

Overhead went a great escort of fighters to protect us from attack and a very comforting and impressive sight it was too, but what was still more impressive was that as far as the eye could see were hundreds and hundreds of ships of all shapes and sizes, and you knew that beyond the horizon were more and still more.

Sergeant Richard W. Herklotz, 110th Field Artillery, US 29th Infantry Division

There were so many vessels, so many ships, that there was nowhere on the horizon that you could look and not see some type of vessel. Everywhere in the air there were barrage balloons on cables from each ship. It seemed that they filled the sky.

Alan Melville, RAF war correspondent

We weighed anchor just after half-past six. The great mass of ships slipped very quietly away. At sea, they formed up in their own convoys and forged steadily out to sea, bearing almost due south. The minesweepers went ahead of us and cleared narrow lanes in the minefields right up to the beaches – a magnificent job superbly carried out. The armada thinned and ships which had been lying almost alongside our own sheered away to port and starboard to keep to their

own courses. I went up on the boat-deck and stayed there all
night, with a disc ready on my recording gear in case we ran
into any excitement. The navigating officer told me with a
gloomy satisfaction that the number of our convoy was
thirteen. 'They don't usually do that,' he said. 'They usually
miss out thirteen. I don't like it.' He showed me the charts of
our crossing: where we would be at each hour, what ships
would be lying near us, at what points we would alter course.
Everything happened exactly as it had been set down on
paper. When we reached the minefields, the lanes through
them were marked. At eleven, when we were due to find the
battle-wagons of His Majesty's Navy on our port bow, there
they were . . . *Ramillies, Warspite, Frobisher, Mauritius, Dragon,
Arethusa*. It never got really dark that night; you were always
able to make out grey shadows and have a guess at what type
of craft they were. And it was certainly one of the quietest
nights I have ever experienced: the last quiet night I was to
enjoy for many weeks. I recorded nothing; there was nothing
to record. The mightiest invasion armada of all time was
crossing the Channel to smash an entrance into Europe, and
we might have been enjoying a day trip to Margate.

About nine o'clock the captain had asked me to read the
farewell messages from Admiral Ramsay, Admiral Talbot
and from General Eisenhower over the ship's broadcast
system. I put them over as well as I could, but all the time
I felt – quite wrongly, I know – that they were somehow
unreal and out of touch with the actual situation. They were
big pronouncements by big men, but it was our own little
convoy with its own escort and its own load of troops that
mattered most at that moment. We were well out to sea by
then and rolling quite a bit. The one padre on board held a
service on the quarter-deck; the rhino (a sort of mobile raft
with an outboard motor attached) which we were towing
ploughed through the swell thirty yards behind us. The men,
in their lifebelts and steel helmets, crowded round the padre
and we sang the same old hymns . . . 'Abide with me' and 'O

God our Help in Ages Past'. The padre had hoisted himself on to a packing case near the galley doorway and twice, when we took an extra heavy roll, he had to be steadied by the men round him to stop him taking a header in the middle of his prayers.

As the armada made its way slowly across the Channel, the men aboard the transports and landing ships were in muted, reflective mood.

Trooper Peter Davies, 1st East Riding Yeomanry
We were told to get our heads down, and to sleep. I don't think many did, I certainly didn't and the lads who were seasick certainly didn't. We talked about everything to pass the time – everything bar the thing we were going to do.

W. Emlyn 'Taffy' Jones, 1st Special Service Brigade
It took us a little while in the cramped conditions to settle down, sorting out our equipment, rucksacks, wireless sets, mortars, etc. and the smell of nauseous fumes of diesel and the time we would have to spend on board wouldn't make this trip very comfortable . . . Sleep was out of the question. Everyone to their own thoughts. A little joking and singing but with a certain apprehension of what tomorrow would bring. What would be their thoughts at home? – our families, wives and children, when they switched on the radio tomorrow morning? Hope they don't worry too much.

Alfred Leonard, Merchant Navy, aged 16
You were very aware that what was about to happen was going to be important. The atmosphere was full of that. I think the older men felt more fearful, but being young you don't look at the fear side of it so much, you just thought it's a big thing you're being part of.

Sombreness was not universal. On some ships there was something approaching a party spirit.

Frederick Wright, RN

Diary, 5 June

We have aboard our lovely fast steamship a lovely body of men, all in fine physical condition – Canadians – all in grand spirits, and all psychologically minded, for they all know what they are going to France for. Tonight I shall be playing dice with them, for that is their famous pastime.

Wright and his Canadian friends played dice until four the next morning. Even the wave of seasickness which swept over the armada as it hit mid-Channel did nothing to spoil the game. The troops and sailors on the small boats had a particularly rough and nauseous passage.

George Collard, 1st RM Armoured Support Regiment

The LCIs wallowed in the rough sea – the added armour to their sides, and the weight of the tanks, made them very low in the water. We slung hammocks where we could, sometimes between the tanks. Many were seasick, including the sailors. Most of the Marines had never served afloat, but I had experience of Northern Patrols on HMS *Diomede* and knew that hard-tack army biscuits taken in large amounts would act like concrete in the stomach and you never became seasick. No seasick tablets were given the Marine as was given to other troops – a point of pride I suppose.

William Seymour, RN

We had been postponed a day, but the sea did not seem much better to me on the day we sailed. The waves were coming over the side of the ship. Some of the tanks on the landing craft had broken their chains and were moving about in the very rough seas. A few had to turn back. But on we went, rocking from side to side.

I wasn't scared. If you're being seasick you feel like you're dying anyway.

G.G. Townsend, Combined Operations

Nearer and nearer we crept towards the enemy-held coastline as, in the eerie silence, anxious eyes scanned the agitated water for drifting mines and hostile German E-boats while the rest of us hurriedly removed the caps and inserted the fuses in the thousand rockets which lay patiently in their well-greased ramps, awaiting the electric charge which would send them soaring on their flight of destruction. There was a heart-stopping moment when the lookout on the fo'c'sle spotted something and, after a slight change in course, a large dark object floated past the port side, but we were never sure what it was, for this was no time for investigation, and so we plodded on.

Long before the armada reached this stage of its journey, back in the dying afternoon of the fifth, the parachutists and glider troops who would be the first Allied invaders to land in Normandy, and who were charged with seizing the left and right flanks of the invasion area, had paraded at their camps in the Midlands and the south of England prior to emplaning.

The Times war correspondent, attached to 6th Airborne Division

I watched the unit go to war at dusk on D–1 (the day before D-Day), parading with everybody from its brigadier downwards in blackened faces and wearing the camouflage smocks and rimless steel helmets of the airborne forces.

Each of the black-faced men appeared nearly as broad and thick as he was tall by reason of the colossal amount of equipment which the parachutist carried with him.

The brigadier and the lieutenant-colonel made brief speeches. 'We are history,' said the latter; there were three cheers, a short prayer and in the gathering of darkness they drove off to the aerodrome with the men in the first lorry singing, incredible as it seems, the notes of the Horst Wessel Song at the top of their voices.

At Welford aerodrome the men of the American 101st 'Screaming Eagles' Airborne Division were reviewed by Eisenhower himself, gaunt-faced, burdened with worry but still able to turn on his famous popular touch. Passing along the line of men, he asked one man:

'What is your job, soldier?'
'Ammunition bearer, sir.'
'Where is your home?'
'Pennsylvania, sir.'
'Did you get those shoulders working in a coal mine?'
'Yes, sir.'
'Good luck to you tonight, soldier.'

The parachutists of the US 101st and 82nd Airborne Divisions had enormous quantities of equipment stashed around their bodies to carry into battle. One US parachutist listed his load.

Donald Burgett, US 101st Airborne Division

My personal equipment consisted of: one suit of ODs, worn under my jump suit – this was an order for everyone – helmet, boots, gloves, main chute, reserve chute, Mae West, rifle, .45 automatic pistol, trench knife, jump knife, hunting knife, machete, one cartridge belt, two bandoliers, two cans of machine-gun ammo totalling 676 rounds of .30 ammo, 66 rounds of .45 ammo, one Hawkins mine capable of blowing the track off of a tank, four blocks of TNT; one entrenching tool with two blasting caps taped on the outside of the steel part, three first-aid kits, two morphine needles, one gas-mask, a canteen of water, three days' supply of K rations, two days' supply of D rations (hard tropical chocolate bars), six fragmentation grenades, one Gammon grenade, one orange smoke and one red smoke grenade, one orange panel, one blanket, one raincoat, one change of socks and underwear, two cartons of cigarettes and a few other odds and ends.

Unsurprisingly, Burgett could hardly walk and had to be helped into the plane by Air Corps personnel. On the flight over, Burgett and his comrades knelt on the floor and rested the weight of the gear and parachutes on the seat behind. The British paratroopers were only slightly less encumbered.

James Byrom, 6th Airborne Division

Fantastically upholstered, our pockets bulging with drugs and bandages, with maps and money and escaping gadgets, we stuffed ourselves into our jumping jackets and waddled, staggering under the weight of stretcher-bundles and kit-bags, to the lorries waiting to take us to the airfield. And there formidably arrayed on the tarmac runway was a line of camouflaged Dakotas, stretching away into a yellow sunset streaked with bars of black cloud. We had already met the crew of our aircraft, and they had assured us that the flight would be 'a piece of cake' – a little flak over the French coast, but really nothing to worry about. Now I thought they looked less confident, their Air Force charm a little strained.

Conscious of themselves as an elite, these airborne troops' morale was especially high (although veterans of most units report morale as 'good' in the twenty-four hours before D-Day). To be young and at war was even exciting. And the fear which came was mostly the fear of letting others down.

Corporal Ted Morris, 225 Para Field Ambulance, 6th Airborne Division

Before midnight on the fifth we went to the airport for parachute inspection, before the take off. There was a big lance-corporal with us, Taff Rowlands, a Welshman. He was a lad for a bit of fun and he kept kicking our parachutes and saying 'That bloody thing won't open.' That was the mood. You were young, you lapped it up.

Captain Philip Burkinshaw, 12th Yorkshire Parachute Battalion

Shortly before 11.30 p.m., the converted Stirling bomber of 38 Group which was to transport us to Normandy roared down the runway at RAF Keevil . . . and as the wheels of the heavily laden plane ceased to roll and became silent and I knew we were airborne, my mind was awhirl with mixed emotions and, I must confess, some fears, particularly the fear of being afraid. Would we be dropped on or near to the dropping zone, or perhaps due to change in the weather or wind speed, or a fault in navigation, well behind enemy lines; would I find the rendezvous; how would I shape up in front of my platoon in the stark reality and unaccustomed horrors of battle, and would I command and guide them as they deserved. The moment of reckoning was inexorably approaching for me, as it was for thousands of others in the air, on land and on sea.

As fleet after fleet of planes passed over the south coast of England, people left dance floors, pubs and beds to watch. Among those watching the first waves of British parachutists depart was Major-General Richard Gale, Commander of the

British 6th Airborne Division, and about to emplane himself for France.

Major-General Richard Gale, 6th Airborne Division

That night the moon shone. The sky was clear as one by one the great aircraft, boosting up their engines, roared down the runways. Next to go were the two parachute brigades and the engineers accompanying them. Then our turn came. My glider number was 70. I was accompanied by my ADC, Tom Haughton, David Baird my GSO 2, my personal escort, my signaller and my driver, and Rifleman Grey, Tom's batman. In the glider also were my Jeep with wireless set and two motor cycles. There were twelve of us in all. Before us lay an hour and a half's flight. We were to land just north of Ranville in the area captured by Nigel Poett and his brigade. We hoped that the sappers would have cleared away sufficient of the stakes to give us a reasonably safe landing zone.

During the few days I had been on the station I had got to know the station commander and his staff very well. I remember I had once said that I liked treacle very much indeed. It was a thoughtful, friendly, and very charming gesture, therefore, when Group Captain Surplice handed me a tin of treacle to take to France just as I was emplaning.

In the glider we all wore Mae Wests, and taking our places we all fastened ourselves in and waited for the jerk as the tug took the strain on the tow-rope. Soon it came and we could feel ourselves hurtling down the smooth tarmac. Then we were airborne and once again we heard the familiar whistle as the air rushed by and we glided higher and higher into the dark night.

At the same time as Gale's glider was being towed through the night, across the sky to the west General Matt Ridgway of the US

82nd Airborne Division sat with his 'stick' (a planeload of parachutists) aboard a C-47 transport.

General Matt B. Ridgway, US 82nd Airborne Division

We flew in a V of Vs, like a gigantic spearhead without a
shaft. England was on double daylight saving time, and it
was still full light, but eastward, over the Channel, the skies
were darkening. Two hours later night had fallen, and below
us we could see glints of yellow flame from the German anti-
aircraft guns on the Channel Islands. We watched them
curiously and without fear, as a high-flying duck may watch
a hunter, knowing that we were too high and far away for
their fire to reach us. In the plane the men sat quietly, deep
in their own thoughts. They joked a little and broke, now
and then, into ribald laughter. Nervousness and tension, and
the cold that blasted through the open door, had its effect
upon us all. Now and then a paratrooper would rise, lumber
heavily to the little bathroom in the tail of the plane, find he
could not push through the narrow doorway in his bulky
gear, and come back, mumbling his profane opinion of the
designers of the C-47 airplane. Soon the crew chief passed a
bucket around, but this did not entirely solve our problem. A
man strapped and buckled into full combat gear finds it
extremely difficult to reach certain essential portions of his
anatomy, and his efforts are not made easier by the fact that
his comrades are watching him, jeering derisively and
offering gratuitous advice.

Wing to wing, the big planes snuggled close in their tight
formation, we crossed to the coast of France. I was sitting
straight across the aisle from the doorless exit. Even at fifteen
hundred feet I could tell the Channel was rough, for we
passed over a small patrol craft – one of the check points for
our navigators – and the light it displayed for us was bobbing
like a cork in a millrace. No lights showed on the land, but in

the pale glow of a rising moon, I could clearly see each farm and field below. And I remember thinking how peaceful the land looked, each house and hedgerow, path and little stream bathed in the silver of the moonlight.

It was now midnight. Within minutes the first parachutists would be jumping out over Normandy.

D-Day

6 June 1944

I'm glad I'm here. I'd hate to miss what is probably the biggest battle that will ever happen to us.

Anonymous Allied soldier

Gefreiter Werner Kortenhaus of the 21st Panzer Division stared into the Normandy night above him. On patrol north of Falaise he and his four comrades had become alarmed by the sounds of aircraft flying overhead. Usually aircraft passed high above them but these were flying low, much lower than usual, then zooming up. They suspected that agents or supplies were being dropped for the French Resistance and decided to investigate. They found nothing, but still they could hear aircraft. Worried, Kortenhaus and his patrol turned back to their tank harbour.

Gefreiter Werner Kortenhaus, 21st Panzer Division

As we got close to the village where our tanks were dug in, the moonlight was coming through the clouds, and we could see that the crews were at their tanks. This was unusual because most of them would normally have been asleep. 'What's going on?' I asked. It occurred to me that it might be some sort of night exercise. They said, 'No, it's an alarm.' This was about 00.45. As the others prepared the tank, I remembered that my laundry was still with the French woman who did our washing. I woke her and said, 'I need my clothes straight away.' She said, 'But they're still wet.' I said, 'I must have them anyway,' and paid for them, and ran to my tank.

As Kortenhaus hurried back to his tank, the first of the Allied airborne troops, parachutists and a small glider force from the British 6th Airborne Division, had already landed near the Orne River. As the minutes passed more and more British parachutists descended on Normandy, like so much confetti in the night. Nearly 5000 of them had landed by 1 a.m.

Report: RAF 296 Squadron

At 23.00 hrs [5 June] the first aircraft took off, followed closely by the other aircraft of Phase I. All aircraft followed the same route to LITTLEHAMPTON and from there to the French coast. The first aircraft encountered little opposition while carrying out the drop.

Adventures in the rear of the machine delayed F/Lt. WHITTY'S drop. The first man of the stick collapsed and fell on the doors over the jumping hole. The aircraft circled off the coast while he was lifted and one door opened. This meant a delay of 10 minutes before he was thrust out and 7 troops dropped on the first run over the DZ [Drop Zone]. On the second run the other two men jumped. For the other two aircraft of this phase everything went according to plan. A little light flak was experienced after dropping but was easily evaded.

Parachutists falling over and blocking the jump doors was to be a surprisingly common occurrence during the Normandy drop. Mostly it was occasioned by the pilots taking action to avoid flak.

Corporal Ted Morris, 225 Para Field Ambulance, 6th Airborne Division

The green light went on and we started to jump . . . about two or three did so, but when Bud Abbott went to jump he fell over because the plane lurched and he became wedged across the door. We had to drag him away before we could jump. I got out, but they sat Bud Abbott in the corner of the plane – it was too late for him to jump. But Abbott came back to Normandy that night, hitching a ride on a glider, and landing with the ruddy glider reinforcements. The best of it was that Abbott was a conscientious objector. We had about a dozen of them in the para field ambulance unit – they wouldn't shoot or fight, but they acted as orderlies.

One of the more bizarre adventures of the drop happened aboard an Abermarle aircraft of RAF 296 Squadron.

Flight Lieutenant J.G. Hayden, RAF

In one of the aircraft there was a dog which belonged to one of the paratroopers, but the dog didn't want to drop. The crew had an awful difficult job chasing it around the aircraft to get its parachute fastened to the static line and then to throw it out after the paratroopers.

For some of the human British parachutists the drop was relatively straightforward, landing near their DZs and quickly finding friendly company in the darkness.

Captain Philip Burkinshaw, 12th Yorkshire Parachute Battalion

At approximately ten minutes to one, with some assistance from Cockcroft beside me, I got up and made my way over to the long hole at the back of the Stirling. The chaps followed and stood behind me in their jumping order. The hatches had been raised by the RAF despatchers and the blast of air flowing up into the plane was fresh and invigorating. I stood on the edge of the hole, parachute static line trailing behind me inside the fuselage. At about 500 ft it was possible as I looked down to make out the dull grey sea below in the light of the moon which was occasionally visible through the scurrying clouds. Suddenly, as our pilot cut back on his engines, a white line of cliffs passed by underneath and I realized that this was at last the Normandy coast. Almost immediately afterwards a patchwork of fields and hedgerows cut by narrow white lines was clearly visible. Moments passed – the 'Action Stations' red light was switched on up front by our pilot, followed quickly by the green, and the command 'Go' from the RAF despatcher. I stepped off into space, the verse from the poem, 'Paratroops', vividly coming to mind:

> Out of the hatch we are hurled, and the body that bore us
> fades to a shadow, its murmur a breath of the breeze,
> weather and earth and the passage of arms are before us,
> battle may blaze before half of us rise from our knees.

During the next few moments I fell, aware of nothing apart from a rush of air until the comforting jerk on my back and shoulder webbing told me that my chute had opened. I then became aware of aircraft overhead and my chute canopy swelling out above me as I lazily drifted down to earth. My first positive action was to pull on the pin to release the kitbag, containing the wireless and reserve ammunition, secured to my right leg. I pulled but nothing happened and soon I realized that the bag and I were inseparable! By this time I was nearing *terra firma* and it was obvious that the defences were coming to life – tracer crisscrossing up into the sky and some on the ground. I hit the ground with a fair bump and crumpled up. Although the kitbag was still on my leg I was none the worse for that. A tap on my quick release box and I was out of my parachute harness and on my feet. Shortly, I came across two other figures walking in the same direction as myself and challenged them with my Sten at the ready. To my great delight they were two of the lads from my platoon, and having briefly exchanged mutual congratulations, we moved on together. After about a quarter of a mile or so we ended up at a small copse where I found three other chaps.

Corporal Ted Morris, 225 Para Field Ambulance, 6th Airborne Division

I dropped near Ranville church, about a quarter of a mile from it across a field. It was the usual thing when we landed, there was a password and God knows what. Someone came out of the darkness as I landed and I never used the password – they could have been German, anybody at all for all I could see. I said, 'Who's that?' He said, 'It's me.' It was a bloke named Cooper. He'd actually jumped next to me, so the drop system worked for us.

James Byrom, 6th Airborne Division

A shadow darted from a nearby tree, and I was joined in the open by the huge Sten-gunner with the black face. The whites of his eyes gleamed in the moonlight, and for all my weariness I found myself on the verge of giggles.

'You speak the lingo, tosh? All right then, you go up and knock on the door, and we'll give you coverin' fire. I'll stay 'ere and my mate'll creep round the other side of the yard so's to cover you proper.' I knocked once and nothing happened. I knocked again, louder this time. Suddenly there was the clamour of French voices. Footsteps approached the door, withdrew, hesitated, then approached again. The door opened.

On the way I had been searching for suitable words with which to introduce ourselves – some calming, yet elegant, phrase worthy of the French gift of expression and of their infallible flair for the dramatic moment. But at the sight of the motherly, middle-aged peasant the gulf of the years disappeared, and I might have been back in 1939, an

English tourist on a walking tour dropping in to ask for a glass of cider and some camembert.

'*Excusez-nous, Madame. Nous sommes des parachutistes anglais faisant partie du Débarquement Allié.*'

There was a moment of scrutiny, then the woman folded me in her arms. The tears streamed down her face, and in between kisses she was shouting for her husband, for lamps, for wine. In a moment I was carried by the torrent of welcome into the warm, candle-lit kitchen. Bottles of cognac and Calvados appeared on the table, children came clattering down the wooden stairs and we found ourselves – an evil-looking group of camouflaged cut-throats – surrounded and overwhelmed by the pent-up emotions of four years. The farmer and his wife wanted us to stay and drink, to laugh and cry and shake hands over and over again. They wanted to touch us, to tell us all about the Occupation, and to share with us their implacable hatred of the Boche. It seemed that the moment so long awaited could not be allowed to be spoilt by realities, till every drop of emotion was exhausted. I was nearly as much affected as they were. Warmed by the fiery trickle of Calvados, I rose to this – certainly one of the greatest occasions of my life – so completely that I forgot all about the Drop, all about the marshes and the Battery. It was the sight of my companions, bewildered by all this emotion and talk, automatically drinking glass after glass, that suddenly reminded me of what we had come for. I began politely to insist on answers to questions which had already been brushed aside more than once: Where were we? How far away were the nearest Germans? Once more the questions were ignored. '*Ah, mon Dieu, ne nous quittez pas maintenant! Ah, les pauvres malheureux! Ils sont tous mouillés!*'

Sixty miles across Normandy to the west, the Airborne's American comrades began jumping from their Dakotas at 1.30 a.m.

General Matt B. Ridgway, US 82nd Airborne Division

Beside the door, a red light glowed. Four minutes left. Down the line of bucket seats, the No. 4 man in the stick stood up. It was Captain Schouvaloff, brother-in-law of Fëdor Chaliapin, the opera singer. He was a get-rich-quick paratrooper, as I was, a man who had had no formal jump training. I was taking him along as a language officer, for he spoke both German and Russian, and we knew that in the Cotentin Peninsula, which we were to seize, the Germans were using captured Russians as combat troops.

A brilliant linguist, he was also something of a clown. Standing up, wearing a look of mock bewilderment on his face, he held up the hook on his static line – the life line of the parachutist which jerks his canopy from its pack as he dives clear of the plane.

'Pray tell me,' said Schouvaloff, in his thick accent, 'what does one do with this strange device?'

That broke the tension. A great roar of laughter rose from the silent men who were standing now, hooked up and ready to go.

'Are we downhearted,' somebody yelled.

'HELL NO!' came back the answering roar.

A bell rang loudly, a green light glowed. The jumpmaster, crouched in the door, went out with a yell – 'Let's go!' With a paratrooper, still laughing, breathing hard on my neck, I leaped out after him.

John Houston, US 101st Airborne Division

Left foot forward, on the edge of the door to push off, swing the right leg out to make a half turn, and get your back to the prop blast, feet together, knees bent, arms on the reserve chute, head down. The static line jerks and the chute snaps open perfectly. We are so close to the ground that there is no time to do any sightseeing on the way down. Hands on the risers to pull up against the shock of landing. The ground is coming fast. Thump, one roll. This is France.

A cow stands looking from a few yards away. She seems curious but not excited. There is no wind, so the chute collapses quietly. Unsnap the harness and get the rifle out of its boot. This is done quickly, then the question 'Where am I and where is everyone else?'

Each man in the division had been issued a little cricket snapper to use in place of a password. One click is the challenge and two clicks the answer. I hear someone moving along the hedgerow and click the cricket. Two clicks come back, and Shedio and Spitz come out of the shadows. We whisper together for a minute. There is no firing nearby, but we don't want to announce that we are here. Mac hears us and joins the group. We move along in the direction of the flight of our plane, and soon gather fifteen men. This is everyone from our plane except Bray, who, as Number 16, jumped last.

General Matt B. Ridgway and Private John Houston were among the lucky that night, for the American drop, centred on the village of Ste Mere Eglise, threatened to assume the proportions of a disaster. A bank of cloud disorientated the pilots, some of whom were anyway panicked by the necklaces of incandescent flak and tracer shooting up from the German defences. There had been some dispersement on the British drop, but members of the US 101st and 82nd were dropped too high, too low, over the sea and as much as 30 miles from their objective. Many of them were in action almost as soon as their boots hit the earth.

Donald Burgett, US 101st Airborne Division

I lay on my back shaking my head; the chute had collapsed itself. The first thing I did was to draw my .45, cock the hammer back and slip the safety on. Troopers weren't issued pistols, but my father had purchased this one from a gun collector in Detroit and sent it to me in a package containing a date and nut cake. Captain Danes kept it in his possession for me and let me carry it on field problems. He had returned it to me when we entered the marshaling area.

The pilots were supposed to drop us between 600 and 700 feet, but I know that my drop was between 250 and less than 300 feet. The sky was lit up like the Fourth of July. I lay there for a moment and gazed at the spectacle. It was awe inspiring, I have never seen anything like it before or since. But I couldn't help wondering at the same time if I had got the opening shock first or hit the ground first; they were mighty close together.

The snaps on the harness were almost impossible to undo, and as I lay there on my back working on them, another plane came in low and diagonally over the field. The big ship was silhouetted against the lighter sky with long tongues of exhaust flame flashing along either side of the body. Streams of tracers from several machine guns flashed upward to converge on it. Then I saw vague, shadowy figures of troopers plunging downward. Their chutes were pulling out of the pack trays and just starting to unfurl when they hit the ground. Seventeen men hit the ground before their chutes had time to open. They made a sound like large ripe pumpkins being thrown down to burst against the ground.

'That dirty son of a bitch of a pilot,' I swore to myself, 'he's hedgehopping and killing a bunch of troopers just to save his own ass. I hope he gets shot down in the Channel and drowns real slow.'

Small private wars erupted to the right and left, near and far, most of them lasting from fifteen minutes to half an hour, with anyone's guess being good as to who the victors were. The heavy hedgerow country muffled the sounds, while the night air magnified them. It was almost impossible to tell how far away the fights were and sometimes even in what direction. The only thing I could be sure of was that a lot of men were dying in this nightmarish labyrinth. During this time I had no success in finding anyone, friend or foe. To be crawling up and down hedgerows, alone, deep in enemy country with a whole ocean between yourself and the nearest allies sure makes a man feel about as lonely as a man can get.

For the French civilians watching the 13,000 American parachutists come down over the Cherbourg peninsula the drop presented a remarkable spectacle. The American parachutist himself was no less interesting a phenomenon.

Alexandre Reynaud, Mayor of Ste Mere Eglise

All around us, the paratroopers were landing with a heavy thud on the ground. By the light of the fire, we clearly saw a man manipulating the cables of his parachute. Another, less skillful, came down in the middle of the flames. Sparks flew, and the fire burned brighter. The legs of another paratrooper contracted violently as they were hit. His raised arms came down. The giant parachute, billowing in the wind, rolled over the field with the inert body.

A big white sheet hung from an old tree covered with ivy. A man was hanging from the end. Holding onto the branches, he came slowly down, like a snake. Then he tried to unbuckle his belt. The *Flak* were only a few yards away. They saw him. The machine guns fired their sinister patter; the poor man's hands fell, and the body swung loosely to and fro from the cables.

A few hundred yards in front of us, near the sawmill, a big transport plane crashed to the ground, and soon there was a second fire raging.

The belfry sounded the alarm once again.

Now we were directly in the line of fire of the machine gun in the belfry. The bullets hit the ground right near us.

It was a lovely night, lit by large swaths of moonlight.

Meanwhile, a paratrooper appeared suddenly in the midst of the group at the pump. He pointed his machine gun at us, but when he realized we were French, he didn't shoot. A German sentry hiding behind a tree let out a yell and ran away as fast as he could. The paratrooper tried to ask a few questions, but since no one in the group could speak English, he crossed the road and disappeared into the night.

Above the fire, the big planes glided by uninterruptedly, dropping their human cargoes on the other side of the cemetery

. . . .

Around 3 o'clock, on the square under the trees, the flash of lighted matches appeared, followed by the red glow of lighted cigarettes, then an electric light on the body of a parachutist. By the light of that lamp, it looked as though men were lying at the base of the trees. We whispered about it for a long time: were they Germans or British? Given the situation, we didn't think Germans would be lying on the ground, but standing up or ambushed in houses.

Little by little, the night began to dissolve, and a milky dawn began to filter through. As the contours became more precise, we were astonished to see that the town was occupied neither by the Germans nor the British, but by the Americans. The first thing we recognized were the big round helmets we had seen illustrated in the German magazines. Some of the soldiers were sleeping or smoking under the trees; others, lined up behind the wall and the town weighing building, stood with arms in hand, watching the Church still held by the enemy. Their wild, neglected look reminded us of Hollywood movie gangsters. Their helmets were covered with a khaki colored net, their faces were, for the most part, covered with grime, like those of mystery book heroes.

The more enthusiastic and *sympathique* French civilians proved useful to American parachutists still wondering exactly where in hell they were.

Donald Burgett, US 101st Airborne Division

Just then three young girls, about eighteen or so, came out of a doorway and ran to me yelling, 'Vive les Americains.' Then, with a lot of hugging and kissing, they offered me a jug of wine, which I refused. Not that I don't like wine, but I just didn't feel like being poisoned, and at this time I didn't trust anyone. The Lieutenant had arrived by this time, and asked if anyone could speak English. The girls said, in very poor English, that there was an old woman who could; she used to teach it in school. One of the girls brought her to us. Muir asked her where we were, and even though she told us we still didn't know. The Lieutenant brought his map out and the old woman pointed to the coastal town, 'Ravenoville', and told us there were other Americans here, but also many Germans all around and even in the town itself. We thanked her, then Lieutenant Muir cussed and swore as he examined the map, for we were about twelve miles from our drop zone and our objectives. Muir let out a string of oaths that ended with the Air Corps; 'They dropped us all over the whole damned Cherbourg Peninsula,' he said. 'Who the hell's side are they on anyway? Now we've got to fight through nine towns and twelve miles of enemy country just to get to where we were supposed to land and start fighting in the first place.'

All that night spats of violence erupted over the Cotentin as US airborne troops fought their way to their objectives, and fought Germans wherever they found them.

General Matt B. Ridgway, US 82nd Airborne Division

My own little command group of eleven officers and men set up division headquarters in an apple orchard, on almost the exact spot we had planned to be before we left England. Hal Clark's boys had not failed us. They had put us down on the button.

The Germans were all around us, of course, sometimes within five hundred yards of my CP, but in the fierce and confused fighting that was going on all about, they did not launch the strong attack that could have wiped out our eggshell perimeter defense.

This was in large part due to the dispersion of the paratroopers. Wherever they landed, they began to cut every communication line they could find, and soon the German commanders had no more contact with their units than we had with ours. When the German commander of the 91st Division found himself cut off from the elements of his command, he did the only thing left to do. He got in a staff car and went out to see for himself what the hell had gone on in this wild night of confused shooting. He never found out. Just at daylight a patrol of paratroopers stopped his car and killed him as he reached for his pistol. The lieutenant commanding the patrol told me the story with great glee.

'Well,' I said, 'in our present situation, killing division commanders does not strike me as being particularly hilarious. But I congratulate you. I'm glad it was a German division commander you got.'

Donald Burgett, US 101st Airborne Division

'What's your plan?' one of the men asked. After a little thought the Lieutenant answered, 'A head-on attack and the sooner the better, so let's go.' He jumped up and started running toward the group of houses across the field, yelling as he went. We all jumped up and followed him, yelling and screaming at the top of our lungs. We automatically spread out and fired as we ran through the fields, apple orchards and right up to the houses themselves. I saw my first Kraut running through the trees on an angle toward our right flank. I stopped, took a good sight on him and squeezed the trigger. The rifle bucked against my shoulder. I don't remember hearing the shot or feeling the recoil, but the

German spun sideways and fell face first out of sight in the grass. Another Kraut stepped around the corner of a building, stopped and just stood there looking down at the spot where the first soldier fell. He was facing me. I had a good straight-on shot at his chest and took careful aim. Again the rifle bucked against my shoulder, and he too fell face forward.

Fighting was at a fever pitch now. All around, men were running between buildings, through yards and over fences. Three troopers ran through a gate in a hedge surrounding a house and almost immediately there came a long ripping burst of a Kraut machine gun. The three Americans died in the weed-choked front yard. Automatically other troopers shunned the yard but moved on the double on all fours down the hedges on either side until they were in throwing distance of the house and grenaded it. One trooper leaped through a side window, fired several rounds from his M-1, then stepped to the front door and motioned that it was all clear. Running through the open gateway, past the dead and into the house, I saw a German machine gun, a lot of empty shells and a couple of boxes of ammo under the window to the left of the door. No Germans or bodies were in the house. Evidently they had cleared out when the first grenades hit, leaving their gun behind. The trooper who went through the window said they went out the back way just as he entered. He fired at them but none of them went down. We left the house and rejoined the others in clearing out the remaining houses.

Two troopers came out of one of the buildings carrying a case of German hand grenades between them. They ran down the street throwing potato mashers into windows and apertures in the walls. German soldiers were pulling out of town by the back way and disappearing into fields and woods surrounding the town. German dead were scattered about in the houses, ditches and fields. I don't know how many I hit. The ones that fell when I fired would have dropped anyway if a bullet had passed close to them.

After occupying the enemy positions we wondered why they had given up so easily, for the walls were all of stone and two feet thick, with small rifle apertures to fire out from, and many of the rooms were filled with food, ammo, and weapons. Over 200 Germans had vacated these positions, leaving behind thirty dead and about seventy-five prisoners. Four of our men had been killed. Phillips could speak some German and he questioned the prisoners as to why their comrades had pulled out. They said that when we came running at them yelling, hollering and shooting across the open fields, they figured the whole invasion was directed right at them and never dreamed that only twenty men armed with rifles would attack over 200 well-armed soldiers in stone fortifications.

If the British and American parachutists had a tough time of it, few of them would have swopped positions with the airborne troops arriving in Normandy that night by glider, crash-landing in tiny fields all too frequently occupied by 'Rommel's asparagus' and other anti-landing devices.

The Times war correspondent, attached to 6th Airborne Division

Our glider was a Horsa, which looks almost like a normal aeroplane except that its wings are set farther back to compensate for the lack of engine weight forward. It is generally used as a troop-carrier. Heavy weights are carried in Hamilcar gliders, which look like nothing on earth except possibly streamlined pantechnicon vans.

Our trip to France was made in almost complete darkness, and we had seen few signs of *Flak* or of firing from the ground when the pilot of our tug aircraft slipped the tow rope and we headed down. Gliders, just before they land, usually put their noses down through 45 degrees and then pull them up sharply to land in as short a space as possible. Parachutist pathfinders had been before us to clear away as many obstacles as they could, but even if the obstacles had not been removed we should have been able to get down safely provided the fuselage itself did not strike one of the iron or wooden posts which the Germans had compelled the French farmers to put up all over their open fields.

Ours, however, was in no way a normal landing. We hit a telegraph pole, and crashed in such a way as to break the back of our glider in two places. Our business then was to get out as quickly as possible and scatter because, for all we knew, we might have landed right in front of a German position, and if they had opened fire immediately we should all have been trapped.

The crash had jammed fast the door in the fuselage, but after some kicking and banging against the glider's plywood walls we got out into the night air. Immediately fire was opened on us, and we had several casualties. I was slightly hurt and later went off in search of divisional headquarters and of stretcher-bearers for our wounded.

Those landing by glider included Major-General Gale of the 6th Airborne, arriving as part of the division's reinforcement in the early hours of the morning.

Major-General Richard Gale, 6th Airborne Division
We were flying at about five thousand feet and we soon knew the coast was under us, for we were met by a stream of flak. It was weird to see this roaring up in great golden chains past the windows of the glider, some of it being apparently between us and the tug aircraft. Looking out I could see the canal and the river through the clouds; for the moon was by now fairly well overcast and the clear crisp moonlight we had hoped for was not there. Nevertheless here we were.

In a few moments Griffiths said, 'We are over the landing zone now and will be cast off at any moment.' Almost as soon

as he had said this we were. The whistling sound and the roar
of the engines suddenly died down: no longer were we
bumping about, but gliding along on a gloriously steady
course. Away went the tug aircraft with Crawford in it back
to England. Round we turned, circling lower and lower;
soon the pilot turned round to tell us to link up as we were
just about to land. We all linked up by putting our arms
round the man next to us. We were also, as I have said,
strapped in. In case of a crash this procedure would help us
to take the shock.

I shall never forget the sound as we rushed down in our
final steep dive, then we suddenly flattened out, and soon
with a bump, bump, bump, we landed on an extremely
rough stubble field. Over the field we sped and then with a
bang we hit a low embankment. The forward undercarriage
wheel stove up through the floor, the glider spun round on its
nose in a small circle and, as one wing hit one of those
infernal stakes, we drew up to a standstill.

We opened the door. Outside all was quiet.

Captain Philip Burkinshaw, 12th Yorkshire
Parachute Battalion

One glider, which just missed the copse, floated down almost
on top of us like some giant bat and ground to a halt after a
very rough landing in the field beside us. It proved to be the
one which carried the Divisional Commander, Major-General Richard ('Windy') Gale. Apparently slightly stunned
and somewhat shaken up by the heavy landing, he lumbered
up to me and bellowed in his customary direct manner:
'Where the hell am I?' I tried to enlighten him with my
assessment of our position and told him where the CO could
be found, but I must confess my confidence momentarily
suffered a setback! I hasten to add that 'Windy' was the
nickname for our respected Divisional Commander because
of his surname and in no way implied any weakness of nerve;

in fact, the opposite was very much the case.

About this time we had our first encounter with the enemy. A staff car containing, it was subsequently discovered, the officer in command of the bridge defences, came at speed down the road from the direction of Ranville, followed by a motor-cycle escort. The armoured car somehow survived the fusillade of small-arms fire directed at it, but the motor cyclist was killed, his machine careering off the road into the ditch. The armoured car proceeded on its way to the bridge and was taken care of by Major Howard's men. When captured, the German officer, a Major Schmidt, who was fairly badly wounded, apparently asked to be shot as he had let his Führer down by failing to hold the bridges. He made it plain, however, that he was confident that we would all soon be thrown back into the sea!

After this brief initial encounter, the battalion proceeded on down the road to Le Bas de Ranville, taking it with little difficulty and being joined there by other members of the battalion who, having landed outside the dropping zone, had not managed to reach the rendez-vous. Digging in furiously and encouraged the while by some mortaring and shelling from the direction of Caen, we were in position by 4 a.m.

Some hours previously the news of the airborne landings had been passed to the headquarters at St Lô of one of 'Windy' Gale's opposite numbers, General Marck of the Wehrmacht. The news arrived during a small surprise birthday party for the general, a veteran of the Eastern Front.

Major Friedrich Hayn, Wehrmacht Staff Officer

At 01.11 hours – an unforgettable moment – the field telephone rang. Something important was coming through: while listening to it the General stood up stiffly, his hand gripping the edge of the table. With a nod he

beckoned his chief of staff to listen in. 'Enemy parachute
troops dropped east of the Orne estuary. Main area Bréville–
Ranville and the north edge of the Bavent forest. Counter-
measures are in progress.' This message from 716 Intelligence
Service struck like lightning.

Was this, at last, the invasion, the storming of '*Festung
Europa*'? Someone said haltingly, 'Perhaps they are only
supply troops for the French Resistance?' . . . The day
before, in the St-Malo area, many pieces of paper had been
passing from hand to hand or had been dropped into the
letterboxes; they all bore a mysterious announcement: *La
carotte rouge est quittée.* Furthermore, our wireless operators
had noticed an unusually large volume of coded traffic. Up
till now, however, the Resistance groups had anxiously
avoided all open action; they were put off by the danger
of premature discovery and consequent extermination.

Whilst the pros and cons were still being discussed, 709
Infantry Division from Valognes announced: 'Enemy para-
chute troops south of St-Germain-de-Varreville and near
Ste-Marie-du-Mont. A second drop west of the main
Carentan–Valognes road on both sides of the Merderet
river and along the Ste-Mere-Eglise–Pont-l'Abbé road.
Fighting for the river crossings in progress.' It was now
about 01.45 hours.

Three dropping zones near the front! Two were clearly at
important traffic junctions. The third was designed to hold
the marshy meadows at the mouth of the Dives and the
bridge across the canalized Orne near Ranville. It coincided
with the corps boundary, with the natural feature which
formed our northern flank but would serve the same purpose
for an enemy driving south. It is the task of parachute troops,
as advance detachments from the air, to occupy tactically
important areas and to hold them until ground troops, in this
case landing forces, fight their way through to them and
incorporate them into the general front. Furthermore in
Normandy they could, by attacking the strongpoints im-

mediately west of the beach, paralyze the coastal defences. If it really was the task of the reported enemy forces to keep open the crossings, it meant that a landing would soon take place and they were really in earnest!

Erich Marck proved to be an exception among German Generals that June morning. He mobilized his 87th Corps almost immediately. Other senior German commanders proved sluggish, their bewilderment and indecisiveness improved by the Allied ruse of dropping several thousand dummy parachutists. Worse still for the German Army, numerous of its commanders were away from headquarters. General Dollman and others were in Rennes for a *kriegspiel* (ironically enough with the scenario that the Allies would land in Normandy), and General Edgar Feuchtinger of the crack 21st Panzer Division was nowhere to be found. Rommel himself was in Germany, convinced that the weather was too bad to allow an invasion. It was a frustrating experience for German troops ready and willing to encounter the enemy.

Gefreiter Werner Kortenhaus, 21st Panzer Division

I would say we were ready to march at 2 a.m. at the latest. As well as the earlier alarm, news of an airborne landing at Caen had meanwhile come through on the telephone, and we were ready to go. The engines of the tanks were running, but we didn't receive any marching orders. We thought, 'If we have to march, let's go now while it's dark and the enemy planes can't see us.' We waited for orders, and we waited. Just stood there, inactive by our tanks. We couldn't understand why we weren't getting any orders at all.

As Kortenhaus waited by his tank, and night began to pass into grey dawn, the largest armada of ships ever assembled had crossed the Channel and lay off the invasion beaches of Normandy. The sea was crammed with ships from the Cherbourg peninsula to the mouth of the Orne. The Americans were to land first, the H-Hour (landing time) for their two beaches in the west, codenamed Omaha and Utah, being 06.30. The British and Canadians were to land an hour later, at 07.30, on beaches Gold, Juno and Sword, the landing priority dictated by the tide conditions. Contrary to German expectations, the Allies would go in at low tide. Aboard the Allied ships there were last-minute pep talks, breakfast (for those who could eat it), and farewells. The first of the assault waves began clambering into their beaching craft. By 05.25 they were well on their way to shore, launched, in some cases, over eleven miles away.

At that same moment warships in the British sector began a mighty bombardment of German coastal defences, lobbing enormous shells at batteries and pill-boxes. Ships in the American sector began a bombardment of coastal positions at 05.45. Allied rocket ships rushed in and released salvo after salvo at German positions. From the air RAF and USAAF bombers released hundreds of tons of explosives. The noise was enormous, the sight awesome.

Ken Wright, 1st Special Service Brigade
Up at 4.15 a.m. Breakfast 4.45. It was quite unpleasantly rough, and I did not feel much like eating. Went on to the upper deck about 5 o'clock just in time to see a destroyer blow up and sink within 5 minutes, a mile or two to port: I think through striking a mine. It was rather appalling. The ship just cracked in half, and the two ends folded together as if it were a pocket knife closing.

Frederick Wright, RN
Diary, 6 June
The big battleships have opened up a heavy bombardment – the air is absolutely full of planes. I have just been up on our gun turret – a fine view from there. Our lads are singing 'You are my sunshine' – full of good spirits . . . What a wonderful sight – clear visibility . . . Still the big battleships are banging

away like Hell . . . All I can hear is Bang! Crash! Bang! Crash!
– We are all amazed! Cannot realize the truth – not one
German plane to be seen. I can still see our invasion barges,
pitching and tossing, almost turning over.

Lieutenant-Commander R.C. Macnab, RN, aboard HMS *Glasgow*, supporting 2nd American Army

One six-inch gun battery on Pointe du Hoc in particular
came in for a terrible time; enormous explosions rent it
continuously for about 20 minutes and later it received
many broadsides from the US battleship *Texas*. Almost
the entire point is now crumbled into the sea, and the
battery never fired a shot . . . Our orders contained the
positions of every gun, machine gun, mortar, beach obstacle
etc. on the shore – we almost knew what the Huns were
having for breakfast – if we hadn't interrupted them. Some
new guns and smoke throwers were installed two days
previously – but we had them lined up as targets and
destroyed them before the landings. Two towers had been
removed the day before, but we had been tipped off not to
look for them as landmarks!

Able Seaman R.E. Hughes, aboard HMS *Glasgow*
Diary, 6 June
05.45 I said a few prayers and am thinking of you all at home.
We started shelling the beaches and approaches. RAF still
bombing. Y turret is the first to open fire, our targets being
gun batteries and insistent smoke mortars. Continued patrol
by RAF gives us a grand feeling.

Anne de Vigneral, Ver-sur-Mer
Diary, 6 June
I quickly wake the children – we take clothes and blankets
(prepared and ready at the foot of each bed for a month or

more) and beneath a frightful noise run towards the trench
and tumble in. The house trembles and the windows dance –
we pile into the centre and stay crouched. Eight people in
this narrow pipe 5 m long by 0.5 m wide! . . . from this
moment we are dumb with terror and deafened; the whole
sky is lit up, flashes, fires, tracer bullets, shells fall all around
us and we hear windowpanes fall out. Fires break out some
way away (it was the Château de Courseulles). Sometimes
we no longer see the nearby house because so much dust and
soil is flying around . . .

M. Leveel, aged 19

Everything was exploding into violent action. It is impossible
to imagine the noise, and suddenly in the direction of
Vierville we saw this strange orange-red light. At first we
thought it was the sun, but there were many lights, changing
colour and shape. We decided to leave the house to go and
take cover in some trenches we had dug, but everyone kept
getting in each other's way as we rushed about. There were
about ten people in the house, my parents, some friends, a
couple of cousins etc., and we just couldn't think straight.
There was a certain amount of nervousness and apprehension too. Then we heard another strange noise, a sort of
swoosh, and out to sea we saw something rising high in the air,
rather like giant fireworks. There were thousands of them. I
didn't find out till some years later what they were. They
were rockets fired from ships. Even 20 km away the noise was
unbelievable.

Marine Stanley Blacker, RM

As we went in to land the noise, the noise was deafening.
Behind us the *Rodney* was firing ten-ton salvos, which almost
shattered your ears. In front, I could see all the coast and
villages in smoke and flames.

G.G. Townsend, Combined Operations

I received and passed to the Captain a message informing us
that H-Hour had been delayed by a matter of minutes,
which did nothing to calm down the feeling of excitement,
until, at last, we were aiming ourselves at the target area
which was exactly as depicted on the photographs removed
from our briefing package, the church spire of the village of
Bernieres-sur-Mer clearly visible. We thundered in, full
speed ahead, because there were no sophisticated adjust-
ments to be made, the only range finder being the craft itself.
With the command, *'Fire One'*, we launched our first salvo
over the heads of the assault craft in front of us, our own craft
almost shuddering to a halt from the thrust of the rockets as
they sped skywards. Each successive salvo bombarded the
bridge with base plates, and spray from the water cooled the
deck, and the whole craft, now completely enshrouded in a
great pall of choking smoke, was shaken and subjected to so
much strain that she seemed to be in danger of falling apart.

Donald S. Vaughan, 79th Armoured Division

There was an awful lot of noise going on, planes were going
over, the Germans were firing, and there were big warships
behind us firing 15-inch shells over the top – I'd never heard
them before, and they sounded like locomotives going
through the air.

William Seymour, RN

You could see the coastline on fire for miles. I thought we'd
never make it in alive.

For the Allied troops on the assault craft the bombardment was the
only cheer on the long journey in. In waves which reached six foot
in the westerly American sector, many of the troops were chron-
ically seasick. They were wet and drenched with spray, and a

number of landing craft floundered or were hit by mines and underwater obstacles.

Ernest Hemingway, war reporter

As we moved in toward land in the grey early light, the 36-foot coffin-shaped steel boat took solid green sheets of water that fell on the helmeted heads of the troops packed shoulder to shoulder in the stiff, awkward, uncomfortable, lonely companionship of men going to a battle. There were cases of TNT, with rubber-tube life preservers wrapped around them to float them in the surf, stacked forward in the steel well of the LCV(P), and there were piles of bazookas and boxes of bazooka rockets encased in waterproof coverings that reminded you of the transparent raincoats college girls wear.

All this equipment, too, had the rubber-tube life preservers strapped and tied on, and the men wore these same grey rubber tubes strapped under their armpits.

As the boat rose to a sea, the green water turned white and came slamming in over the men, the guns and the cases of explosives. Ahead you could see the coast of France. The grey booms and derrick-forested bulks of the attack transports were behind now, and, over all the sea, boats were crawling forward toward France.

As the LCV(P) rose to the crest of a wave, you saw the line of low, silhouetted cruisers and the two big battlewagons lying broadside to the shore. You saw the heat-bright flashes of their guns and the brown smoke that pushed out against the wind and then blew away.

．．．．

The low cliffs were broken by valleys. There was a town with a church spire in one of them. There was a wood that came down to the sea. There was a house on the right of one of the beaches. On all the headlands, the gorse was burning, but the northwest wind held the smoke close to the ground.

Those of our troops who were not wax-grey with seasickness, fighting it off, trying to hold on to themselves before they had to grab for the steel side of the boat, were watching the *Texas* with looks of surprise and happiness. Under the steel helmets they looked like pikemen of the Middle Ages to whose aid in battle had suddenly come some strange and unbelievable monster.

There would be a flash like a blast furnace from the 14-inch guns of the *Texas*, that would lick far out from the ship. Then the yellow-brown smoke would cloud out and, with the smoke still rolling, the concussion and the report would hit us, jarring the men's helmets. It struck your near ear like a punch with a heavy, dry glove.

Then up on the green rise of a hill that now showed clearly as we moved in would spout two tall black fountains of earth and smoke.

'Look what they're doing to those Germans,' I leaned forward to hear a GI say above the roar of the motor. 'I guess there won't be a man alive there,' he said happily.

That is the only thing I remember hearing a GI say all that morning. They spoke to one another sometimes, but you could not hear them with the roar the 225-horsepower high-speed grey Diesel made. Mostly, though, they stood silent without speaking. I never saw anyone smile after we left the line of firing ships. They had seen the mysterious monster that was helping them, but now he was gone and they were alone again.

I found if I kept my mouth open from the time I saw the guns flash until after the concussion, it took the shock away.

T. Tateson, Green Howards

The assault landing craft held about thirty men tightly packed. They were low-lying, flattish boats and we were seated so that our heads were below the level of the gunwale. We were ordered to keep our heads down as we approached the coast to avoid enemy fire. However, our landing craft was disabled by some underwater mine or obstacle and became impossible to steer. One of the other boats was brought alongside and although it was already fully loaded with a similar number of men, we had to clamber aboard and abandon our boat. We were now exposed to enemy fire as well as being grossly overloaded.

As the boats approached the shore they began to encounter German resistance. Many of the Wehrmacht's gun emplacements, made from concrete several feet thick, had withstood the barrage. Unhappily for the GI in Hemingway's boat, not every German was dead – far from it.

Petty Officer J.E. Burton, RN
As we headed towards the beach I could hear the noise of shells exploding and gunfire, above the engine-room noise, and getting louder and louder. We could feel the effects of explosions in the water from near misses. We were both anxious as to what was happening and what we were to be faced with upon beaching. I suddenly became aware that there were hundreds of gallons of high-octane petrol in the fuel tanks in front of me! As we ran in to the beach, the shelling became worse, louder and more frequent. One shell dropped very close to the port side of the engine room and when it exploded all the tins of paint, grease etc. shot off a shelf and the stoker on the port engine leapt across the engine room and into my arms like a trained monkey. I persuaded him to return to his engine.

Trooper Peter Davies, 1st East Riding Yeomanry
Close to us we could see a little landing craft disappear in the trough when one of the great shells would land by it and a

plume would go up in the air. Everybody was saying, 'Oh
they've had it, that's one gone.' And suddenly this one
particular landing craft would bob back up and a cheer
went up, not just from our boat but every boat around.

Lieutenant (jg) Clark Houghton, US Navy

So we were amid sniper fire and machine-gun fire and flak.
When we got to the beach we saw the obstructions that Jerry
had put up, and all became more tense. The skipper picked
his spot and headed in. How close we came to tragedy at this
point. We headed between two stakes on which were
fastened mines. There was just room and we made it. Then
all hell broke loose.

It was H-Hour. At 06.25 the Americans began to land at Omaha
and Utah beaches. One of the first to wade ashore at Utah was the
naval officer in charge of the beachhead.

Commodore James Arnold, US Navy

As the ramp lowered, I was shoved forward up to my
knapsack in cold, oily water.

German 88s were pounding the beachhead. Two US tanks
were drawn up at the high-water line pumping them back
into the Jerries. I tried to run to get into the lee of these tanks.
I realize now why the infantry likes to have tanks along in a
skirmish. They offer a world of security to a man in open
terrain who may have a terribly empty sensation in his guts.
But my attempt to run was only momentary. Three feet of
water is a real deterrent to rapid locomotion of the legs. As I
stumbled into a runnel, Kare picked me up. A little soldier
following grabbed my other arm. Just for a moment he hung
on. Then he dropped, blood spurting from a jagged hole torn
by a sniper's bullet.

The soldier on Arnold's arm was bitterly unlucky, for Utah was to be a comparatively easy landing – at least in the cold terms of casualty statistics – that June morning. By a freak of nature – the strong tide – the bulk of the invasion force on Utah landed south of the designated place in an area which turned out to be very lightly defended. The difficulties of the Utah landing were to come later in the day as the narrow exits from the beach became blocked and troops became bogged down in the marshy area behind the dunes. In the meantime, some GIs landing on Utah even found the experience something of an anti-climax.

Anonymous Pfc, US 4th Infantry Division

You know, it sounds kind of dumb but it was just like a [training] exercise. Easier. We waded ashore like kids in a crocodile and up the beach. A couple of shells came over but nowhere near us. I think I even felt somehow disappointed, a little let down. Can you believe that!

Omaha was a very different affair. It was always going to be the most difficult of the Allied landings, dominated at each end of its long crescent length by cliffs, with the centre overlooked by green bluffs. The advantage at Omaha would always lie with the defence.

Sergeant Richard W. Herklotz, 110th Field Artillery, US 29th Division, aged 22

On Omaha the Germans were looking right down our throats.

And the Germans at Omaha were first-rate troops, unlike most of the Wehrmacht's coastal defence that day.

Captain Edward W. McGregor, 18th Infantry Regiment, US 1st Infantry Division, aged 25

We had a bad break tactically because the German 352nd Infantry Division were on a counter-attack training exercise at Omaha. So instead of a fortress battalion – you know, with kind of second-rate troops – we had a whole damned infantry division in front of us.

The misfortune was compounded by poor judgement, with most of the amphibious DD tanks which would support the landing being released too far from shore and sinking like stones. For the Germans it turned into a veritable turkey-shoot. For the assault waves of the US 1st and 29th Infantry Divisions it was a nightmare.

Don Whitehead, Associated Press war correspondent

The ramp lowered and we waded ashore to the rattle of machine guns and bursting of shells. Bullets cracked over our heads and we flung ourselves on the rocky beach under cover of a gravel embankment.

The enemy on the right flank was pouring direct fire on the beach. Hundreds of troops, pinned under cover of the embankment, burrowed shallow trenches in the loose ground. No one was moving forward. The congestion was growing dangerous as more troops piled in. Snipers and machine-gunners were picking off our troops as they came ashore . . . Wounded men, drenched by cold water, lay in the gravel, some with water washing over their legs, shivering, waiting for stretcher-bearers to take them aboard returning small craft. 'Oh God, lemme aboard the boat,' whimpered a youth in semi-delirium. Near him a shivering boy dug with bare fingers into the ground. Shells were bursting on all sides of us, some so close that they threw black water and dirt over us in showers.

Report: 16th Infantry Regiment, 1st Infantry Division

As the landing craft reached the beach [at Colleville-sur-Mer], they were subjected to heavy artillery, mortar, machine-gun, and rifle fire, directed at them from the pill-boxes and from the cliffs above the beach. Men were hit as they came down the ramps of the landing craft, and as they struggled landward through the obstacles, and many more were killed or injured by the mines attached to the beach obstacles. Landing craft kept coming in with their human cargoes despite the heavy fire and continued to disgorge them on to the narrow shale shelf from which no exits had been opened. Several landing craft were either sunk or severely damaged by direct artillery hits or by contact with enemy mines.

The enemy now began to pour artillery and mortar fire on to the congested beach with deadly precision and effect. Visibility from the enemy strongpoints was such that the assault groups, armed with rocket launchers, flame-throwers, Browning Automatic rifles, and pole charges of TNT could not approach them directly. A few squads and platoons of infantry gradually and slowly crawled forward from the shelf across the minefields between the enemy strongpoints, and made the slope.

Captain Edward W. McGregor, US 1st Infantry Division

My impression of the beach when I landed was, 'This is a rough place to be.'

Anonymous Pfc, US 1st Infantry Division

There were men crying with fear, men defecating themselves. I lay there with some others, too petrified to move. No one was doing anything except lay there. It was like a mass paralysis. I couldn't see an officer. At one point something

hit on the arm. I thought I'd taken a bullet. It was somebody's hand, taken clean off by something. It was too much.

Captain Joseph T. Dawson, 16th Infantry Regiment, US 1st Infantry Division, aged 30

The beach was a total chaos, with men's bodies everywhere,
with wounded men crying, both in the water and on the
shingle. We landed at high tide, when the water was right up
to the shoreline, which was marked by a sharp-edged
crystalline sand, like a small gravel, but very, very sharp.
That was the only defilade which was present on the beach to
give any protection from the fire above. That was where all
the men who had landed earlier were present, except for a
handful who had made their way forward, most of them
being killed . . . The beach sounded like a beehive with the
bullets flying around. You could hear them hit and you
could hear them pass through the air.

Russell Stover, 116th Infantry Regiment, US 29th Infantry Division

The boat stopped. We were on an obstacle. Thank God it
wasn't mined. The ramp went down and we leaped out, into
waist-deep water and three-foot waves. Some lost their
footing, some their weapons. We had more than two
hundred yards to go to the high water mark. Some engineers were working to our left. There was only one tank
ahead and to the left but it wasn't firing or moving. There
were no 'instant fox holes' either; there wasn't one crater for
cover. There wasn't even one DUKW with artillery firing on
the machine-gun placements on top of the bluffs. No Piper
Cubs overhead to direct the naval fire. It was very obvious to
me that many plans were going wrong. There was a boat
burning to our right, heading back out. We waded through
the surf and floating debris. I looked back and saw that we
were in good formation, well spread out, just as we had

practiced dozens of times before. Reaching the sand, I tried
to run, but found it was very difficult, my impregnated pant
legs were filled with water. The extra weight took its toll and
about half way in I fell to the sand exhausted. I thanked the
Good Lord for the smoke that still covered the bluffs. A shell
had started a grass fire. If not for that smoke, we would not
have made it in. Recovering, I started running again. The
man to my right didn't follow, I think he was our first
casualty.

For the GIs waiting to land it was an unedifying scene.

Sergeant Richard W. Herklotz, US 29th Division

As we got closer to the beach we saw that casualties were
floating in the water just like refuse in a harbour. There was
this and that equipment floating, soldiers, sailors – it was very
disheartening. For hours off the coast we watched the tide
bring out the debris and the bodies of those who had died.

At one point the battle for Omaha was going so badly that General
Bradley, waiting offshore on the *Augusta*, 'gained the impression
that our forces had suffered an irreversible catastrophe.' Hundreds
of the initial assault waves lay dead – there were to be over 2000
casualties on the beach that day – and the landing schedule was in
turmoil. And yet force of numbers, determination, and individual
example began to get the GIs off the beach and forcing routes up
the hill to the rear.

Sergeant Mike Rehm, US 5th Rangers

We were pinned down by heavy fire for about an hour.
General Cota, who was the executive officer, came along and
saw us crouched behind a wall. He said, 'Who are you
people?' We said, 'Sir, we're Rangers.' He said, 'Godda-
mit, if you're Rangers get up there and lead the way.'

Captain Joseph T. Dawson, US 1st Infantry Division

We landed at H + 30 minutes and found . . . both the assault units rendered ineffective because of the enormous casualties they suffered. Fortunately, when we landed there was some let-up in the defensive fire from the Germans. Even so the boat containing assault unit Company G, which I commanded, took a direct hit from the artillery of the Germans, and I suffered major casualties. I lost about twenty men out of a total complement of 250 from that hit on my boat, and this included my naval officer who was communications link with the Navy, who were to support us with their fire from the battleships and cruisers some 8000 yards out in the water.

As soon as we were able to assemble we proceeded off of the beach through a minefield which had been identified by some of the soldiers who had landed earlier. We knew this because two of them were lying there in the path I selected. Both men had been destroyed by the mines. From their position, however, we were able to identify the path and get through the minefield without casualties and proceed up to the crest of the ridge which overlooked the beach. We got about halfway up when we met the remnants of a platoon of E Company, commanded by Lieutenant Spalding. This was the only group – somewhere less than twenty men – we encountered who had gotten off of the beach. They had secured some German prisoners, and these were sent to the beach under escort. Above me, right on top of the ridge, the Germans had a line of defences with an excellent field of fire. I kept the men behind and, along with my communications sergeant and his assistant, worked our way slowly up to the crest of the ridge. Just before the crest was a sharp perpendicular drop, and we were able to get up to the crest without being seen by the enemy. I could now hear the Germans talking in the machine-gun nest immediately above me. I then threw two grenades, which were successful in eliminating the enemy and silencing the machine gun which had been holding up our approach. Fortunately for me this action was done without them having any awareness of my being there, so it was no hero . . . it was an act of God, I guess.

. . . .

I had only one thought and that was to get to the enemy. My feelings at the time were completely subordinate to the moment in hand, where my responsibility was to get off the beach and approach the enemy. That was my main objective, and that was the only thing I could possibly think at that time.

Don Whitehead, Associated Press war correspondent

Then the brigadier began working to get troops off the beach. It was jammed with men and vehicles. He sent a group to the right flank to help clean out the enemy firing directly on the beach. Quietly he talked to the men, suggesting next moves. He never raised his voice and he showed not the least excitement. Gradually the troops on the beach thinned out and we could see them moving over the ridge.

Captain Edward W. McGregor, US 1st Infantry Division

We hit the sand and found ourselves behind the bodies of the amphibious engineers, who had taken a terrible beating. Eventually we started moving up a draw, where some engineers had been and which was marked with tape. We had several casualties, and I know at least one officer right near me was killed, stepping on a mine. We came up to the top of the ridge and tried to advance a bit, but there was a large German bunker in front of us, and its machine-gun fire hit us every time we tried to move. At this point we didn't have any communication with the American destroyer behind us because within five minutes of landing on the beach the naval ensign officer had been killed – his driver too – and the radio set destroyed by a shell which landed right on top of them. So we planned an assault against the bunker. I volunteered to take some troops with me but before we could get organized there were huge demolitions around the bunker. Thank God we hadn't moved out yet. An American destroyer had moved in and was firing direct with 4-inch guns into the bunker.

Captain Albert H. Smith, 16th Infantry Regiment, US 1st Infantry Division, aged 25

When we were just 500 yards from the shore everything changed. We were now boat to boat, only five inches apart, boats banging side by side. We could see a lot of burning, and a lot of firing from the bluffs. Just as our landing-craft bottom hit the hard sand we took machine-gun fire on the ramp of our LCVP. I yelled to the coxswain, 'Hold the ramp!' For one time the Navy obeyed the Army and he held the ramp. When the machine-gun fire switched to the boat which was just to our left, I said 'Drop the ramp!' and the coxswain dropped the ramp. Thirty-four of us got into the Channel about waist deep, sometimes chest deep, but the last two who were trying to get out were hit as the machine gun swung back . . . As we waded through the Channel our clothing, which was impregnated against a German gas attack, became like a board. We were overloaded, all of us. Finally, we made it to the soft sand. We saw people lying down back of the stone wall – not a concrete wall, just a wall of stones which had been rolled by the tide up on to the beach. Shingle. I said to Captain Hangsterfer, who was under me as the adjutant of the battalion, 'Hank, I think there is some movement off to the left of the beach. I can just see it. We should head left' – which is where we were supposed to land. That we did with the thirty-four men with us, and we went four or five hundred yards to the left, parallel to the sea. On the way we saw some people we knew, they were still there from the first wave. They were rather dazed, and had taken a lot of fire. As we were going left we saw a column of men going up through the minefield, past the barbed wire and up into the high ground behind the beach. I said to Hank, 'We'll follow them and leave the company in a little protection and see what's going on and then bring them on up.' So we in fact got into the column which was composed of other soldiers of the 1st battalion, mainly Bravo Company. As soon as we were off the beach the fire we had been taking became less and less. We had no casualties at this time. We followed the column up and we had only one adventure as we were starting to get to the higher ground. I said to Hank, 'Let's bypass this column, let's make a little more headway, let's go a little faster.' So we made a sharp right turn and went into an area which turned out to be swamp area, just off of the beach. We sank, and the only way we survived was to pop our life preservers, the Mae West preservers. They popped up, and we made our way back to dry ground. I said, 'Hank, we're going to stay here with the column. We're going to take the slow pace forward.' At this time we saw, in the edge of the minefield, two US soldiers who had apparently tried to make it earlier in the day and had blown up. We had to pass over these two bodies so as not to disturb the other mines that were there. All this was in a sector called Easy Red. Well, it wasn't easy, and it was only red with blood. But we still got up out of it.

Russell Stover, 116th Infantry Regiment, US 29th Infantry Division

We reached the high-tide mark only to discover that the first and second waves were still on the beach. Some had dug fox holes which gave some protection from the fire coming from the bluff. The barbed-wire had stopped them. There were three rolls of concertina, then a staked fence, then three more rolls of concertina, about twenty feet wide. Sgt Ritter pointed to a location, and we set up our gun and began firing at the top of the bluff. We were in action! Suddenly I recalled advice from veterans of the Africa and Sicily landings – we could expect mortar fire within three minutes of starting to fire a machine gun.

Our boat load was not equipped with bangalore torpedoes as the wire was to be blown by the first wave of men, but evidently the squad responsible had mislanded or been killed. Word was passed up and down the beach to pass any bangalore torpedoes on to us. After what seemed an eternity, we had four. Sgt Ritter yelled to increase my fire. We were going to try to blow the wire. About this time the Germans fired a rocket from on top of the bluff to my right. I heard the sound of a large gun firing in back of me. I looked back and could not believe what I saw. There was a destroyer, so close I thought it would go aground. Finally we had something larger than a bazooka on our side. But as all our radios had drowned out on the way in, we could not contact the destroyer to coordinate our attack. The fire from the top of the bluffs slackened. I believe that the German machine-gunners up there did not want to disclose their position to the destroyer.

There was a heavy explosion directly in front of me. We had blown the wire. Our riflemen rushed through the gap. Some didn't make it.

Yet, even 'Bloody Omaha' had its lighter moments.

Captain Albert H. Smith, US 1st Infantry Division

I'm moving along [the beach] to my left and I meet standing there and directing some of the troops, Brigadier-General Bill Wyman. He was the senior commander in that area. He said, 'Smitty' – which was my nickname – 'are you advancing by fire and movement?' That was the correct way, in any army: to lay down fire and move quickly while you were protected by your own fire. But I looked at him and I kind of smiled, and I said, 'Yes, sir. They're firing, and we're moving.'

. . . .

When we got up to the top of the bluff and the column slowed down, Hank and I moved off to a little grassy knoll there. And I said, 'We're going to take a five-minute break,' and I reached into my knapsack and brought out a bottle of Johnnie Walker Red, which was a gift from a wonderful old lady in Lyme Regis. So Hank and I, sat on top of our first objective, had a nip of Scotch and an apple.

It was about 10.30 a.m. when Captain Al Smith sat down on top of the bluff above the Easy Red sector of Omaha beach, aside the route forced by Joe Dawson. By that time the Americans had found ways up the bluffs in other sectors and were fighting their way inland. The morning on the US beaches had also seen one of the most epic actions of D-Day, the assault by the Rangers on the Pointe du Hoc, a headland which jutted out between Omaha and Utah and was the site of a German gun battery.

Lieutenant Hodenfield, *Stars and Stripes* reporter

As the morning light grew brighter, we could see hundreds of other boats all making for the shores of Normandy. But those boats were landing on beaches, while ahead of us were sheer cliffs that had to be scaled before we could come to grips with the Germans. Personally, I was less scared of the Germans than of those cliffs; I had been shot at before, but I had never had to climb a rope ladder first.

Those rope ladders were the secret weapon of this expedition. Lt.-Col. James Rudder, former Texas football coach, and Capt. Harold Slater had worked out a system by which

grapnel hooks were shot over the cliffs by rockets, trailing
ladders and single lines. The grapnels were to bite into the
bomb-blasted earth on Pointe du Hoc, and when the slack
was taken up, the ladders would be ready to climb.

The entire success of this operation depended on those
ladders. Pointe du Hoc is accessible from the sea only by
scaling the cliffs, and the Germans, believing that not even
'military idiots' would dare to come from that direction, had
placed all their defenses facing inland. They knew that
Pointe du Hoc was an extremely important target, but they
thought our attack would be made from the flank, so they
had placed a ring of defenses around the inner arc of the
point.

Soon we were able to see on the horizon the dim outlines of
the coast of France, and about that time a terrific naval
barrage started. The naval barrage was not primarily
intended to destroy the German guns – they were too well
casemated for that – but the barrage would drive the
Germans into their deep tunnels.

The plan was that the Rangers were to land at exactly six-
thirty in the morning, just five minutes after the lifting of the
barrage. By the time the Germans would dare to come out of
their holes, the Rangers would be over the top of the cliffs,
spiking the big guns. And then, after the guns had been
spiked, the Rangers would be able to devote their full time to
killing Germans.

Gradually we drew nearer, and some of us raised ourselves
partially out of the boat to take our first real look at
Normandy. It looked very much like England, which we
had just left the night before, and for some reason we felt
disappointed.

But we weren't disappointed in our Navy. The *Texas*,
bulking heavily against the horizon in the half-light of early
morning, was sending shell after shell screaming into Pointe
du Hoc, the sound of the firing reaching us long after we
could see the blast of flame from the gun muzzles.

As we watched the coast of France draw nearer and nearer, it didn't seem possible that this was really the invasion, the second front for which so many men had trained for so long. It looked too peaceful, too quiet. But suddenly we heard a sharp rat-ta-tat, and we saw machine-gun bullets fall into the water ahead of us.

'Hey, boss!' yelled one man. 'Those jerks are trying to hit us!'

They were, too.

The wind was blowing at least fifteen knots, and the heavy seas, with waves reaching four feet, had pushed us off our course. A check with charts and watches showed we were well behind our carefully planned timetable. The naval barrage stopped, as scheduled, five minutes before we were to make our touchdown, but we were far off the course and we had to give up the idea of surprising the Germans. So we kept bucking and bobbing about, getting closer and closer to Pointe du Hoc, but likewise getting closer to the cliff defenders, who had taken positions along the top.

We kept our heads ducked low below the gunwales of the LCA, and we jumped each time a burst of machine-gun fire rattled against our sides. When we dared to look up, we could see men floating around in the water after their boats had been overturned. One man gave us a cheery wave of his hand. It was Captain Slater, who had helped devise the rope-ladder-launching idea. After two hours in the water, he was picked up by the Navy in a fit of high temper at the fate which had robbed him of his chance to see his own weapon in action. He didn't reach France until a week later.

I suppose that we all should have been scared when we finally nosed up to the narrow beach to make our touchdown, but we all were too excited. I was sitting next to Capt. Otto ('Big Stoop') Massney, a company commander. Together, we watched rockets being launched from other craft on our right, and he cursed roundly when he saw that some had been fired too soon and had fallen far short of the cliff top.

'Don't fire those things until I give the word!' he yelled. 'We've got plenty of time!'

When the nose of our LCA ground against the sand, we stopped: he gave the word, and, with a loud roar and whooshing sound, our rockets sailed over the top of the cliffs.

I had ducked my head when the first series of rockets exploded, heeding Massney's warning that we could be blinded if we didn't, but then I looked up to see what had happened. I was lost in admiration of the pretty picture the rockets were making, when the second and third series went off. The explosions were so startling that I fell over backward into the bottom of the boat, but as I rose shamefacedly, Massney patted me on the back and said, 'If that scared you, whatinhell you think it did to the Germans?'

But there was no time for further conversation, for the ramp had been lowered and our men were scrambling ashore with lethal weapons ranging from pistols and knives in small hip cases to big bazookas and trench mortars.

Snipers and machine-gunners were on the cliffs all around us, so we scrambled to the base of the cliff for safety. Sgt. Bob Youso and Pvt. Alvin White had already started up the ladders which were hugging the face of the cliff, and others were lined up, waiting their turn, while Massney stood at the bottom, yelling advice and encouragement.

Those of us not so useful had to wait nearly an hour for our turn to start climbing, so, for lack of anything better to do, I lit a cigarette. Then the thought struck me, *This is a helluva way to invade France, sitting down in the shade with a cigarette.*

I saw Lt. Amos Potts, Army photographer, who was fuming mad because here he was, in the middle of the greatest picture story of his life, and all his equipment had been water-soaked in the landing. He and I were too nervous to sit still, so we started digging some ammunition out of the sand, where it already was being partially buried by the incoming tide. Later, we had reason to be very thankful that we had salvaged that ammunition.

Over on our right, Capt. Walter ('Doc') Block, of Chicago, the medical officer of our battalion, had set up a first-aid post for those men wounded by snipers on the trip in to the beach. He had an impressive number of patients already.

My trip up the ladder was interrupted only by numerous stops to catch my breath. We were able to hear the firing of small arms and occasional loud roars from the top of the cliff, but we had no way of telling what was going on, because Massney had become impatient and had gone up earlier than scheduled, taking the field telephone with him.

Finally I tumbled over the top of the cliff into a shell hole left by a previous bombardment from our Air Force, and I asked some of the men in the shell hole what the score was. But I could learn only that two of the six guns in Target No. 1 had been destroyed by the Air Force, prior to D-Day, and that the remaining four had been removed.

Raising my head carefully over the edge of the shell hole, I got my first real look at Pointe du Hoc. Just picture it as a huge letter V, jutting into the Channel, with sides formed by cliffs 150 feet high. The Rangers had landed on the left side of the V, with our group at the extreme upper end.

Straight ahead of me for a mile was nothing but shell holes from the air and naval bombardments. At my left was a series of small fields with hedgerows extending to the cliffs. On the far right was the English Channel on the other side of the V, and along the cliff was a concrete observation post which controlled the fire of all six German guns. I moved over to the left-flank troops and stayed there until late that evening.

Meanwhile, other units which were also assaulting the cliffs had been having various sorts of trouble. The Germans had come to the edge of the cliffs and had rolled hand grenades down the ladders. Later, as a sort of afterthought, they started cutting the ropes, but by this time the Rangers had gone up and over and were pushing the jerries back.

And then came the last great assault from the sea of the morning of 6 June 1944. Four years after Dunkirk the British sailed back to France, touching down at 07.30, an hour after the Americans, on the eastern half of the invasion coast, some 20 miles of flatness backed by dunes and marshes and dotted with fortified villages. With them came the Canadians whose 3rd Division were to land at beach Juno, in between the British beaches of Sword and Gold. The British landings would prove a curiously mixed affair. Many would find the myriad sea-obstacles and the getting ashore itself the most terrifying part of the process. Others – like the men of the East Yorkshire Regiment – would be mown down as they left the water in a slaughter reminiscent of the Western Front in 1916.

Lieutenant K.P. Baxter, 2nd Battalion, Middlesex Regiment

Steadily the flotilla of LCAs pressed onwards towards the beach. Four hundred yards from the shoreline and the Royal Marine frogmen slipped over the side to start the job of clearing underwater obstacles. This would be sufficiently hazardous at the best of times, but add to it the risk from all those churning propellers – with many more following – and their task became most unenviable.

Closing to the shore rapidly, eyes scanned the clearing haze for familiar landmarks. There were none. A burst of machine-gun fire uncomfortably close overhead brought curses upon those in following craft for their enthusiastic 'covering fire'. Suddenly a burst ricocheted off the front of the craft, telling us that this was no covering fire. The opposition was very much alive and well.

We had still been unable to identify our position but we were by now right on top of the beach. The protective steel doors in the bows were opened and everyone waited, tensed for the soft lurching bump. 'Ramp down!' – and out into knee-deep water. Ahead, a line of prone figures just above the water's edge and, some 200 yards beyond, a tank was nosed up against the small strip of dunes at the head of the beach.

The first impression was that the tank had got in ahead of the first wave and they, following the same instructions as given to the Beach Exit Teams, were holding back until the explosive charges had been detonated.

I had not gone far when I was tripped by some underwater wire, and, with no hope of retaining balance with the heavy Assault Jacket pack that had been issued to us, went flat on my face. Attempting to rise, I was struck a heavy blow on the back which flattened me again. Then suddenly the machine gun opened up on us once again.

The fire came from dead ahead and we could now make out the shape of a heavy embrasure in the low silhouette of some concrete fortifications at the top of the beach. We then realized that, by the narrowest of margins, we had landed immediately in front of Strongpoint 0880, code word COD.

Sergeant Leo Gariepy, 3rd Canadian Division

More by accident than by design, I found myself the leading tank. On my way in I was surprised to see a friend – a midget submarine who had been waiting for us for forty-eight hours. He waved me right on to my target and then made a half turn to go back. I remember him very very distinctly standing up through his conning hatch joining his hands together in a sign of good luck. I answered the old, familiar Army sign – to you too, bud!

I was the first tank coming ashore and the Germans started opening up with machine-gun bullets. But when we came to a halt on the beach, it was only then that they realized we were a tank when we pulled down our canvas skirt, the flotation gear. Then they saw that we were Shermans.

It was quite amazing. I still remember very vividly some of

the machine-gunners standing up in their posts looking at us with their mouths wide open.

To see tanks coming out of the water shook them rigid.

Commander Phillipe Kieffer, French Commandos, attached to British 1st Special Service Brigade

Our two landing craft advanced as on exercise – straight for the coast. The 4th Commandos (British) were in their LCI on our left flank. We couldn't see the coast, which was obscured by a thick cloud of smoke, but the radio contact between the craft on the sea was perfect. The smaller British ones danced on the short waves. At 700 m to port a Polish destroyer had hit a mine and was sinking by the prow. We had to be very close to the coast, the enemy shells enveloped us increasingly. Were we in fact in front of our objective? My watch said 7.25. The two landing craft with the French commandos on board navigated at the same level, fifty metres apart. Suddenly, through a gap in the smoke, the submarine defences, stakes and barbed wire entanglements surged up in front of us. We had arrived. A shock – a bump – we were aground. At this exact moment the sea bed seemed to rise in a rumble of thunder: mortars, the whistle of shells, staccato fire of machine guns – everything seemed concentrated towards us. Like lightning the ramps were thrown down. Wearing their green berets, a first group rushed to the beach but a few seconds before the second group flung themselves forward a 75-mm shell tore away the ramps in a scream of metal and wood. A second's hesitation – the vessel must be cleared and the beach reached at all costs. Speed became the vital factor. The commandos jumped into 6 feet of water with their 35-kilo packs, their weapons making even more weight, and they gained a footage in a few strokes. The other craft, more fortunate, was able to put down its troops by way of its ramps.

Lieutenant H.T. Bone, 2nd East Yorkshire Regiment

In the Mess decks we blacked our faces with black Palm Olive cream and listened to the naval orders over the loud-hailer. Most of us had taken communion on the Sunday, but the padre had a few words to say to us. Then the actual loading into craft – swinging on davits – the boat lowering and finally 'Away boats.' While this was going on, all around could be seen the rest of the convoy, with battleships and cruisers firing their big guns every few minutes and destroyers rushing round. One had been hit by something and only the up-ended part of its bows remained in view. As our flotilla swung into line behind its leader we raised our flag, a black silk square with the white rose of Yorkshire in the centre . . . It was some distance to the beaches, and it was a wet trip. All of us had a spare gas-cape to keep us dry and we chewed our gum stolidly. Mine was in my mouth twelve or fourteen hours later and I usually hate the stuff and never touch it. Shielding ourselves from the spray and watching the fire going down from all the supporting arms and the Spits [Spitfires] overhead, the time soon passed . . . Suddenly there was a jarring bump on the left, and looking up from our boards we saw one of the beach obstacles about two feet above our left gunwale with a large mine on top of it, just as photographs had shown us. Again a bump, on the right, but still we had not grounded. The Colonel and the flotilla leader were piloting us in, and for a few brief minutes nothing happened except the music of the guns and the whang of occasional bullets overhead, with the sporadic explosions of mortar bombs and the background of our own heavy machine-gun fire. The doors opened as we grounded and the Colonel was out. The sea was choppy and the boat swung a good bit as one by one we followed him. Several fell in and got soaked through. I was lucky. I stopped for a few seconds to help my men with their wireless sets and to ensure they kept them dry. As we staggered ashore we dispersed and lay down above the water's edge.

Stuff was falling pretty close to us and although I did not see it happen, quite a number of people from my own boat were hit. Instinctively where we lay we hacked holes with our shovels. The Colonel moved forward. I tried to collect my party of sets and operators, but could only see a few of them. I began to recognize wounded men of the assault companies. Some were dead, others struggling to crawl out of the water because the tide was rising very rapidly.

Sergeant H.M. Kellar, Devonshire Regiment

When we were about 200 yards from our landing point I could see heavy-machine-gun bullets cutting up the sand and making a noise like a huge swarm of bees.

I thought, 'My God, we are going to be slaughtered!' Then we were on the beach and the ramp was down and I do not know why but the firing stopped. Had it not done so I had my eye on a huge crater in the sand in front of a pill-box. On coming down the ramp I spotted our Company Commander staggering about with blood streaming down his face.

Anonymous Private, East Yorkshire Regiment

It was like a bloody skittle alley. The lads were being bowled over right left and centre. I thought to myself, 'You'll be a lucky bugger if you make it up there.' Christ, it were bad.

W. Emlyn 'Taffy' Jones, 1st Special Service Brigade

Looking over the side we saw many craft broken down and some sinking and still no sign of the beach – too much smoke. Columns of water were now shooting up between our landing craft and the sound of battle grew louder. Can't be long now, I can hear the small-arms fire; then suddenly, the beach appeared before us, tanks and landing craft on fire, men moving up the beach as quickly as possible, no doubt remembering Lord Lovat's words: 'If you wish to live to a ripe old age, keep moving.' There were those lying there that just didn't make it. Only seconds to go now before we hit the beach; the noise, the smell of gunpowder, flashing of guns. The naval ratings both port and starboard were firing guns at the enemy targets oblivious of the enemy fire which was now raining down on us. Landing craft to left and right had been hit and were now on fire. This is it – ramp down, let's move, we're a sitting target. Naval personnel scamper back to the rear of the bridge for safety. What's the hold-up? Let's move. Bren gunner has frozen at the top of the ramp, won't move. Hit him out of the way. It seemed like hours before we got moving, then we found that only one ramp could be used. The other had broken away from its stanchions. To make matters worse, the only way we could land was to scramble down this one ramp on our backsides.

Ken Wright, 1st Special Service Brigade
There was a terrific jar, and all the first half of the party in the craft fell over on top of each other. I felt quite numb in my right side – no pain, just a sudden absence of feeling really, and a feeling of being knocked out of breath. At the same moment, the doors of the craft were opened and the ramp lowered, and the naval bloke said 'This is where you get off.' So I got off, after a bit of preliminary gasping for breath and struggling free from all the others. Doughty kept on saying 'Go on, sir,' and it seemed ages before I got myself up and off the boat. There were quite a few who could not follow me off, including our padre. I got off into about three feet of water. It was nearly 7.45 . . . We had about fifty or sixty yards to wade and what with the weight of the rucksack and the water to push through, I was nearly exhausted by the time I got clear. I realized that I had been hit and was therefore less mobile than usual (which is saying something!) so when I got on the beach I just sat down and dumped the

rucksack with all my belongings in it. That beach was no
health resort, and I thought I'd be better off away from it,
even without a change of underclothing!

Driver John Osborne, 101 Company General Transport Amphibious

As I went into the beach there were little spurts in the water; it
took a little while for me to realize they were made by bullets.
There were still a number of Germans in the houses and pill-
boxes along the front. Suddenly between the waves right in
front of my DUKW there was a pole sticking up with a shell
tied to the top. That's when all sense of adventure disappeared.

Private Islwyn Edmunds, South Wales Borderers, aged 19

I was very frightened, not only because of the shot and shell, but
the fact that I could not swim troubled me greatly. Not that it
would have made any difference with the weight of equipment
I was carrying. I was also ordered to take a bicycle off with me,
but I declined by saying I had enough trouble getting myself
off. However, while I was arguing with the sergeant a sailor
from our craft swam to the shore and attached a rope to a
disabled tank, and we were able to work along this line.
Unfortunately as I was proceeding along this rope, the buckle
of my pack got caught in the rope . . . with the waves coming in
I couldn't keep my head above water. I was going under for the
third time, when a hand pulled me out. It was my friend, who
was aware of my fear of the water and had kept a look-out for
me. He dragged me to the beach, where I lay exhausted, shells
exploding everywhere.

Private Robert Macduff, Wiltshire Regiment

The landing craft drew up towards the beach. The infantrymen, who had their small packs on their back, gas-mask in

front, pouches full of ammo and their rifles, jumped in the
water and partly swam ashore. I had a number 18 communication set on my back, on top of it was my small pack, a
number 23 communication set below my gas-mask, a telephone set on one side, on the other the new telephone
equipment and spare batteries – all waterproofed – and a
Sten gun in my hand. Off I jumped from the landing craft –
straight down into the water. With the weight I was carrying
swimming was out of the question. As the water closed over
my head sheer panic gripped me and I began to run as fast as
I could until my head was above water.

Sergeant J.H. Bellows, Hampshire Regiment

I said we were in deep water and was stuck on an obstacle.
The ship officer said it was only four feet six deep. He had his
way and ordered the vehicle to disembark. I ordered all the
men to get on the turrets of the tanks and on the trailer of the
bulldozer. The first tank went off and went to the left, the
water was deep, only the top of the turret and the exhaust
was showing and two men clinging on for dear life. The other
tank went to the right. He foundered, he went deeper. Next
to go was the armoured bulldozer, it went down the ramp,
fouled the chain of the ramp and capsized pulling the trailer
which broke from the bulldozer and floated on its side. The
left hand tank got ashore the other didn't. The bulldozer
never stood a chance. Some of the men still clung to the
trailer and were OK. Quite a few died.

Alfred Leonard, Merchant Navy

There were dismembered personnel in the water which was
upsetting. From a young man's point of view, up to then D-
Day had been exciting, with all the guns going off, everything on the move and nobody getting killed. It was pure
excitement. But when you see dead chaps in the water, you
think 'Crikey, what is this all about?'

George Collard, 1st RM Armoured Support Regiment

The tanks slid into the sea at some depth. Water was pouring in through the turret ring causing some trouble. I found out that the troop sergeant could not get out through his hatch. I could, so it fell to me to give directions to the driver. Exposed in the turret hatch I had some thoughts about being shot between the eyes, but I looked with some admiration at the sight of the shells landing on the concrete stongpoints. Giving orders – 'drive right', 'drive left', 'forward' – I got the tank onto the beach between the anti-invasion obstacles, when we were suddenly in an explosion which blew off the left track. Under cover of the dunes we managed to shorten and correct this, and keep going.

Corporal L.E. Richards, 50th Division, Signaller to Brigadier Sir Alexander Stanier

I asked Corporal Davidson whether he thought the carrier and the Jeep could be driven ashore. He replied that the back axle of the Jeep was broken but that the carrier seemed all right. The carrier had been fitted with extra plates which extended eighteen inches or more above its normal height. These plates were held together by string at the top corner and all the joints had been made waterproof. Knowing Corporal Davidson would try to land the carrier, I volunteered to stay on the front and give him steering instructions, because he was unable to see from his driving seat. Before starting I drew his attention to two mines on a pole slightly to the right of the craft and about eight feet away. To avoid these I told him to bear left when he felt himself on the run or when I should tell him.

Corporal Davidson started the engine and we began to move. I grasped the string, holding the front and side plates together, and stood on the front, with my back to the carrier. As we were moving onto the ramp the carrier hit the side of the craft and I felt myself falling sideways. By this time the carrier was going down the ramp and I must have entered the water at the same time. For a split second I did not know what had happened, and I felt myself being dragged along beside the carrier. In falling, I had hooked two of my fingers round the string and the back of my left hand rested on the top of the side sheet. We were now making for the shore. My fingers pained me intensely but I realized that if I attempted to move them I should, to say the least, lose my tow ashore. My right hand was free and I brought it across my chest and held the set above the water, at the same time kicking my legs. I did this for two reasons, first and foremost to try and keep my feet away from the tracks of the carrier and secondly to propel myself along to ease the weight on my left arm.

Corporal Davidson stopped when he got into shallow water and I stood up and disengaged my fingers. He looked at me and said that he thought I was dead, and wanted to know what had happened. He could hardly believe it when I told him. Neither of us to this day can say how close we must have been to the two mines. They must have been barely inches away. I followed the carrier as it moved onto the beach. We joined up with our party who were already on the beach and I learned that the tanks and vehicles on the beach were unable to leave because of a huge crater in the road near the beach exit.

Alan Melville, RAF war correspondent
It was the first time I had driven anything – waterproofed or not – through any depth of water, and it is a terrifying experience. You can't hear a sound from your engine, and the natural thing to do is to panic and assume that you have stalled. For weeks I had had the one golden rule drummed into me about one's behaviour on such occasions: don't use your clutch – never, never, *never* use your clutch. I had the most maddening temptation to get at that damned clutch: my toes itched to get near it. But to my intense surprise, I

realized that we were still moving. Water was surging round
the sides of the windscreen, and we were leaving a fair-sized
wash behind us. Someone shouted something after us from
the rhino, but whether it was advice, good wishes, or just the
usual blasphemy I never knew.

Captain Peter Young, 1st Special Service Brigade

Land ahead now – a hundred yards away a column of water
shoots into the air. Away to port a tank landing craft burns
fiercely, ammunition exploding as the crew go over the side.
Ashore is a line of battered houses whose silhouette looks
familiar from the photographs. They must surely mark our
landing-place. On the beach a few tanks creep about and fire
occasional shots at an unseen foe. Ouistreham is not much
more than a thousand yards to port now. Somewhere on the
front are the guns that are shelling us; the flashes are plainly
visible every few seconds. The craft slows down.

'What are you waiting for?'

'There are still five minutes to go before H + 90,' the
Captain, a young RNVR officer, replies.

'I don't think anyone will mind if we're five minutes early
on D-Day.'

'Then in we go.'

In fact, most landing craft were ordered in by the beachmasters in
strict succession, and had to wait their turn, milling around
offshore in huge herds. This not only made the craft vulnerable
to German shells, but the unpleasant motion on an anyway
choppy sea produced yet more seasickness.

Major F.D. Goode, Gloucestershire Regiment

As we drew nearer we could see the distinct coast a mass of
smoke and flames. At this time the Colonel joined us on the
bridge and the Captain said that we were too early and we

would have to circle offshore until we were called in to the beach. So we started to circle slowly and the motion became very unpleasant. Nearly all the troops were seasick and those who had managed to find a place on deck looked very grey and miserable. One of the naval ratings brought me a mug of cocoa. Until that moment, although queasy, I had not been sick, but almost immediately after I threw up into a bucket, placed for that purpose on the bridge . . . As we neared the beach we could see some activity by our troops and guide parties and a number of bodies lying about and broken-down tanks and DD tanks. However, by this time we were all feeling so seasick that the one thing we wanted to do was get ashore.

Naturally, being British they had to assume an air of nonchalance. There were some who even pulled it off.

Captain Peter Young, 1st Special Service Brigade
No. 3 Troop comes ashore in grand style and almost unscathed. In the bows Troopers Osborne and Jennings make mock of the German gunners: 'Put your sights up, Jerry!' 'Down a little.' 'Give her more wind-gauge,' and much nonsense besides, as each shell flies past and, as luck would have it, misses their craft – except for the wireless aerial. The first man ashore is Slinger Martin, our veteran Administrative Officer, whose first campaign in France lies thirty years in the past.

Among the most surprising receptions on reaching the sands of Normandy was that granted a company of the Royal Berkshire Regiment.

Captain Peter Prior, Royal Berkshire Regiment
There was a hell of a battle going on further up the beach, but in our sector the opposition quickly crumpled. As we

went ashore we were met by a lovely blonde French girl shouting 'Vive les Anglais.'

This, though, was an exception. The most common welcome was that provided by the Wehrmacht. After touching down on the Normandy shore, the men of the British and Canadian Armies still had to make it across the sand and shingle into the hinterland. Their ease in doing this was largely dictated by the local calibre of the German coastal defences and troops. On Gold beach the British 1st Hampshire Regiment fought a bitter eight-hour battle against the defences at Le Hamel. Several hundred yards to the left the Green Howards moved inland and secured their first objective in under an hour.

Private Jim Cartwright, South Lancashire Regiment

As soon as I hit the beach I wanted to go, get away from the water. I think I went across the beach like a hare.

George Collard, 1st RM Armoured Support Regiment

A number of wounded and dead were on the beach, including some killed where our own [not the Royal Marines'] tanks had run over them, pushing – it appeared – the bile in the liver up to the faces.

Howard Marshall, BBC war correspondent

When they got ashore they seemed to be in perfectly good order because the troops out of that barge immediately assembled, went to their appointed places and there was no semblance of any kind of confusion. But the scene on the beach, until one had sorted it out, was at first rather depressing because we did see a great many barges in difficulties with these anti-tank screens. We noticed that a number of them had struck mines as ours had struck mines. But then we began to see that in fact the proportion which had got through was very much greater and that troops were moving all along the roads and that tanks were out already and going up the hills. That in fact we were dominating the situation and that our main enemy was the weather, and that we were beating the weather. We had our troops and tanks ashore and the Germans weren't really putting up a great deal of resistance.

Donald S. Vaughan, 79th Armoured Division

I was in an AVRE, our job being to lay a coconut matting over any soft spots on the beach. This wasn't necessary, so when we got to the top of the beach we stopped and Corporal Fairley, the demolition NCO, and myself got out to erect a windsock so as to show anybody behind that it was a clear lane. We'd finished erecting the windsock and were re-mounting the tank when we were hit. Corporal Fairley was killed. The tank itself was damaged so badly – tracks were blown off, bogeys as well, the petrol tank was pierced – that we abandoned it. What was left of us.

Ken Coney, Royal Corps of Signals

Diary, 6 June

07.55. We have landed in two feet of water and take cover on the beach. Bullets are zipping through the sea, two Sherman tanks go up in flames. We move along the beach.

08.30. Now we have dug in before a Jerry strong point. A CEP is there. Dead and dying are everywhere. I can't understand why I am not frightened. The shelling is getting worse. MG [machine-gun fire] opens up from the flank. I see a few POWs huddled in the sea, terror-stricken of their own fire. I have exultation at the sight.

10.00. Still hell on the beach

Driver John Osborne, 101 Company General Transport Amphibious

Leaving the sea I saw a young soldier about my age lying half in the water. I was looking down, feeling sorry for him, when I heard a loud explosion in front. I jerked my head around and saw a large piece of something floating down towards me – it was the hatch-cover off the engine compartment of the DUKW in front, the bows of which were now curved up. The driver, Stan Hall, was nowhere in sight but his co-driver George Burton came running towards me yelling like hell. He had actually been blown out of the DUKW! I stopped and pulled him aboard. He was unhurt, except that both his ears had been completely skinned. I later learned that Stan Hall was still alive, but had had his bottom jaw blown off.

James Gallagher, RE

The German artillery piece had been put out of action and replaced by a British gun which the RA boys were operating to good effect. On the outside wall of the encampment were chalked the words: 'UNDER NEW MANAGEMENT – DAY AND NIGHT SERVICE.'

Anonymous Sergeant, RE

We got to the top of the rise [when] I saw my first German. He was alive, but not for long. These two Canadians behind me . . . went up through this opening in the sea wall . . . The Jerry came out of the emplacement with a Schmeisser. I thought, Christ! They haven't seen him . . . But they just didn't stop running. They just cracked their rifle butts down on the German and that was that.

T. Tateson, Green Howards

The beach was in a state of organized chaos with tanks, guns, Jeeps, trucks, personnel carriers and every type of vehicle, some of which had been hit and knocked out. The heather or grass off the beach was burning and clouds of smoke prevented a view of what lay beyond. Wounded men, including some Germans, were sitting at the top of the beach, and stretcher-bearers were carrying others down to the boats from which we had landed. We walked along the top of the beach to reach our intended landing place, which was the road leading inland from le Riviere to Ver-sur-mer.

Major F.D. Goode, Gloucestershire Regiment

I concentrated on following the taped guys to my left through the dunes marked by a wrecked Sherman flail tank . . . I stopped for a while to look at my map but we were off it and my best bet was to find the lateral road and turn right in the direction of Le Hamel. We were now in an area of the main German beach defences, which had been heavily plastered by the Navy and RAF. Pill-boxes and blockhouses were shattered and I have a clear recollection of one embrasure out of which a German officer had tried to climb; it had descended on top of him and squashed his top half, leaving his legs with a pair of well-polished boots protruding.

W. Emlyn 'Taffy' Jones, 1st Special Service Brigade

I remember Sergeant Ian Grant, cameraman of the Army Film and Photo Unit – 'Jock' as I affectionately called him – attached himself to me. We'd had a few words together on the way over. He was a cool customer. The enemy fire didn't seem to bother him, he wanted pictures and on a few occasions I had to tell him to get his head down before he had it blown off. As we came off the beach we again came under heavy fire and we dived into the nearest ditch. On looking up, I noticed 'a piece of steak' on the rear of his shoulder and without a word I pulled out my commando dagger and quickly flicked the offensive piece of meat away.

'What's up?' said Jock, feeling a little nudge. 'I don't know, but I think somebody is trying to hit us,' I replied.

Trooper Peter Davies, 1st East Riding Yeomanry
On the way [off the beach] we passed about in all a dozen French civilians. They were mostly old and didn't look very excited – if they'd had to go through the preliminary bombardment that is hardly surprising.

Ken Wright, 1st Special Service Brigade
There was a huge pill-box right in front of us as we landed, and there was a lot of fire coming from there and from the chateau behind it. I think I must have walked through a machine-gun arc at this time, though I noticed nothing then, for a little later I found bullet holes in my right thigh and left calf. I certainly was in luck that day!

Captain Peter Young, 1st Special Service Brigade
We trot down the inland side of the dunes, dash across a road and a tram-line, and hurl ourselves over a wire fence, no great obstacle. The soldiers come swarming down the slope. Away to the left a quick-firing gun opens up. A shell smacks into the soft ground behind us, and something like the kick of a mule hits me on the right shoulder-blade.

'That was a near one,' shouts RSM [Regimental Sergeant-Major] Stenhouse.

'Near one be damned, it hit me!'

This marsh is not the place to linger in. We push on. Progress is slow, floundering and leaping across deep slimy ditches. But the soft ground minimizes the effect of the German shells. Even so Lieutenant Cowieson, of 5 Troop, has a nasty wound, and Sergeant King takes over his section. No. 3 Troop has lost Sergeant Dowling, wounded by a shell that landed within a yard of him.

At length we reach the forming-up place. Except for 6 Troop the Commando is still more or less intact. Donald Hopson comes up and reports. Then Cowieson appears, assuring me that he is all right, but he seems to be pretty hard hit and I tell him to go back. John Pooley, my Second-in-Command, has also been hit. He soon appears, however, not much the worse for a near miss, though he has a gash on his lip. I move my right arm about and find that it is still in working order; a clod must have hit my equipment.

Near our forming-up place a company commander of one of the assault battalions sits under a hedge with his CSM [Company Sergeant-Major] and two others, waiting for his men whom we last saw digging-in on the beach a thousand yards behind him . . .

Suddenly there comes an unearthly, blood-chilling, bellowing noise like a gigantic cow in agony and six bombs land in the next field in a cloud of black smoke – our first meeting with 'Moaning Minnie', the German six-barrelled mortar.

'Ah, *Nebelwerfer*', says Donald Hopson in his usual cool manner, as if it were some sort of military curio that he has been wanting to add to his collection.

Taking a quick look round to check whether everyone is present, I see Captain Martin again.

'All up, Slinger?'

'Aye, aye, sir.'

'Good. *Vörwats!*' and the advance begins again.

The Allies had broken through Hitler's Atlantic Wall. By midday the Canadians, British and Americans were everywhere on the move inland, plodding up narrow lanes, wading through marshes, edging through Norman orchards bounded by high hedges and along village streets. In the east the British struck out towards their D-Day objectives of Caen, Bayeaux and, in the case of the commandos of Lord Lovat's 1st Special Service Brigade, the reinforcement of the flank on the Orne held by the 6th Airborne Division.

Report: 79th Armoured Division
The [AVRE] crew made their way to Hermanville on foot, led by the crew commander, Sgt Kilvert. Reaching a high farm wall they were checked by heavy small arms fire, which they answered with Brens. Then Sgt Kilvert burst open the farm door and, covered by his crew, raked the farmhouse with fire killing eleven Germans. They later routed an enemy patrol on the same road and handed over to the infantry.

Lieutenant H.T. Bone, 2nd East Yorkshire Regiment
The move inland was not much fun since, although we had cleared the beach defences, Jerry was mortaring us pretty badly from his rear positions. Besides, we had to cross a marsh and in places we were up to our armpits in muddy water and slime. The mortars had our range and as I helped my people through the deep parts (why are all Yorkshire signallers only 5 ft 2 in?) they were bursting only 50 yards behind us. We had just got across the deepest drain when Jerry hit. Then for about half an hour we had a rest while the companies fought the next battle and the commandos streamed through us to do their job . . .

We could not get away, neither could we dig. The ground was hard and tangled with roots, the bombs were bursting literally everywhere all the time. I laid on my face for a few moments then, seeing the Provost sergeant hit five yards away, I pushed over to him and shoved my field dressing on the back of his neck. He had a piece through his shoulder, but it was not serious, and we got him out of it. (Curious how everyone turns yellow when hit.) We all had to get out of it, and we did. The attack went in the rear instead and was successful, lots of Jerry prisoners being captured, but Dicky was killed and Hurch wounded, as well as a good many others.

W. Emlyn 'Taffy' Jones, 1st Special Service Brigade

I saw Sergeant-Major Harry Larkman legging it over a barbed wire fence into a field. 'Harry,' I shouted, 'What the Hell do you think you're doing? Can't you read German? Look between your legs' and when he did there was a notice saying 'Achtung Minen'. He gave a wry smile and waved then took another route. Now it was open country and we had broken through the 'Atlantic Wall' – marshland lay ahead. There was no cover and progress was slow. Shells and mortars came raining down but luckily the soft ground minimized the effect of the bombardments. Into a copse at the top of the rise, a slight rest and then on to Colleville where we were met by enemy small-arms fire; many enemy snipers around but progress had to be made – time was of the essence. The airborne troops who landed during the night of 5/6 June were holding the bridges at Benouville and the Commando Brigade had promised to relieve them by mid-day. Through Colleville and on to St Aubin D'Arquenay where we met with very little resistance, though one had to be aware of snipers. From there on to Benouville where once again we had trouble with snipers. While on our way to Benouville we heard what we thought could only be a tank coming from our road. This would be a great help to us but, unfortunately, it turned out to be one of our bulldozers. We warned the driver to stay put as the area wasn't cleared yet, but he insisted he'd had his orders. We were to meet again a few hundred yards down the road – he was slumped over his wheel, a bullet through his head. Now lay the approach road to the bridge – now known as Pegasus Bridge. A halt was called and we were thankful for the break but still couldn't relax as the enemy were keeping up a relentless bombardment.

The time came for us to cross the bridge which was under a smoke haze. Lord Lovat was standing in the middle of the road, just a few yards from the bridge, oblivious of the enemy fire which came raining down from the Chateau de Benouville on the west bank of the canal a few hundred yards to the south. A number of dead Germans lay around, obviously victims of the airborne assault. To the east side of the canal lay the gliders which had landed during the night. Lord Lovat standing there reminded me of a policeman on traffic duty, urging us on. 'Don't run across the bridge – walk' was his orders. Then it was my turn to go, passing some airborne lads who were dug in at the side of the bridge. 'Good luck, keep going, there's another bridge' they shouted. I think it must have been one of the fastest walks I have ever undertaken, feeling so vulnerable with bullets pinging off the steel girders and a fair amount of mortar fire. Soon I was across and into a ditch on the other side – a slight breather.

Platoon commander, Canadian Scottish
An LMG which sounded like a Bren opened up from a position about 150 yards away. We hit the dirt and I shouted. 'This must be the Winnipegs. When I say "UP" – all up together and shout "WINNIPEGS".' We did, and to our surprise two enemy infantry sections stood up just 125–150 yards ahead. They too were a picture of amazement. Their camouflage was perfect and it was no wonder we did not see them earlier. But the stunned silence did not last long. There was only one course of action, and to a man the platoon rushed the enemy positions. It was a bitter encounter with much hand-to-hand fighting.

T. Tateson, Green Howards
Without warning, a salvo of gunfire landed right in the middle of the troops to our immediate left, followed by a second shortly afterwards. From messages being passed on the radio, I learned that no one knew who was responsible except that it was coming from behind us. When a third salvo descended with the most enormous *crack* my signal training deserted me and I sent the unauthorized message,

'Stop this fucking barrage.' By complete coincidence, but to the flattery of my ego, the firing ceased. We later learned that it came from the Navy lying off shore, who did not realize we had advanced so far.

The speed of the British advance also caught German units unaware.

Anonymous German Private

Right in the middle of all this turmoil I got orders to go with my car for a reconnaissance towards the coast. With a few infantrymen I reported to a lieutenant. His orders were to retake a village nearby. While he was still talking to me to explain the position, a British tank came rolling towards us from behind, from a direction in which we had not even suspected the presence of the enemy. The enemy tank immediately opened fire on us. Resistance was out of the question. I saw how a group of Polish infantrymen went over to the enemy – carrying their machine guns and waving their arms. The officer and myself hid in the brush. When we tried to get through to our lines in the evening British paratroops caught us.

At first I was rather depressed, of course. I, an old soldier, a prisoner of war after a few hours of invasion. But when I saw the material behind the enemy front, I could only say, 'Old man, how lucky you have been!'

In the meantime the 'Tommy' advance went resolutely on.

Major F.D. Goode, Gloucestershire Regiment

Our advance was to be supported by rocket-firing Typhoons of the RAF. The enemy was holding the hedge on the opposite side of the field some 150 yards away. At this point I took the time to change my shirt and vest for dry ones from

my pack as I was soaked with sea water and sweat. I am
vague as to the time but it must have been after midday, as
the sun was high. We heard the roar of the engines of the
aircraft as they swept over us at almost ground level. They
released their rockets behind our position and we could hear
these swish over our heads. The whole line of the hedge
opposite burst into flames with a thunderous bang and we
clambered through our hedge and advanced through the
dead cattle. There did not seem to be any firing from the
direction of the enemy and when we arrived at their position
it was deserted.

. . . The colonel called another 'O' Group to meet in the
village of Ryes and we sat in the ditches by the roadside. The
village had been heavily shelled and most of the trees were
cut down, some across the road. There were a number of
dead Germans lying about and there was a sickly smell of
death in the air. It was hot, sunny and smelly. Colonel Biddle
had a bad cold and could smell nothing, but I for one was
glad to get back to my company.

.   .   .   .

As D Company we brought up the rear of the battalion. We
were marching with some fifty yards between companies and
the transport was in the rear of the company. The roads were
bordered with trees and grass verges which we presumed
were mined. There was a certain amount of sniping and one
who was firing at us turned out to be Japanese.

The sniper was probably recruited from the many Japanese
students at German universities. A significant proportion of the
Wehrmacht's army was made up of non-German nationals including, aside from Japanese, Poles, Russians, Mongolians, Tar-
tars and Uzbeks. Often they surrendered to the Allies with
alacrity.

With the Allied advance came the liberation of the first French
villages.

Anne de Vigneral, Ver-sur-Mer

Diary, 6 June

12 noon. Relative calm, but we all run to find boards and branches to cover our trench. We fetch rugs, mattresses etc. On the last foray we meet a German officer who says to me, 'The sleep is ended.' He was naive! We try to have a disjointed lunch, but it is interrupted continually. The German officer stations himself in a farmer's hedge and forbids them to betray him . . . In any case bursts of fire are everywhere, the children run back into the house. I hadn't realized that in the field where we collected our wood the English were in one hedge, the Germans in the hedge opposite and they were shooting at each other!!

1 p.m. I beg everyone to eat, but the noise gets worse and when I open the window I see all the Germans bent double going over the village bridge. We take our plates out, scuttle across the terrace and fall into the trench. The terrace is covered with bullets, the little maid feels one scrape her leg . . . we found it afterwards . . . We see lots of Germans in the area between the property and the river. We don't know what to think.

1.15. We pop our heads out of the trench and see soldiers, but we can't recognize them. Is the uniform khaki or green? They are on their stomachs in the leaves . . .

1.30. To reassure myself I go to the kitchen to get some coffee (we had lunched in the trench) and come back quietly but very obviously carrying a coffee pot . . . and then the soldiers hidden in the laurels by the bridge come out. Hurrah, they are Canadians. We have lumps in our throats, we all speak at once, it is indescribable. Some laugh, some cry. They give the children chocolate; they are of course delighted. Themselves, they arrive calmly, chewing gum. (Isn't that typically English.)

- 2.00. Their officer arrives and tours the house with me looking for delayed action bombs. I, without a thought of danger, and all in a rush, open doors and cupboards. We find some bottles of champagne which we bring down. We sit on the steps and all drink. Even Jacques, 7 years old, has a glass and drinks a toast with us. We all have already been given Capstan and Gold Flake cigarettes. Oh, don't they smell lovely!!

Trooper Peter Davies, 1st East Riding, Yeomanry

When we stopped outside Colleville there were two infantry-men, one standing guard on the corner of the road and one digging a trench. Two young French girls came out, walking around, from this house and stopped and chatted to these infantrymen. The first thing I saw that made me smile that day was their emergency ration of chocolate being handed over to these two French mesdemoiselles that were chatting to them. It proved we were in France.

As the first invasion forces fought and fraternized, tens of thousands of other GIs and Tommies continued to pour across the Channel, along with ship after ship of material.

Nevin F. Price, USAAF 397th Bomb Group

Flying back from a bombing raid behind Omaha it occurred to me that if we had to ditch there were so many ships in the Channel we could have walked back to England bow to stern.

Included in this cross-Channel traffic was a bizarre procession of gigantic concrete objects (caissons, or 'Phoenix units'), later to be metamorphosed into the purpose-built Mulberry Harbour. Sitting on top of one of the caissons was an anti-aircraft gunner of the Royal Artillery.

Bombardier Richard 'Dickie' Thomas, RA

As the tug pulled us out, we could see these flags on small buoys. Slowly but surely we started swaying from side to side

– there was no steering mechanism on the caisson, it was just a concrete box. As we went along we caught up the flags and started pulling them out. Anybody following us didn't know where they were going. Apparently a lot of ships mislaid their route because of the lost guide flags.

The departure of the thousands of Allied troops left English ports in an eerie silence.

Mary J. Thomson, Tilbury

We woke, it was a bright sunny day, and the troops had all gone. Everything had gone. The tents had gone – we didn't hear anything. The men had just disappeared. Strangely enough there was no litter. There was just flattened grass where the tents had been.

Even though the worst of the fighting on the Normandy beaches had subsided after the breakthrough by the first invasion waves, the beaches continued to have their horrors and dangers.

Colonel H.S. Gillies, King's Own Scottish Borderers

Signs of earlier fighting were abundant on the beach. The turf and sand were ripped up by tank tracks, barbed wire and beach obstacles were targetted together among broken glass and debris from the houses, and here and there a few bodies lay around covered with gas-capes.

By this time the beach was not under direct enemy small-arms fire, but spasmodic mortar and gun fire were taking a continuous toll.

Alan Melville, RAF war correspondent

I stopped the Jeep to ask someone if he had seen anyone else in RAF uniform; at that moment something – I never found out

what – dived out of the sky and seared along the beach with
its machine guns blazing. There was a half-dug slit trench
right in front of me and I threw myself into it head first. My
legs were sticking out and I remember lying there thinking
that I would rather be shot in the legs than anywhere else. I
wanted to push my steel helmet back to protect my neck but I
was too frightened to move. My face was pressed tightly down
into the sand, and I must have pushed the top layer of sand
away, for it was wet and clinging. It got in my mouth, and it
was a taste we were all to get to know very well.

Driver John Osborne, 101 Company General Transport Amphibious

During the afternoon the bodies had been collected off the
beach and stacked up outside the beach dressing station.
They were like a wall about three or four bodies high.

Lieutenant H.T. Bone, 2nd East Yorkshire Regiment

The Colonel was getting a grip on the battle and I was sent
back on the beach to collect the rest of us. I did not feel
afraid, but rather elated and full of beans. There were some
horrible sights there and not a few men calling out for help. I
wanted to pull a body out of the waves, but he looked to be
dead and I had no time or duty there, the beach medical
people would gradually get round to them all. Under the
sides of a tank that had been hit I saw a bunch of my people
and I bawled at them to get up and get moving since they
were doing no good where they were and could quite safely
get along to HQ. I felt a little callous when I found that
nearly all of them had been hit and some were dead.

Bombardier Harry Hartill, RA

Unfortunately the ramp of the liberty ship had been lowered
at the edge of a bomb crater and the first vehicle off promptly

vanished in ten feet of water. The ramp was resited and the ship's captain ordered the next vehicle down. But there were no John Waynes among us – better to be a live coward than a dead hero, we thought, and we waited for someone to drive off. The Captain drew his revolver and shouted 'I'll shoot the first bastard that disobeys my orders,' and fired over our heads. Reluctantly we drove down that awesome ramp onto the beach at Normandy.

. . . .

We were ordered to dig in and my four cable laying signallers and myself dug a 12-foot long and 2-feet deep trench for our protection. A couple of enemy shells came over and we dug deeper. More shells brought more digging, making it difficult to climb in and out.

Leading Aircraftman Gordon Jones, Combined Operations

Everything on the beach was was laid out so beautifully: there were tapes where we were supposed to go, there was a beach master giving directions, so up we went in our Chevrolet four-wheel drive trucks. Wonderfully easy. When we got to our designated area we were supposed to dig slit trenches, but we thought, 'What the hell do we want to dig slit trenches for? This is an absolute cakewalk.' So we didn't. Then three Heinkels – I think it was Heinkels – came over at about 100 feet, parallel to the beach from further up in France, and they were so low that I could see each gunner in his perspex cupola. They sprayed machine-gun fire everywhere. No one in our group was killed but it was certainly an eye-opener.

This Heinkel raid was one of the very few appearances by the Luftwaffe on D-Day. In the weeks beforehand numerous Luftwaffe planes and pilots had been withdrawn from France to protect the skies of the Fatherland itself against USAAF and RAF bombing. In the morning of 6 June, the Luftwaffe made only one raid on the Allied invasion forces, a low-level streak along the beaches by Josef 'Pips' Priller and his wingman Heinz Wodarczyk in their FW-190 fighters, a piece of outrageous bravery in a sky filled with Allied planes which drew admiration from the most anti-German of the invaders. Luftwaffe pilots still in France faced the most mundane but disabling problems in flying in to help their Normandy-based comrades, as in the case of this Me109 pilot proceeding from Perpignan via a refuelling stop near Paris.

Gunther Bloemertz, Luftwaffe

Our destination lay somewhere south of Paris, and no one but the Kapitän knew which airfield it was.

As the Eiffel Tower thrust itself needle-like out of the mist over the French capital, we climbed higher and then, with the squadron-leader ahead, dived with increased speed.

'We land here,' he called through to us as we flew low across the dry earth of an airfield.

'Still much too far from Paris,' grumbled one of the night-birds. But we landed all the same.

The shining hulls of American bombers were drawing across the sky above us.

'Where's our Sprit, Herr Major?' called the Kapitän from his cockpit as the Airfield Commander approached. This elderly officer could scarcely have seen a single aircraft land on his field in the whole war. Now he pointed significantly at the bombers.

'*There's* Sprit,' he said.

'We've got to have Sprit, Herr Major, *Sprit* – I repeat – otherwise we give up!' The Chief jumped angrily from his machine.

'I have orders to fly operational sorties against the invasion from your airfield. Your field has eighty thousand litres of petrol in its tanks for this purpose. My aircraft must be tanked up within an hour. We are armed for the sortie, and Le Bourget is sending ammunition for subsequent operations.'

'Yes, I have eighty thousand litres of A3 here. You can have that.'

'What! A3? Eighty thousand litres of A3? That's crazy! You can drive your car with A3, Herr Major, but our aircraft won't get off the ground with it.'

We stood round in dismay, thirsty men standing before a pool of poisoned water.

So we didn't fly on.

The absence of the Luftwaffe over Normandy was a particular curse for those Wehrmacht and Waffen SS units making their way to the front, left completely at the mercy of Allied airpower. These units included the crack Panzer divisions, Lehr and 12th SS, which Berlin, after much prevarication, had agreed to mobilize in the afternoon. For Panzer Lehr it was a sacrificial journey.

General Fritz Bayerlain, Panzer Lehr
I was driving in front of the middle column with two staff cars and two headquarters signal vans along the Alençon–Argentan–Falaise road. We had only got to Beaumont-sur-Sarthe when the first fighter-bomber attack forced us to take cover. For once we were lucky. But the columns were getting farther apart all the time. Since Army had ordered radio silence we had to maintain contact by dispatch riders. As if radio silence could have stopped the fighter-bombers and reconnaissance planes from spotting us! All it did was prevent the division staff from forming a picture of the state of the advance – if it was moving smoothly or whether there were hold-ups and losses, and how far the spearheads had got. I was for ever sending off officers or else seeking out my units myself.

We were moving along all five routes of advance. Naturally our move had been spotted by enemy air-reconnaissance. And before long the bombers were hovering above the roads, smashing cross-roads, villages, and towns along our line of advance, and pouncing on the long columns of vehicles.

Much the same fate was befalling the 12th SS Panzer, as its legendary leader describes, somewhat breathlessly, here.

Brigadefuhrer Kurt Meyer, 12th SS Panzer Division, aged 33

A chain of Spitfires attacks the last section of the 15th Company. Missiles and cannon reap a devilish harvest. The section is travelling through a narrow pass; it is impossible to get away. An elderly French woman is coming towards us and screaming, 'Murder, Murder!' An infantryman lies on the street. A stream of blood comes out of his throat – his artery has been shot through. He dies in our arms. The munition of an amphibious vehicle explodes into the air – high tongues of flame shoot up. The vehicle explodes into pieces.

Amazingly, Werner Kortenhaus and the 21st Panzer Division had escaped an air attack on their march forwards all morning. On reaching Caen in the afternoon, however, they encountered the terrible results of Allied bombing.

Gefreiter Werner Kortenhaus, 21st Panzer Division

The long road from Falaise to Caen rises to a hill where one can suddenly get a view over Caen, and as we drove over this hill we got a shock because the city of Caen was burning. I had never seen the city before, never been there at all, and all I could see was a huge black cloud over

Caen, as though oil had been burnt. At that point, I
realized for the first time that I was at war. As we got
closer to Caen our tanks had difficulty getting through the
city because the streets were covered with rubble. So we
lost a lot of time while some tanks went west around the
city and others went east.

Consequently, the 21st Panzer Division, the Wehrmacht's best
hope that day of pushing back the British and Canadians, lost
valuable hours. Finally, at around 5 o'clock in the afternoon 21st
Panzer was ready to make its armoured dash to the sea. At the
start-line, three miles to the north-east of Caen, General Marcks
had a final word with Herman von Oppeln-Bronikowski, who
would lead the panzer charge: 'Oppeln, the future of Germany
may very well rest on your shoulders. If you don't push the
British back to the sea, we've lost the war,' said Marcks. Only
minutes later as Bronikowski's tanks raced towards the sea they
were met by heavy fire from Sherman Fireflies of the Staffordshire Regiment. Thirteen panzers were knocked out almost
immediately. A handful made it through to Lion-sur-mer,
but not enough even to embarrass British operations. It was
too little, too late. Perhaps fortunately for Werner Kortenhaus,
his company did not take part in the dash, having been detailed
to hold the line on the Orne against the British 6th Airborne.
Yet, if the 21st Panzer Division had failed to throw the Allies
back into the sea, it also prevented the British from reaching
their D-Day objective of Caen. It would do so for many days to
come.

Off Omaha and Utah beaches the Americans, like the British
and Canadians, were moving inland. At Utah the progress was
spectacular, with the US 4th Infantry Division rolling out into
Normandy to link up with the US 82nd and 101st Airborne, as
groups of the latter continued to hold Ste Mere Eglise and fight

toward their buddies arriving by sea. Probably the biggest problem at Utah in the afternoon of 6 June were jams in the traffic of thousands of men as they left the narrow beach exits.

At Omaha too, the Americans were moving inland, but here they had to fight savagely for every inch. Having reached the top of the bluffs behind the beach, the US 1st and 29th Divisions found a lattice-work of hedges, narrow fields and hamlets that made ideal defensive territory for the determined remnants of the 352nd and 716th Divisions of the Wehrmacht. It was a bitter foretaste of the fighting in the *bocage* that was to come. And the beach itself was still coming under heavy shell fire.

Sergeant Richard W. Herklotz, US 29th Division

It [Omaha] was no summer resort. It was really a chaos, people were wounded, bodies were being piled up, equipment which had been destroyed was being pushed out the way because of the continued flow of landing craft coming in. If they were blocked on landing they would have been dead targets, because the Germans could look right down the cliffs and shoot the craft right out of the water. By the time we landed the engineers had opened up the obstacles on the draw which went up to Vierville and St Laurent, but we were, I guess, not fifty yards off the beach when we got shelled by a heavy weapon which hit our ammunition truck, and there was a fire. Of our battery of sixty-eight men we lost seventeen right there. At moments like that you cope, you endure because of the training that you have received, the repetition of it, so you do everything naturally, on the spur of the moment. You just do what you were trained for so many months to do, and keep going.

Captain Joseph T. Dawson, US 1st Infantry Division

The Germans were now retreating, we were advancing and although we had some contact with them we didn't experience any more active resistance from them until we had got across a small open field some 100 yards wide and entered into a wooded area which led to the town of Colleville. We had a very fierce battle all the way into the village, which was about a mile and a half from the crest of the ridge [at Omaha beach] ... It was a long narrow little village commanded in a meaningful way by a church with a steeple which the Germans were using as an observation point, to direct artillery fire at the beach itself. I entered the church along with a sergeant and an enlisted man and we encountered Germans in there, just as we entered the door. They were trying to get out, as we came in. I lost my enlisted man and my sergeant was wounded; however, we were able to overcome the Germans. After we cleared that, we were able to secure and stabilize the village itself, so that subsequent troops landing were able to pass through us at approximately 3.30 in the afternoon.

Shortly after the contingent of the following force of the 18th Infantry had passed through us our Navy started firing on us, on the village, and literally levelled it. During this time we suffered the worst casualties we had experienced in the whole day's work. Fire from our own Navy; 'friendly fire' it was called. It happened due to the fact that I had lost communication with the Navy back at the beach when I lost my naval officer. The Navy didn't realize we were in the village. I was frantically throwing smoke grenades up in the air to identify us as friendly, but it was too late for the barrage to not take effect. What was very disturbing to me was that they had waited until 15.30 to level the town and we had been there two hours by that time. Later when we brought an inquiry the Navy contended that their orders were to fire at H + 60 and again as visibility would permit. They contended that the smoke and firing on the beach obscured their opportunity to see any targets until the pall of battle lifted sufficiently for them to have

visual observation, which happened to be 15.30. I feel that
the Navy's interpretation of their orders was, shall we say,
a little far-fetched. I was very bitter about it, but time
has permitted me to mellow my feelings. We lost over
eighteen men dead, and several wounded – I never did
count them all. I'd suffered casualties throughout the day.
Out of the day's run we were over 50 per cent depleted
by the end.

Captain Albert H. Smith, US 1st Infantry Division

I recall testing German defences south of the hedgerow along
our dirt road [on top of the bluffs at Omaha beach]. Several
rifle teams attempted an advance across the hedgerows –
only to receive heavy arms fire from three directions. Somewhat later, a helmet raised on a stick just above the hedgerow vegetation drew immediate sniper fire. It was not
difficult to conclude the enemy was in strength just to the
south – in fact, right next door . . . Towards late afternoon I
was happy to see Lieutenant-Colonel Joe Sisson and his 3rd
Battalion, 18th Infantry, approaching our location. It was a
great feeling to know reinforcements were at hand. I passed
along what little I knew about friendly and enemy disposi-
tions. Shortly thereafter, two lead companies were deployed
from east to west along our dirt road; bayonets were fixed,
and men charged south across the hedgerow. That bayonet
charge – to the best of my recollection – was made sometime
around 17.00. Initially, German small-arms fire was heavy;
then, it seemed to fade as attacking companies moved further
south to other hedgerows and fields.

Donald Burgett, US 101st Airborne Division

All the troopers were firing now, and some of the ones closer
to the road were lobbing grenades as fast as they could on
the other side. It became a pitched battle with only a
narrow black-top road separating the two forces. Actions

became automatic, firing at fleeting shapes, crawling to different positions and firing, reloading and firing again and again.

The Germans were in the ditch on the other side of the road while we were in the ditch on this side. A distance of not more than fifteen yards separated us. At times, just as I slipped my rifle through the foliage to fire, I could feel the muzzle blasts from the enemy rifles as they fired toward us. The Germans usually dropped back into the ditch while working the bolt of their rifles, but we could nearly always get off one to three shots before ducking back down. We were so close together that our faces were being blackened by the enemy's muzzle blasts. They used a smokeless powder and were hard to locate, whereas our weapons spewed out billows of smoke that gave our positions away and kept us moving to keep from getting our brains blown out. There was very little wind and the smoke hung close around us. The smell of powder burned deep into our nostrils, leaving the backs of our throats and the roofs of our mouths dry, along with a taste like sucking an old copper penny.

Lt. Elliott Johnson, US 4th Infantry Division

We weren't the only ones that got across the water. There was an anti-aircraft crew. This was the dangedest thing. You can't imagine all this noise and all these shells exploding and fellows being hurt and killed, and here's this crew sitting smoking cigarettes and reading a comic book. I couldn't believe it. We stopped a hundred feet from them. I could see them out of the corner of my eye.

All of a sudden – wham! – they were galvanized into action. I looked up and nobody had to say anything. All of us dove out of that thing and crawled under, 'cause here came these three German aircraft. These guys didn't do any hiding. We did. It's a good thing we did. The Germans hit that thing with those .50-caliber machine guns. And these guys hit every one of those three German airplanes and knocked them down. Every one of them.

Pfc P.J. McCall, US 4th Infantry Division

As we pushed inland from Utah I was sent ahead to check the road we were going along. I cautiously went around a corner, and everything seemed OK, but after I cleared the corner I suddenly knew someone had their sights on me. I could just feel it. I was about to dive to the ditch when this voice – in the other ditch – said, 'Hey soldier, can you give me a light?' A head popped up slightly, and it was grinning. I wasn't sure for a moment whether it was a German playing a trick, but he had the drop on me anyway – and his voice was pure Bronx. He was 101st Airborne, and walked his way towards the beach through the night and morning.

Sergeant Richard W. Herklotz, US 29th Division

We were always told to have nothing in our gas-masks, always to have it ready because you'd have just 30 seconds to don it if gas came. I remember going around this churchyard above Omaha just after we got shelled, and I got tied up with communication wire. Somewhere along the line the Air Force had dropped yellow smoke, and the yellow smoke was knitting through the area and somebody shouted '*Gas!*' I had my gas-mask all tied up with the wire, and I couldn't get to it and when I got to it I had oranges in there, I had cigarettes – everything I wasn't supposed to have. I never did get the gas-mask out, so if it had been gas I'd certainly still be there.

. . . .

Off the beach there was a church surrounded by wire or some sort of wrought-iron fence. And there was a German in the tower and I think every GI on the beach shot at this German guy in the tower. We came to find out later that the

German was tied in the tower, everybody shot at him figuring he was alive, but he'd been shot many times and had been tied so that he would not fall out.

Able Seaman R.E. Hughes, aboard HMS *Glasgow*, off Omaha beach

Diary, 6 June

17.00. Urgent call for fire from beach.

17.15. Troops had a sticky time being shelled by mobile AA. We cannot get range because they keep moving.

Donald Burgett, US 101st Airborne Division

The officer had a bullet in his neck. The bullet had passed almost all the way through from the right side to the left and was lying pretty close to the surface, forming a big lump. He brought the tank to a stop and said he didn't feel good, so we helped him from the tank and placed him on the grass under the trees. The other troopers said I had done a good job setting the arm earlier, so they elected me to remove the bullet. I didn't want the job but someone had to do it.

After building a fire from one of the German packing crates, I heated my trench knife while another trooper gave the officer a shot of morphine. He was cold and clammy-feeling, and his tan skin had suddenly taken on a pallor that looked kind of sickly, but he did not pass out, even when I cut in his neck. The bullet did not come out easily and when the ordeal was finally over, he looked up at me and said in a weak voice, 'I don't think I'm going to make it.'

It was the first thing he had said. All through the operation he hadn't even groaned. We covered him as best we could to keep him warm against shock. The last time I saw him he was still living and looked as though he was getting better.

Tom Treanor, *LA Times* war correspondent

'Watch yourself, fella,' someone said, 'that's a mine.' A soldier sprawled on the bank was speaking. He had one foot blown half off and tied with a crude bandage. Pain had sucked his face white but still he remained conscious and still he took care lest someone should step on a live mine a few feet from his elbow. As each man edged up the path, he repeated the warning in a weak voice: 'Watch yourself fella, that's a mine.'

He knew what a mine could do. He'd stepped on one a couple of hours earlier.

I can stand the dead, but the wounded horrify me, and I only looked at him to thank him. He looked very tired but perfectly collected. 'What you need is a medico,' I said. 'I will get one for you when I go back down.'

'Yeah,' he said, 'but how are they going to get up here?'

He was right. The pathway was so clogged with men and so heavily mined that it was impossible for stretcher-bearers to get up to him. The engineers would have to get up first.

Sergeant Richard W. Herklotz, US 29th Division

Well, when you stand there and you've been with an individual – your sergeant, your right-hand man, say – and he's gasping for his last breath and he's speechless, it leaves you speechless. What would you say to him? What could you say?

It was now evening on 6 June, 1944. In the brilliance of the sinking sun the business of war continued.

Driver John Osborne, 101 Company General Transport Amphibious

In the evening I was sent out again to pick up some of our airborne chaps who had been caught in a flamethrower. They were in a bad way. Four of them were on stretchers

placed across the DUKW. There was also a German who
had been shot in the leg; he was the only one who complained. He kept on about losing his boot. (I later found the
German's damn boot in the DUKW; I don't know if it was
given to him.) With me too was a young chap from
Ordnance Corps. He had been bombed by something in a
house and was bomb happy. I gave him my home address
and asked him to write to my mother to tell her I was
allright. I learned later that he played on this and had
money and food from her.

Able Seaman J.H. Cooling, RN, aboard HMS *Scorpion*

All that day we bombarded the coast without a break, but it
was not until the evening that the gliders came over. We
watched them come along thick and fast, towed over the
beaches and away out of sight. It seemed almost impossible
to count them. It was a wonderful sight indeed.

Alan Melville, RAF war correspondent

There was a wonderful sunset that evening. I was standing
at the entrance to our dug-out during a lull in the shelling
when the most almighty roar of aircraft brought everyone
up from their holes. Two great waves came in from the
sea; the first of glider-towing bombers, the second of
paratroops. They went through exactly the same moves:
they roared in majestically as though this was just one
more exercise over Salisbury Plain, the bombers released
their gliders and the gliders slipped down between our own
position and the first rising slopes of the ridge of hills. The
bombers swept majestically round – quite slowly: you
would have thought they were lingering on purpose in
the hope that the Luftwaffe or the enemy ack-ack guns
would have a crack at them. Then, somewhat disappointed, they turned out to sea and went home for their

suppers. The paratroops who followed did just the same;
their aircraft swept over our heads and the parachutes
began to drop just at the foot of the ridge. They opened
and billowed out – hundreds of them. Pure white against a
lovely sky: we use white parachutes for men, and coloured
for supplies, and it was men that we were wanting that
night. They disappeared from our view behind the clumps
of trees, and it was days later when some of them filtered
back to the beaches that we learned what had happened to
them that night. Their aircraft, too, swept round and tore
back home. The troops forgot all about the shelling and
the snipers. They stood on the edges of their trenches and
waved and yelled themselves silly. It was the greatest
hoister of morale which anyone could have provided
and it came at precisely the right minute. I talked next
morning to some German prisoners, and the arrival of
those two waves of aircraft seemed to have had an equally
great effect on them. They said they had never imagined
that we possessed so many aircraft, and that when they
saw them – the first formations three miles inland and the
tail of the armada still out on the horizon – they knew that
it was hopeless.

Lieutenant C.T. Cross, Oxford and Buckinghamshire Light Infantry

The glider flight was bloody! It was, of course, longer than
most we'd done before because of the business of getting into
formation, collecting fighter escort and so on. After about
quarter of an hour I began to be sick and continued until we
were over the Channel where the air was much calmer. The
Channel was a wonderful sight – especially the traffic this
end – Picadilly Circus wasn't in it.

The landing was ghastly. Mine was the first glider down
though we were not quite in the right place, and the damn
thing bucketed along a very upsy-downsy field for a bit and

then broke across the middle – we just chopped through those anti-landing poles (like the ones I used to cut down during my forestry vac.) as we went along. However, the halves of the glider fetched up very close together and we quickly got ourselves and our equipment out and lay down under the thing, because other gliders were coming in and Jerries were shooting things about at them and us – so it wasn't very healthy to wander about. Our immediate opposition – a machine gun in a little trench – was very effectively silenced by another glider which fetched up plumb on the trench, and a couple of Huns – quite terrified – came out with their hands up.

Donald Thomas, 53rd Airlanding Light Regiment, RA

On the way over in the glider one of my colleagues was very nervous. I was sitting between him and somebody else in the tail end. I remembered that the major . . . in his briefing of the day before [5 June] had promised an umbrella of fighters flying above us. Half-way across the Channel I went to look through the window for these fighters and this nervous chap pulled me back saying, 'Sit down, you'll affect the balance of the glider!' (He stayed very nervous, and was sent back to England after four or five days. I was glad because he was making me nervous as well.) We landed in a cornfield, hit one of the posts planted there and finished up at a bad angle . . . Getting out we could hear machine-gun fire and we went down to the ground. I always remember the smell of the ground – a sweet, scented smell. After all, I had my nose in it.

As well as delivering airborne reinforcements, the Allied air forces continued their bombing of targets in Normandy.

Odette Lelanoy, Vire

My father had found on his way to work that morning
in Vire – we lived about 1.5 km away, in the countryside – lots of pamphlets on the roadside path. The
pamphlets had been dropped by the Allies, and had
written on them, 'URGENT, townspeople leave the
town quickly because you are going to be shelled' –
something like that. So my father, at the factory where
he worked, gave out these pamphlets to everyone, telling
them to 'head for the countryside, don't stay where you
are.' He went to see friends to convince them and tried
to convince everyone, but no one listened. Not even our
friends. It was awful because on 6 June at 8 o'clock in
the evening, when we were still outside in the garden,
we heard aeroplanes coming in high overhead, Flying
Fortresses at a height of about 3000 feet in tight
formation. The next thing, in a space of a few seconds, there was a ripping sound – as though silk was
being torn. After that there followed a whistling and
then explosions. They had dropped bombs from these
Flying Fortresses which, at 3000 feet, looked really tiny.
They looked like fleas, no bigger than that.

We began to see dust and flames as more and more
waves passed over us. We hid for cover in the house
behind the thickest walls and stayed there throughout,
in the thick of it, this fire, this deluge. I don't know
how long we stayed there. It seemed like an eternity. It
terrifies me even now as I look back. Afterwards my
father, who had been in the 1914–18 war, told my
mother and I to leave for a farm about 1.5 or 2 km
away where we knew the farmer, and we set off for it
on foot. My father went into town to see if our friends
were still alive. He went to all the places we had lived.
Our old flat was destroyed, everything opposite was
destroyed. All he found there was a fragment of thread
hanging in a tree, which he recognized from the smock

of a child. He stayed in the town all night, helping the wounded.

By the fall of night, 100,000 Allied troops had landed in France. More than 12,000 of them had become casualties of war. A similar number of Germans had died or been wounded trying to stop them. Now, over 60 miles of front, soldiers tried to snatch some sleep, planned their next moves, or nervously scanned the darkness. And the diarists among them made their last entries of the day.

General Matt B. Ridgway, US 82nd Airborne Division

I was in fine physical shape, but never in all my life have I been so weary as I was at the end of that first day in Normandy. Just before midnight, tottering on my feet as was many another soldier who had fought there on that day, I rolled up in a cargo chute and lay down for the first sleep I'd had in forty-eight hours. I crawled into a ditch, for the town of Ste Mére Eglise was only a short distance away, and all that night German airplanes were overhead, dropping five-hundred-pounders, and German artillery was shelling the city heavily.

Captain Albert H. Smith, US 1st Infantry Division

At about midnight we thought we would be able to get a little sleep. You know the hours were such that daylight lasted almost until 11 p.m., 23.00 hours? We were dead tired then. Everyone was dead tired. I said that I was walking around like a zombie. It got very cold, it went down to about 30 to 40° Fahrenheit. Two of us, another officer and myself, got under his raincoat and tried to get some sleep leaning against the hedgerow. It was a very bad physical feeling, but nevertheless we knew we had landed and were going to hold

our position on the bluffs, and troops were moving inland. So
it was a feeling of cold, miserable tiredness, but mentally we
were feeling, 'God, we did it.'

Corporal G.E. Hughes, 1st Battalion, Royal Hampshire Regiment
Diary, 6 June
06.00 Get in LCA. Sea very rough. Hit the beach at 7.20
hours. Murderous fire, losses high. I was lucky T[hank] God.
Cleared three villages. Terrible fighting and ghastly sights.

Able Seaman R.E. Hughes, aboard HMS *Glasgow*
Diary, 6 June
23.30. Bombs are dropping near us now and everyone
standing to. Several enemy planes fly low over the ships –
terrific reception for them.

Major F.D. Goode, Gloucestershire Regiment
It was now night, my servant Private Morris had blown up
my Lilo and put it in a farm cart that sloped slightly and was
under an open shed. It faced north towards the beaches.
Here I set up my company HQ and being by this time very
tired settled down on my Lilo . . . there was a steady noise of
aircraft going to and coming from the beaches. It was a clear
night and the beaches represented a fantastic firework
display as the Germans tried to bomb them and all the
ships and AA opened up with coloured tracers. Watching
this I fell asleep.

Lieutenant-General Edgar Feuchtinger, CO, 21st Panzer Division
About midnight, Kurt Meyer arrived at my headquarters.
He was to take over on my left and we were to carry out a
combined operation the next morning. I explained the

situation to Meyer and warned him about the strength of the enemy. Meyer studied the map, turned to me with a confident air and said, 'Little fish! We'll throw them back into the sea in the morning.'

D-Day was over, and the Allies had secured a bridgehead. The Battle of Normandy, however, was only just beginning.

Soldiering On

Combat, Life and Death in the Battle of Normandy, 7 June – 20 August 1944

Sometimes I wondered if the battles would ever end. We seemed to be fighting all day, every day. We couldn't see an end to it.

Trooper Peter Davies, 1st East Riding Yeomanry

Everyone who took part in the Battle of Normandy that summer was struck by the particular loveliness of the countryside they marched and fought through. Its hedges, orchards and meadows were almost a painful reminder of home for the men from England's shires, while Americans were struck by its verdancy.

Ernie Pyle, war correspondent
29 June 1944
All the American soldiers here are impressed by the loveliness of the Normandy countryside. Except for swampy places it is almost a dreamland of beauty. Everything is green and rich and natural looking.

There are no fences as such. All the little fields are bordered either by high trees or by earthen ridges built up about waist-high and now after many centuries completely covered with grass, shrubbery, ferns and flowers.

Normandy differs from the English landscape mainly in that rural England is fastidiously trimmed and cropped like a Venetian garden, while in Normandy the grass needs cutting and the hedgerows are wild, and everything has less of neatness and more of the way nature makes it.

Yet, if it was beautiful, the Normandy landscape was also deadly. The *bocage*, with its medievally small meadows and high farm hedges, was the perfect defensive country, where every hedge could hide a tank, every roadside ditch a heavy machine gun. The *bocage* was perhaps densest in the American sector, the Cotentin and the western half of Normandy. To fight in the hedgerows took a special kind of combat.

Anonymous US Infantry Officer

I want to describe to you what the weird hedgerow fighting in northwestern France was like. This type of fighting was always in small groups, so let's take as an example one company of men. Let's say they were working forward on both sides of a country lane, and the company was responsible for clearing the two fields on either side of the road as it advanced. That meant there was only about one platoon to a field, and with the company's understrength from casualties, there might be no more than twenty-five or thirty men.

The fields were usually not more than fifty yards across and a couple of hundred yards long. They might have grain in them, or apple trees, but mostly they were just pastures of green grass, full of beautiful cows. The fields were surrounded on all sides by the immense hedgerows – ancient earthen banks, waist high, all matted with roots, and out of which grew weeds, bushes, and trees up to twenty feet high. The Germans used these barriers well. They put snipers in the trees. They dug deep trenches behind the hedgerows and covered them with timber, so that it was almost impossible for artillery to get at them. Sometimes they propped up machine guns with strings attached so that they could fire over the hedge without getting out of their holes. They even cut out a section of the hedgerow and hid a big gun or a tank in it, covering it with bush. Also they tunneled under the hedgerows from the back and made the opening on the forward side just large enough to stick a machine gun through. But mostly the hedgerow pattern was this: a heavy machine gun hidden at each end of the field and infantrymen hidden all along the hedgerow with rifles and machine pistols.

We had to dig them out. It was a slow and cautious business, and there was nothing dashing about it. Our men didn't go across the open fields in dramatic charges such as you see in the movies. They did at first, but they learned better. They went in tiny groups, a squad or less, moving yards apart and sticking close to the hedgerows on either end of the field. They crept a few yards, squatted, waited, then crept again.

If you could have been right up there between the Germans and the Americans you wouldn't have seen many men at any one time – just a few here and there, always trying to keep hidden. But you would have heard an awful lot of noise. Our men were taught in training not to fire until they saw something to fire at. But the principle didn't work in that country, because there was very little to see. So the alternative was to keep shooting constantly at the hedgerows. That pinned the Germans to their holes while we sneaked up on them. The attacking squads sneaked up the sides of the hedgerows while the rest of the platoon stayed back in their own hedgerow and kept the forward hedge saturated with bullets. They shot rifle grenades too, and a mortar squad a little farther back kept lobbing mortar shells over onto the Germans. The little advance groups worked their way up to the far ends of the hedgerows at the corners of the field. They first tried to knock out the machine guns at each corner. They did this with hand grenades, rifle grenades and machine guns . . .

Usually, when the pressure was on, the German defenders of the hedgerow started pulling back. They would take their heavier guns and most of the men back a couple of fields and start digging in for a new line. They left about two machine guns and a few riflemen scattered through the hedge to do a lot of shooting and hold up the Americans as long as they could. Our men would then sneak along the front side of the hedgerow, throwing grenades over onto the other side and spraying the hedges with their guns. The fighting was close – only a few yards apart . . .

This hedgerow business was a series of little skirmishes like that clear across the front, thousands and thousands of little skirmishes. No single one of them was very big. Added up over the days and weeks, however, they made a man-sized war – with thousands on both sides getting killed. But that is only a general pattern of the hedgerow fighting. Actually each one was a little separate war, fought under different circumstances. For instance, the fight might be in a woods instead of an open field. The Germans would be dug in all over the woods, in little groups, and it was really tough to get them out. Often in cases like that we just went around the woods and kept going, and let later units take care of those surrounded and doomed fellows. Or we might go through a woods and clean it out, and another company, coming through a couple of hours later, would find it full of Germans again. In a war like this everything was in such confusion that I never could see how either side ever got anywhere.

Anonymous US Infantry Officer

There were just three ways that our infantry could get through the hedgerow country. They could walk down the road, which always makes the leading men feel practically naked (and they are). They could attempt to get through gaps in the corners of the hedgerows and crawl up along the row leading forward or rush through in a group and spread out in the field beyond. This was not a popular method. In the first place, often there were no gaps just when you wanted one most, and in the second place the Germans knew about them before we did and were usually prepared with machine-gun and machine-pistol reception committees. The third method was to rush a skirmish line over a hedge-row and then across the field. This could have been a fair method if there had been no hedgerows.

Usually we could not get through the hedge without hacking a way through. This of course took time, and a German machine gun can fire a lot of rounds in a very short time. Sometimes the hedges themselves were not thick. But it still took time for the infantryman to climb up the bank and scramble over, during which time he was a luscious target, and when he got over the Germans knew exactly where he was. All in all it was very discouraging to the men who had to go first. The farther to the rear one got the easier it all seemed.

Of course the Germans did not defend every hedgerow, but no one knew without stepping out into the spotlight which ones he did defend.

In truth the Allies were badly prepared for fighting in the *bocage*. Somewhat naively they had expected to punch through the Atlantic Wall and simply march on Paris. The *bocage* would not be a problem because the Allies would not be in it long enough for it to be a problem. As this American infantry officer points out, ironically enough the Allies had prepared for the invasion amid countryside uncannily like that of Normandy.

Captain Albert H. Smith, US 1st Infantry Division

We did our training in the middle of beautiful British hedgerows. And if somebody had said, 'You're going to run into this sort of thing' – narrow roads, with high mounds of dirt on either side and all – we'd have practiced and found a way through them without casualties. But that wasn't done as part of our training. We were trained to eliminate pill-boxes, we were trained to eliminate bunkers, to get out of landing craft and move quickly – that we could all do.

It was not just the Normandy landscape which encouraged a long, slow war of hard fighting. It became official Wehrmacht policy.

War diary, Wehrmacht 7th Army
10 June 1944
The Chief-of-Staff Army Group 'B' presents the views of the Supreme Commander of the armed forces (Hitler) . . . that there should be neither a withdrawal, fighting to the rear, nor a disengagement rearward to a new line of resistance, but that every man will fight and fall, where he stands.

This order, the diametric opposite of the Fuhrer's usual insistence on counter-attacks to destroy the enemy, was occasioned by brutal necessity. On 7 and 8 June, the two days following the Allied landing, Kurt Meyer's 12th SS Panzer Division (Hitler Youth) tried to drive the British and Canadians into the sea. Meyer's Panzers and fanatical teenage soldiers – the members of the 12th SS were as young as 16 – drove back the Canadians for two miles, but failed to break through. In turn, the British and Canadians tried to take Caen but were unable to breach the line held by the 12th SS, although they did manage to seize the village of Cambes on 9 June. These three days saw some of the fiercest fighting of the war.

Emil Werner, 25th Panzergrenadier Regiment, 12th SS Panzer Division
Until Cambes, everything went well. So far as we were concerned, the village looked fine. But on the outskirts we came under infantry fire and then all hell broke loose. We stormed a church where snipers had taken up positions. Here I saw the first dead man from our company; it was Grenadier Ruehl from headquarters platoon. I turned his body over myself – he'd been shot through the head. He was the second member of our company to die. Dead comrades already; and we still hadn't seen any Englishmen. Then the situation

became critical. My section commander was wounded in the arm and had to go to the rear. Grenadier Grosse from Hamburg leapt past me towards a clump of bushes with his sub-machine gun at the ready, screaming 'Hands up! Hands up!' Two Englishmen emerged with their hands held high. As far as I know, Grosse got the Iron Cross, second class, for this.

Lieutenant-Colonel J.M. Meldram, report No. 1, Canadian War Crimes Investigation Unit

Some [German] tanks continued forward to Bretteville to within about 300 yards of battalion headquarters. There they remained for one and a half hours shelling and machine-gunning the town. About midnight two Panthers entered the town. One came opposite battalion headquarters and was struck by a PIAT bomb fired from behind a low stone wall at 15 yards range, safe from the tank's huge gun. It halted for a moment, started again and after 30 yards was hit again by a second PIAT bomb. It stopped, turned around and headed out of town. A third PIAT hit finished it off so that it slewed around, out of control, running over a necklace of No. 75 grenades which blew off a track. The crew dismounted and attempted to make off, but were killed by small-arms fire. During this incident the second Panther had remained further up the road. Seeing the fate of its companion it commenced to fire both 75 mm and MG [machine gun] wildly down the street, 'like a child in a tantrum,' doing no damage whatsoever except to set fire to the first Panther.

Altogether twenty-two Panthers circled about battalion headquarters and A Company's position during the night, and it is hard to picture the confusion which existed. Contact with all but D Company was lost. Fires and flares lit up the area, and the enemy several times appeared to be convinced that opposition had ceased.

Sergeant Leo Gariepy, 3rd Canadian Division

The morale of the men was very low indeed. So many of their long-time comrades had stayed behind on the battlefield, the battle itself had been so savage, so furious, that every man felt that the 12th SS Panzer had a personal grudge against our tanks. Silently, grimly, we were looking at each other, knowing exactly what was in the other man's mind. They simply lay there, not sleeping, eyes opened, just staring into space. A poet or a writer would have found the proper words to describe this vacant look and what was going through their minds, but other than a few comforting words from the padre, Major Creelman, not much was said. Mostly, everyone was rather vindictive, and silently swearing revenge.

Colonel H.S. Gillies, King's Own Scottish Borderers

The attack entailed crossing a distance of about one thousand yards of open cornfield which fell away from Cambes Wood. We had barely crossed the start-line when the enemy reacted fiercely, with well-sited machine gun and intense mortar fire which enfiladed the companies as they moved forward. It was a situation almost reminiscent of some First World War battlefield . . . We could see the tracer bullets flicking off the corn. Casualties began to mount as we pressed forward, but the grave situation in which we found ourselves was suddenly retrieved by the decisive action of my company second-in-command, who organized a very effective 2-inch mortar smoke screen to cover our open flank. This allowed us to complete the remainder of our advance without prohibitive casualties and to establish contact with the Royal Ulster Rifles. After a sharp battle at close quarters, the village was cleared at dusk, but we were then subjected to an intense barrage of gun and mortar fire, which caused many more casualties. At best, it was only possible in the pitch darkness to establish a tentative defence system and we fully expected the enemy to launch a counter-attack at the first opportunity. They had now been identified as the notorious 12th SS (Hitler Youth) Panzer Division.

Cambes as it was revealed in the dismal light of dawn was one of the less pleasant sights of the campaign. The trees had been shredded and the paths and open spaces were littered with branches. The chateau was blasted and gutted and the village wrecked and empty, and over everything hung the sickening odour of rotting bodies. Bloated cattle lay on their backs with stiffened legs pointing skywards and our own and enemy dead lay where they had fallen, sprawling and grotesque . . . It took hours to collect the dead and then burial was a long and dangerous process under the constant shell fire. However, this was to be our home for a considerable period and we gradually accustomed ourselves to life in digging trenches.

The failure to take Caen was a major setback for the Allies. The city was strategically important, for behind lay the open plain – tantalizingly good tank country – and the short route to Paris. But by 9 June the German shield around Caen had been strengthened by the arrival of the outstanding Panzer Lehr division, taking their place alongside 21st Panzer and 12th SS Panzer. For nearly six weeks, these and other German divisions would, *pace* Hitler, 'fight and fall' in defence of Caen. For the British and Canadian infantry the names of the villages around Caen, places such as Tilly-sur-Seulles and Villers-Bocage, would henceforth always be remembered with a shudder of horror.

*

Private Robert Macduff, Wiltshire Regiment
Normandy
One of the scenes which will live forever in my mind is the arms and legs on the roadside covered in maggots. The smell was vile. Someone had been killed, someone had gone for ever. The thought in my mind was 'There but for the grace of God go I.' In the major scheme of things I was a little

unknown who would probably end up like that, someone who will never know what their contribution had been, and never know the outcome. It was very depressing.

*

Across in the west of Normandy the US Army was meanwhile attempting to roll back the Wehrmacht on the Cherbourg peninsula, and capture the port of Cherbourg itself. It proved heavy going – 'The goddamn Boche just won't stop fighting,' one officer complained to General Bradley – especially for troops untested in battle. To help keep their cutting edge the Americans were obliged to retain the battle-hardened airborne divisions in the *bocage* for over a month, although it was initially intended to withdraw them in the first week after D-Day. In numerous towns – including Cherbourg – the tenacious Germans were only defeated after massive airstrikes.

General Matt B. Ridgway, US 82nd Airborne Division
There were four of these crossings and by far the toughest was the causeway across the wide and sluggish Merderet. Here the road came down and made a right angle turn through a low cut in the hills about twenty or thirty feet high. It then emerged onto a perfectly open, straight road that stretched five or six hundred yards across the swamp. The Germans naturally concentrated their fire on our end of the defile, and it was the hottest sector I saw throughout the war. We lost a lot of men there and I think the assault unquestionably would have failed if all the commanders from division to battalion had not been there in person to shove the troops across.

We weren't going after that crossing cold, of course. We had artillery support by then, from the battalions of the 4th Division. We had a battalion of 105 self-propelled howitzers, a battalion of 155 howitzers, a platoon of tanks, and every 50-caliber machine gun we could lay hands on. We massed them all there on the river lip, and for ten minutes before the crossing we poured shells into the German positions on the far side. It was a tremendous spectacle – the crash of the guns blended into one great blasting roar of terrific noise, and the smoke and dust and haze soon grew so thick you could hardly see six feet in front of you.

We really poured the fire across, and we were getting plenty in return. I lay up on the crest to the right of the crossing, alongside one of the tanks, whose gun was banging away with a noise to split the head. Off to the left the automatic weapons were going like the hammers of hell, and to the rear our heavier artillery was firing, the shells passing directly overhead.

I lay there watching, peering through the haze and smoke, as the first men came down to the crossing, shoulders hunched, leaning forward as if they were moving against a heavy wind. Some of them began to go down, and the others hesitated. Then they turned and started back, instinctively recoiling from the sheer blasting shock of the concentrated enemy fire. I jumped up and ran down there. The men were milling around in the cut. Jim Gavin, whom I had put in charge of this operation, was there, with the regimental CO Colonel Lewis, and the battalion commanders. And there in the cut at the head of the causeway we grabbed these men, turned them around, pushed, shoved, even led them by hand until we got them started across.

We got across all right in spite of fairly heavy casualties, and cleared the far end of the causeway, so that the 9th Division, which was to take up the attack on the other side, could pass through. The Division Commander, General Manton Eddy, told me a few hours later that he'd never seen so many dead Germans anywhere. I agreed with him. I hadn't either. And I think that fight was as hot a single battle as any US troops had, at any time, during the war in Europe.

After that one, my aide told me, laughing, that back at headquarters they were referring to me as 'The Causeway

Kid'. I didn't see anything particularly humorous in the title, for I saw too many fine youngsters killed at those swamp and river crossings. The fire was always hot along those exposed stretches of straight road. I remember one night I stepped out from behind a farmhouse to the edge of the macadam highway, and saw lights winking in the dark at my feet. I said to the officer with me:

'That's the first time I've seen fireflies around here. Wonder why we haven't seen them before.'

'Fireflies, hell,' he said. 'Those aren't fireflies. They're machine-gun bullets ricocheting off the road.'

John Houston, US 101st Airborne Division

The next morning the order was 'Continue the attack southwest from Carentan.' The third platoon had no officer left and no staff sergeant, so Sergeant Houston was in charge. There were twenty of us left in action out of the fifty who had taken off from England a week before.

It was impossible to make rapid progress because each hedgerow was a natural defense line. Machine guns seemed to be placed at every corner, and their music was punctuated by the *brrrrp* of Schmeissers. We had gained a few small fields along the road toward Periers when a counter-attack came at us about noon. Offense immediately became defense.

Sergeant Cassada had his machine-gun crew, Andy Ritchie and Bill Shumate, set up in the corner of the field that our platoon was holding. Riflemen were stretched along the hedgerow and picked off any Nazi who stuck his head up. Eighty-eight fire was coming in, but it was long and didn't do us any harm. When a light tank came around a corner of the lane in front of us, Langlinais and Milburn Young, who had rifle grenades, fired and the tank pulled back. The earth is a soldier's best friend when fire is heavy. I went back and forth the length of the platoon line without raising a foot off the ground.

Early June, 1944. A woman hangs out the washing in an English south coast town. Behind her the road is lined with vehicles (Photo: Imperial War Museum)

American infantrymen try to find room on a cramped landing ship, 5 June (Photo: Imperial War Museum)

British soldiers aboard a landing craft find some amusement in a travel guide to France (Photo: Imperial War Museum)

Above: Eisenhower addresses troops of the US 101st Airborne Division ('The Screaming Eagles'), as they prepare to take off from Greenham Common airbase on the evening of 5 June (Photo: Imperial War Museum)

Opposite page above: Assault trooops of the US 1st Infantry Division shelter behind beach obstacles and the few tanks which made it ashore at 'Bloody' Omaha, on the morning of 6 June (Photo © Magnum)
Below: Marines of 4th Special Service Brigade landing at St Aubin-sur-Mer, 6 June (Photo: Royal Marines Museum)

Above: Commandos of the 1st Special Service Brigade landing at La Breche, Sword Beach, 6 June (Photo: Imperial War Museum) *Below*: A typical scene from the British beaches on D-Day: men from the 1st Battalion, South Lancashire Regiment, fall wounded at the water's edge, while just a few yards away others march forward without opposition (Photo: Imperial War Museum)

The scene at sea on D-Day, pictured from the US beaches (Photo: Imperial War Museum)

Marines of 46 Commando RM advancing through La Delivrande from Sword Beach to Caen, 8 June (Photo: Royal Marines Museum)

In the middle of the afternoon word came down from regiment that tanks from the Second Armored Division were coming to help us. We soon heard the roar of big Sherman tanks on the road behind us. Each of our squads was assigned to work with a tank, and the action started. Some of the tanks had been equipped with bulldozer blades to cut through the hedgerows.

The two tanks attached to our platoon started across the field, with machine-gun bullets bouncing off them. When the first one got to the next hedgerow, troopers rushed up to finish off the Nazis trying to get away from the tanks. Now that the German front line was broken, we moved along close to the tanks, using them for cover from the burp gun fire. Freddie Brannon was hit during this action, but that was the only casualty third platoon had that day.

Before dark the line had been pushed out about two miles and a half from Carentan, and the tanks left us to go about their business elsewhere. The troopers dug in; it had been another long day.

Company H settled into a defense line for the next three days. Most of the foxholes were developed into two-man dugouts with roofs made of planks from broken buildings. Each soldier soon began to think of a certain spot as his 'home', even though it might be just a hole in the ground. When Chaplain Engle or Father Sampson came around they were shown these homes just as if they had been new houses in the suburbs back in New York. Everything is relative.

We began to get acquainted with a new ration system called ten-in-one. They were meals for ten men packed together and easy to prepare without the facilities of a kitchen. The training that some of the men had in Boy Scouts came in handy, and each squad began to brag about the meals they prepared . . .

Every now and then we were reminded that we were in the front lines by some 88 shells hitting along the road or burp gun fire near the outposts. In the afternoon of June 16

Company H was told to push the outposts farther ahead to give better observation. The whole company would move up to set up the outposts and then bring telephone wire back to our permanent positions. We moved up, using hedgerows for concealment, and, after a couple of brisk fire fights, captured two German outposts a few hundred yards in front of us.

Heavier machine-gun and artillery fire began to come in soon after we took their outposts. Young and I were near the end of a hedgerow and crawled around it to see what was ahead. Shells burst in a line in the field in front of us, and for a split second we knew that the next one would hit our corner. The earth seemed to explode. I was lifted up and slammed down to the ground. Then there was a strange quiet as if they had determined to get us and would stop firing now that it was accomplished.

I turned to look at Young. The shell had landed practically on him, and there was no need to ask a medic if he was dead. 'How come I'm not dead? I can move! No blood! My ankle hurts.' I sat up and looked at my boot. There was a small hole in it, and blood was beginning to ooze out.

Lenny Lloyd called out, 'Are you okay, sergeant?'

'Just hit in the ankle, but Young was killed.'

I limped over to the rest of the platoon, and we got orders to pull back to our defense line. The outpost squads were digging in, and communications men were taking the telephone wire back. Our company medic told me to leave the boot laced tight until we got 'home'.

Andy Ritchie cut a strong stick out of a hedge for me to use as a cane for the quarter-mile hike back to our positions. When we arrived there the company medic came around and helped me take off the boot. He said it wasn't too bad, but he thought there was a piece of shrapnel stuck in the bone just above the ankle.

There is a mixture of feelings in combat soldiers with light wounds. One is of relief that you can rest, sleep in a bed and not have to wonder about machine guns in the next hedgerow. The other is a feeling of guilt for leaving your buddies, so I asked the medic to bandage it up and put the boot back on.

Captain Stanley ordered that the three of us wounded in the action would go to the division hospital in Carentan. That left Sergeant Cassada in charge of third platoon. Two lieutenants, one staff sergeant, and two of the original squad leaders had been killed or wounded between June 6 and June 16.

Harold Denny, *New York Times* **war correspondent**
But the troops even up close to their goal [Cherbourg] could not see the port. It was hidden in the haze of smoke and dust of our bombardment and the air was choking with the smoke of burning wooden emplacements and powder.

I followed our advancing infantry with some mopping-up troops and, on a hill overlooking Cherbourg, found other American infantrymen had fallen into enemy fox holes to rest, some of them asleep as soon as they lay down. They were waiting while our artillery scoured the valley to our right for German batteries that had been shelling our rear.

Here the devastation of our bombs was apparent. German vehicles and guns lay wrecked and wasted. German wire, which had been tied to the pill-boxes, was almost obliterated. In one open field just behind, lay dead cows and chickens . . .

Now we are inside most of the German fortifications [inside Cherbourg] we see how we were helped by bad German guesswork. Most of the fortifications face seaward and the Germans were able to turn only some of their guns landwards when the threat came from the south, making our advance easier. The Germans evidently thought Cherbourg a likely target for an invasion, and the shore all around the northern tip of the peninsula is heavily fortified with beach defences such as our men encountered on D-Day.

Leutnant Poppel, Wehrmacht 6th Parachute Regiment

Diary, 7 June

At first light vast numbers of enemy bombers reappear, bringing death and fire into the French hinterland. Naturally, their targets are the railway junctions, strategic concentration points and channels of communication, as well as our advancing armoured units. They know well enough that if they can eliminate our reinforcements they should be able to achieve their objectives without massive casualties. As for our own pilots – they are nowhere to be seen.

We all reckon that I Battalion has been thrown into battle alone and with no prospects of success. It must already have suffered considerable casualties if it hasn't been wiped out completely – and my friend and comrade Eugen Scherer is with them. During the night, the Regimental Commander has ordered II Battalion to relieve I Battalion. The northeast position of the hills of St Come-du-Mont must be held at all costs, to provide a favourable basis for further counterattacks.

Enormous explosions can be heard in the north and northeast, which must be coming from the enemy's naval heavy artillery. We can also hear the noise of battle from that direction.

13.00 hours. 9 Company has now been moved to St Come-du-Mont to consolidate our positions there.

We have learned that I Battalion has suffered very high casualties after the Americans made further airborne landings by glider to the rear of them in the early hours of the morning. With enemy units ahead of them, with a whole Regiment of elite enemy troops behind them, and with marshland to the south, all that the Battalion could do was to take up a position of all-round defence and defend themselves to the last man. Meanwhile, II Battalion has gone on the attack in the north, but made only sporadic contact with enemy units and has been forced to withdraw to the hills. There it has been reinforced by a fortress construction battalion composed partly of young and old infantrymen but partly of Russians who can't really be relied on.

During the morning, 9 Company advances as far as the foothills of the mountains but is then forced to yield to the enemy's superior force. The Company is now sealing off the hills alongside units of II Battalion and the infantry.

17.00 hours. On the order of the Battalion, second mortar group under Leutnant Schröder is despatched to reinforce 9 Company. I go with my captured French car and the lorry over the 2 kilometres of marshland to St Come-du-Mond so that I can supply the group myself and can discuss tomorrow's plan of attack with Oberleutnant Wagner.

At Regimental headquarters the order reaches me to prepare tomorrow's attack with Oberleutnant Wagner. The plan is to drive the enemy back to St Marie-du-Mont. In the opinion of the men involved, this task can't be achieved with the forces we have available. The Americans, supported by their naval artillery, are already advancing inexorably and our advanced units are already engaged in bitter fighting. Although night is slowly closing in, there has been no let-up in the noise of battle. With Unteroffizier Hiester and my loyal paladin Söser I go to the front to see Oberleutnant Wagner and discuss the situation with him on the spot.

Despite everything we learned in our peacetime exercises, the men are lying in large groups right next to each other. They can only be dispersed with great difficulty and much profanity. A few hundred metres further on, and the shells are landing close by. At once I'm transported back into the old-style warfare. I come across Wagner behind a hedge, in discussion with the infantrymen. Today he doesn't seem as calm and level-headed as he usually is. Messages continue to come in, bringing important information from the command posts.

After a short time the main points of the attack have been

discussed over the map, the ground signals and signals agreed. The leader of his company HQ personnel takes rapid notes and asks some final questions. Then a cry from ahead: enemy attacking with tanks!

The men, particularly the infantrymen, are damned jittery. But even Wagner can't seem to make up his mind what to do. Since I can't help here but can only make things worse, I start to make the journey back with my lads. At the junction I meet my mortar group, which has just got here by truck. Quickly, we organize the unloading of the shells. I give my instructions to Schröder and then travel back in the lorry. The driver races along the narrow dirt road with its high hedgerows like the devil incarnate, and brings us back to Regimental HQ.

A massive operation is under way there. ADCs come and go, messengers hurry past and are quickly dispatched on their way. The lamp is burning in the underground bunker – the Commander and the Battalion Commander are at work. Outside, the soldiers' cigarettes are glowing in the darkness. The Old Man gives Oberleutnant Prive the information about tomorrow's attack, so he discusses the last details with us. He too is less than delighted with the strength of the forces available to him. In particular, he's angry that he has to attack with just two platoons. We can all sympathize with his predicament.

What has persuaded the Commander to depart from the basic principles of his map exercise? Before this he always preached to us to 'Think big!' – but now he's simply tearing this fighting Regiment apart. It's incomprehensible. But perhaps – and more likely – the whole tragedy lay in the fact that the whole Regiment had only about 70 trucks at its disposal, and these were often so old and useless that we couldn't repair them when they broke down. Replacement parts simply weren't available any more. Consequently, most of our elite Regiments had to go everywhere on foot, like in the Middle Ages, carrying all the heavy guns, anti-

tank guns and mortars. The General Staff seems to have
thought that we paratroopers could manage with nothing
more than our knives. This attitude even seems to have
affected Field Marshal Rommel, who was otherwise so
prudent: he had created defences against airborne landings, had ingeniously strengthened the coastline – but little
or nothing was available for the rapid transportation of the
reserve divisions to the coast . . .

8 June
Things get under way before dawn. Only one thing is wrong:
it's not our attack, but the enemy's, hitting deep into our
assembled troops. The attack begins with sustained bombardment from the enemy naval artillery, explosion after
explosion landing on our comrades over there. Using our
field glasses and the battery commander's telescope, we try to
penetrate the thick mist, but without success. We can locate
the line only roughly by listening for the exceptionally rapid
fire of our MG 42s. Our six-barrelled mortars have begun to
fire as well, but there's just no comparison with the enemy's
armoury of heavy guns.

As the day grows brighter, we can see our targets. At one
point there's a large number of Yankees running about,
apparently a supply depot or even a command post. Doppelstein soon works out the firing distances, then we send the
first shells over. After a few shots, we start to make direct hits.
Brick dust whirls upwards from the farmhouse, people come
running out in an attempt to get away from concentrated
mortar fire. Even the cows are jumping around in comical
fashion. Don't forget – we can shoot too.

On the mountains, the sound of battle is moving to the
west – which means that we are retreating slowly. If we could
only get a signal from the infantry, but there's nothing,
absolutely nothing. It makes me want to throw up. We're
desperate to help those poor fellows, but when we've no idea
where the front line is we can't do a thing. Surely it would be

so easy for the infantry to show the position of the front line by sending up a light signal?

It's full daylight now. The enemy's artillery strikes are landing further forward, making thick clouds of smoke drift eastwards over the hedges. More gliders are landing by the church of Ste Mere Eglise . . .

Through the battery commander's telescope we can see the enemy fleet at the mouth of the Vire. An overwhelming spectacle of the power of the Allies. Ship after ship, funnel after funnel – a sight that absorbs everyone with its sheer military strength. Twenty-seven big freighters each with three or more funnels, ten battleships, twenty or thirty cruisers, hundreds of smaller vessels can be recognized and counted. Really, it looks like a naval review in peacetime. We can clearly see the muzzle flashes from the warships, then the heavy stuff screams overhead and tears deep holes in the marshland. There's nothing we can do except suffer and wait.

Once again, the fighter-bomber formations are approaching the town. They're there, their machines scream into the dive. The dreadful crack of bombs on houses, then dirt and dust are thrown into the air and our tower sways. They turn and come in again. Dammit, get down from this scaffold. My God, that only just missed. But it's no good – we have to climb to the top again as it's the only way we can help our hard-pressed comrades in their battle.

After a long time spent in fruitless observation, during which my howitzer platoon leader asks me three times whether he can open fire, we see some units retreating. At first a few men, individually, then whole groups, platoons coming back at the foot of the mountains. The enemy fire is increasing all the time, but we have no real chance of responding effectively. Then, even more bad luck, a barrel burst. Two men – of course, they're the best gunners – are badly wounded and two others less so. A tragic loss considering how few guns we have for the whole Regiment. Now the rest will be even more hard-pressed.

Meanwhile it has turned into a beautiful day, blue sky, the sun burning hot in the sky. On both sides though, the soldiers continue to suffer. Raiding parties search the city for French vehicles and fuel, and my organizers prove themselves extremely competent once again. A wonderful pale grey limousine rolls up, followed by a little blue one, and we also get our hands on a motorcycle and repair it. At first the Battalion made fun of the Company, but now our transport is the envy of them all.

9 June

Now, halfway up the mountain, we can at last see the American infantry units. Well, you fellows, we've been waiting for you for hours. In no time, the order to open fire is given to the howitzer platoon. Shortly afterwards the shooting begins and, after a few corrections, we begin to score direct hits on the Yankees – exactly where we wanted. I lift Doppelstein on my shoulder in sheer joy. Suddenly life on this mountain is fun again as we make the Yankees scatter. How our infantry will celebrate, especially those involved in the rearguard action. It's only a shot in the arm from the rascally artillery, but it brings some relief, especially if we can make every shot count. More groups are working their way to the road. 'Rapid rate of fire.' My poor gunners have had long enough to rest. Their aim is excellent and the range-finder operator is already preparing for new targets.

11.00 hours. Whole columns of infantry appear on the railway line, heading towards us. It's to be hoped that the Americans don't get too far forward, or they'll be able to attack the lads on the flank. To the left and right of the tracks there's marshland, so no alternative route is available to the retreating Germans. Apparently the Americans haven't spotted them yet though, since they aren't directing any artillery fire at the tracks.

Meanwhile the Americans have advanced to the road and

our own infantry has reached the protecting bridge in numbers. Now to send over our heavy stuff. Those fellows really do offer a tempting target. Our six-barrelled mortars, which have found the correct range, open up. The shells land right in the middle of the Yankees. The whole area, including our old command post, is now coming under fire from the guns. Our infantry exploits the situation at once and works its way forward at great speed. It's a miracle that the Americans didn't direct their artillery fire at the road and the railway.

The entire Battalion staff has now joined us up here. The Commander and Oberleutnant Ulmer enjoy the spectacle of this less than glorious retreat by our Regimental Commander. Like us, they're also fascinated by the spectacle of the invasion fleet . . .

We continue to organize ourselves and to drag whatever we can from Carentan. Butter, cheese, real coffee, wine, champagne, socks and shirts – all coveted and needed. The men continue to strengthen the positions, clean their guns and themselves. Ammunition belts are reloaded. 11.00 hours: about twenty Amis can be seen by the old Vire bridges, helping to build footbridges, and there is also considerable activity by supply trucks. Just what our mortars and machine guns have been waiting for. I gladly give permission to open fire, and soon two enemy trucks are in flames. Peters and Domke are the happy marksmen.

11 June

Now the time has come. The artillery has been keeping up a heavy barrage for 15 minutes, the assault guns have been moved forward to the furthest point where the hedgerows offer cover. At the stroke of 06.00 hours our artillery fire creates a fire-screen above the positions to be attacked. Simultaneously the tanks advance, accompanied by the infantry. The enemy line has already been reached, with hardly any shots being fired from there.

My men are fairly well acquainted with the terrain and move towards the old line. Widely spaced and in echelon, they advance from hedge to hedge. As they approach their objective, they come under semi-automatic fire. A sniper in a tree! A burly lance-corporal, a Bavarian or Tyrolean with a neat moustache, brings two men down from the trees single-handedly but is then hit and killed. Two others are wounded. This much we can see from the observation post. Then we gather round the radio equipment to hear the incoming reports and get the details of the situation.

07.30 hours. Report from SS Battalion I/37: Advancing steadily despite very stiff enemy resistance. Americans moving to the north. Enemy groups still situated between our spearheads. Own casualties moderately high.

09.00 hours. Report from the left flank: Have reached outskirts of Carentan, strong enemy groups still in rear. Request artillery fire on Carentan since noise of tanks detectable there.

09.15 hours. Report from the right flank: Unable to prevail against strong resistance without tanks. Approximately 500 metres territory gained by 09.00 hours.

09.50 hours. Report from SS Battalion I/37: Attack at a standstill in front of Carentan. Enemy attacking from Carentan with tanks.

10.45 hours. Forced to withdraw under massive enemy pressure.

Then everything happens with lightning speed. The Commander of the SS troops has realized that only our own position can now be held, and orders a rapid withdrawal to the initial position.

The troops are pouring back, but can still be intercepted and made to reinforce the line of defence.

*

William Seymour, RN
Normandy
Our commanding officer was 29 years of age. We were all youngsters and he was like a father to us.

*

A recurring fear of footsoldiers in Normandy was of sniping. The landscape, with its churches, trees and hedges, was almost made for it. It came with the turf, so to speak.

Ernie Pyle, war correspondent
Here in Normandy the Germans have gone in for sniping in a wholesale manner. There are snipers everywhere. There are snipers in trees, in buildings, in piles of wreckage, in the grass. But mainly they are in the high, bushy hedgerows that form the fences of all the Norman fields and line every roadside and lane.

It is perfect sniping country. A man can hide himself in the thick fence-row shrubbery with several days' rations, and it's like hunting a needle in a haystack to find him.

Every mile we advance there are dozens of snipers left behind us. They pick off our soldiers one by one as they walk down the roads or across the fields.

It isn't safe to move into a new bivouac area until the snipers have been cleaned out. The first bivouac I moved into had shots ringing through it for a full day before all the hidden gunmen were rounded up. It gives you the same spooky feeling that you get on moving into a place you suspect of being sown with mines.

Major F.D. Goode, Gloucestershire Regiment
There was a horse trough alongside the wall separating us from the church and here we washed and shaved. Looking for a 'loo' I went round the wall and found a nice stone outhouse facing the church tower, which was very comfor-

table . . . As I went to emerge from the doorless 'loo' a bullet hit the lintel and it was apparent that there was one or more snipers in the church tower. So I shouted for my Sergeant-Major who was on the other side of the wall to cover me. He opened up with a Bren gun on the tower and I slid around the wall. This episode caused some ill feeling in C Company who were at that moment climbing inside the tower and stalking the sniper, whom they later killed.

Marine Stanley Blacker, RM

The sniping as it was getting dusk every day was terrible, for several weeks after D-Day. You could stand on the beach and see the bullets going in the water not far from you. Where could you go to avoid them? There wasn't anywhere.

Leonard Miles, 168 General Transport Company

The first few days were particularly bad because there was such a lot of sniping. A lot of people were being killed, just out of the blue. It went on until our guns got into position and they were able to knock off the snipers from the high buildings, church steeples and the like. Eventually the snipers were snuffed out, which was good because when they were about you never knew where the next bullet was going to hit.

Alan Melville, RAF war correspondent

The Airborne boys were trudging down the road from the east, to be rested after putting in a hellish day and night. They were dead beat and filthy, and I think they must have been thankful to be told to flop down in the ditches along the side of the road while the entertainment was going on. It was strange to see them crouching there – some of the toughest and best fighters in our whole Army – while a peasant woman and her son marched down the middle of the road completely unconcerned with what was going on around her. We yelled at her to take cover, but as nobody seemed to know the French for either 'snipers' or 'duck', she waddled serenely on. The more we shrieked at her, the more she beamed back and called out, '*Vive les Anglais!*' to each one of us. She had a bundle of washing on her back, and I suppose not all the snipers in the Third Reich were going to interfere with her washing-day. Finally, she disappeared quite safely into her house, only to bob out a few moments later to ask the soldier lying nearest her front door if he had any chocolate. He hadn't, but he flung her a boiled sweet and a bullet zipped past her nose and buried itself in the very centre of the crossing, as if to mark the spot for future firing. She disappeared again with more cries of '*Vive les Anglais!*' and I suppose got on with her smalls.

The snipers in the trees were silenced at last by lobbing a large number of hand-grenades amongst them – a perfor- mance which brought forth shrieks of mirth from the local population, who seemed to be always ready for a good laugh and didn't particularly mind who provided it, or at whose expense. We were left with one last stronghold in the squat square tower of the village church. There seemed no point in holding up the war because of what at the most must have been four over-zealous Germans, and an s.p. gun in a field some distance away was asked to take a hand in the proceedings. It did so most effectively. The church tower had four little turrets, one at each corner, and the first four shells removed one turret apiece as clean as a whistle. The fifth was less tidy: it removed the whole tower. By this time the snipers had wisely decided to move rather nearer ground level, and they marched out smartly and gave themselves up. The villagers went reluctantly back to work. The Airborne boys hoisted themselves wearily on to their feet and tramped off down towards the beach. The four lines of vehicles and the cursing majors moved on. The show was over.

*

Trooper Peter Davies, 1st East Riding Yeomanry
Normandy

I don't think fear came into it. I don't ever remember being frightened. It was as if you were seeing a big screen and you were going into it. You saw everything that happened, the shells, the smoke, the noise – the noise was tremendous. You couldn't think for the noise sometimes.

*

Almost as much disliked as the sniper – by the infantryman at least – was the tank. The infantryman disliked his own tanks because he thought they attracted unwelcome attention from the other side, and the enemy's because they tended to be impenetrable givers of death. For his part, the tank man could hardly conceive of life without his steel shell, even though tank life was often extremely physically uncomfortable. The close country of Normandy may not have been 'classic' tank terrain, but it was a rare day when the menacing clank of a tank track was not heard. And, as the Allies discovered only too quickly – if they did not already know it – the German tank divisions were formidable opponents. Not the least reason for this was that the Germans had, in the Tiger and Panther tanks, armour which out-gunned the Allies' Shermans, Cromwells and Churchills. (The ubiquitous Sherman also had an alarming tendency to 'brew up' when hit.) The Allies, though, had the advantage of numbers. In consequence, the tank fighting in Normandy was often bitterly intense.

Trooper Peter Davies, 1st East Riding Yeomanry

We started off on 7 June and came across a thick hedge, which the driver of our tank shot through – rather foolishly, as it happened: we dropped about eight feet into a sunken road. The effect of almost 30 tons of tank dropping down rattled everything, including us, and smashed every valve in our radio sets. We had a box of spare valves which when I picked them up rattled like a lot of broken crockery. So we could hear nothing and we couldn't pass a message to anybody. A sergeant of another tank came over and said 'You'll just have to plod on, see what you can find and report back.' Off we went again and got to a place called Cazelle, smashed through a cart in a farmyard the Germans had left across the gateway, passed a small wood, and got out into some open country. I would imagine this was sometime after lunch. Previously we had passed a British sniper in a hedge who said, 'There's nobody after me. It's Jerry country from here.' Anyway, off we took across this plain and suddenly I noticed in my periscope in front to the right a spurt of dust. I said to Ben Matthews, who was acting commander, 'Did you see that!' It looked like a dud shell, it didn't explode. I traversed my turret around and there was another one. It dawned on me then that it wasn't shells not exploding but some beggar firing armour-piercing at us. The shots were coming from directly behind us. The driver started to swear and said, 'There's another one, in front of me!' I thought it was our own people. Ben Matthews said 'It's coming from that wood behind us.' Then the driver took it into his head to go like the clappers across this open country, and still there were dust puffs at the sides of us, and we started zig-zagging to avoid them. We hid behind a haystack until the top was blown off, and the haystack didn't seem such a good place to be. We then went on about another 100 yards, zig-zagging, the driver was going like mad, pulling one tiller then the other so we zig-zagged across the plain. Suddenly there was the most almighty bang: a shell had hit the side of the tank and taken one of the bogeys off. But we were still mobile, the driver managed to keep it going – until we were hit again. The explosion was enormous, with a lot of smoke, a lot of smell, and a lot of noise. We must have been hit straight up the rear; it had gone through the exhaust area, smashed through one of the twin engines and up into the tank and punctured the fuel tank. The obvious thing to do was get out, as quickly as we could. Another shell hit, skidded along the top, taking a few bits off. By now we had all leapt out and started to run from the tank, which we felt sure was going to explode, and headed for a thick hedge to try and shelter. I was expecting all the time to be hit by machine-gun fire or other bullets. We got to the hedge and realized that we had just run through a minefield because there was wire at the far end which said 'Achtung Minen!', with a skull and cross-bones on it. Luckily none of us had touched anything. We hid in this ditch for a while and presently a German tank came out of the wood. So it wasn't our own people as we thought. The Germans must have allowed us to pass then attacked us.

We spent the night in the ditch, which was between a sort of double hedge. In front of us was a chateau with German soldiers, and we spent the night trying to keep an eye on them. The following morning we attempted to make our way back to our own lines, and were promptly strafed by a British fighter plane who thought we were Germans. Having survived that we split up, three of us going one way, two the other; we thought a bunch of five of us was too obvious. We stopped at a farmhouse, tiptoed in and there was a German truck full of potatoes in the yard. So we thought we might have a look and see if there was anybody it it, and there was a big fat Jerry in the cab, so we tiptoed away again.

We went on a bit further, came to a village, I'm not sure which one, where we were strafed by a Spitfire – you have to bear in mind we were wearing tight round tank helmets and grey overalls, so we looked like the Germans. I dived one side of the street into a ditch, the two other lads went the other. I landed on two German Teller mines and immediately bounced back out of the ditch. It was only afterwards that I realized that somebody had taken them up, and they weren't buried but had been lifted. I didn't think about that at the time, I just bounced out.

We met a fellow walking up the road and somebody said,

'Go and ask him, Pete, where the Germans are.' I said that I didn't think my schoolboy French was adequate. Anyway I went up to him and asked if he spoke English. He said, 'Yes I do. Are you English?' I said we were, and that he spoke very good English. He said, 'I kept a shop in Hastings for nine years.' So we had picked the right fellow to ask. He informed us that they were on the other side of the village, not here. He took us into his house and gave us a glass of red wine. In the heat of June, and after having no food or water during the night, the red wine got to us a little bit. I felt a bit woozy, so did the others, and we thought we'd better get on.

We did eventually get back, clinging on to the back of a half-track we met, and got to where the squadron was harboured for the night in the middle of a field. Somebody gave me a blanket, but before I went to sleep the Adjutant came across and said, 'It's nice to see you back. I'll talk to you in the morning,' and gave me a drink out of his hip flask. I crawled under a tank and went to sleep. I was woken on the morning of the ninth by a friend who had been my Number 2 gunner for years before but had moved back on to reserves. He had got a mug of tea in his hand and I hadn't realized that the tank I was under had gone, had pulled off me earlier. He kicked me and said, 'You're not dead, you're still alive, get up!' Apparently the message he had received when he landed was that the five of us who had previously been his crew were dead and had been knocked out. But we weren't, and we all survived. We were very lucky.

. . . .

We had a nasty time at a tiny little hamlet of a dozen places called Galmanches (it doesn't seem to be on modern maps). We were mortared all day by German infantry, and shelled by artillery, and we had to hold it without infantry. We fought there for five hours. It was said afterwards that we were lucky we weren't annihilated, that B Squadron had taken the brunt of the battle. We lost a lot of commanders dead or wounded. I think it was eleven out of the nineteen in the one day.

.   .   .   .

The Germans had greater firepower. We were outgunned on a number of occasions. Their tanks were better than ours, their guns were better than ours – I don't think their crews were better than ours. I have to say that, but I believe it was true. We were faster, we could manoeuvre better – we could survive better.

.   .   .   .

It was mostly the 21st Panzer division in front of us. We had fewer tanks than they had, but to kid them we had a lot more we used to stick the barrel through the hedge, stay there for ten minutes, quarter of an hour on watch, pull back and run down the hedge and stick it through somewhere else and kid the Germans there were tanks all along the hedge. Whereas there might have been only two or three.

Donald S. Vaughan, 79th Armoured Division

It was pretty hot and dusty on the roads, and a Churchill tank took all the dust in. And when it was hot weather, the heat inside was terrific. You had a big engine in the back, it's a steel cage and you've got six men inside as well.

Gefreiter Werner Kortenhaus, 21st Panzer Division

My company was under the control of Battlegroup von Luck. We made two attacks, one on the seventh of June and one on the ninth, and had a lot of losses – of our seventeen tanks, only one survived. The rest were destroyed. That had a big effect on us, and we sat around afterwards very crushed in spirits. It was now clear to us that we weren't going to do it, we weren't going to push the Allies back. The Allied attacks were too strong, particularly because of their air superiority. There was hardly any chance of avoiding a bad ending. But when an order came to attack we still did it – it must have been the same on your [the Allied] side – because if a commander says, 'Attack!' or 'Tanks, advance!', no one could say, 'I'm not doing it.'

.   .   .   .

I have one terrible memory. On 9 June we had attacked Escoville, an attack which only lasted a few minutes. There were infantry behind us, under covers, who were wounded and we had to reverse. The driver can only see in front of him and did not know they were there . . . we reversed over them, over our own infantry. Because they were wounded they couldn't move out of the way. One saw some terrible things.

Anonymous British Tank Officer
We all thought that our tanks were deficient, and I believe that this had a highly adverse effect on morale. In the end we all became 'canny', and would obey orders only to the extent that there appeared a reasonable expectation of successfully carrying them out. Thus there was a sort of creeping paralysis in the armoured units; because of the pervading fear of 88s, Panthers, Tigers and Panzerfausts, initiative was lost and squadron commanders tended to go to ground at the first sign of any serious opposition and call up an artillery 'stonk'. With any luck, as the day wore on, the battle died down and that was at least another day got through.

Major F.D. Goode, Gloucestershire Regiment
There were some of our tanks sculling around behind our position and soon the enemy opened up with 88s and the shells were whistling overhead. I reckoned that they were coming from the farm and that the Germans had moved back there. So I called for fire on the farm. My chaps were making tea and I was enjoying a mug when I saw a naval

lieutenant in battle dress coming along the ditch followed by two ratings hauling a huge wireless set. I said, 'Good morning, who are you?' He replied, 'I am a Forward Officer Bombardment.' I said, 'I hear about you chaps at the Staff College. What do you want? Have some tea.' Tea being provided he said that [HMS] *Rodney* was answering my call for fire and asked where was the target. When he saw it he said, 'Christ, that's close!' I suggested calling off the fire but he said he could not, so we dug deeper. The first shells came over with a noise like an underground train and fell about 100 yards from us; the next over and the third hit the target. We had no more trouble with that 88.

Private Robert Macduff, Wiltshire Regiment

A German tank had spied the communications trench and moved its track down the trench, but we managed to pull the equipment to the bottom of the trench and the tracks missed. As it went by, the turret top lifted and a hand grenade was thrown. I was pleased that the thrower was a bad shot. He missed by yards.

. . . .

An amusing thing I saw during a small tank battle was a German Tiger tank in a field with a small British tank running around it. The Tiger tank was trying to shoot the British tank, but the turret of the Tiger tank was hand traversed and he couldn't get it around fast enough. The small British tank was firing its gun into the Tiger tank and destroyed it. It seemed to me like the David and Goliath story.

For three days, 13–15 June, the village of Lingèvres to the west of Caen was fiercely disputed by elements of the British 7th Armoured Division and Panzer Lehr, as the Allies tried to envelop Caen.

Leutnant Ernst, Panzer Lehr

We reached Lingèvres and straightaway joined in the counter-attack. In the narrow village streets the noise of the tracks and engines of our tanks was deafening. Our tracks screeched as we turned just in front of the church, where we came across the hulk of a British signals tank that had been knocked out. Along a stony track, we headed for a small wood about 300 metres away.

'Battle Stations! Close hatches!' came the order from Hauptmann Ritgen. Inside 'Zitrone' there was tension in the air. Now that the hatches were closed, the noise of the engine and tracks was muffled. All that could be seen of the outside world through the vision ports of the cupola was a narrow strip of hedges, fields and the edge of a wood. Ahead of 'Zitrone' three other tanks were moving in single file up the narrow track. They turned off westwards along the edge of the wood and into a field. The wood, although very leafy, was really nothing more than a very thick copse composed of undergrowth, hedges and apple trees that had been allowed to grow wild. Tanks would only get entangled in it.

Suddenly, the gun-layers heard the tank commanders shout: 'Take aim, enemy tank at 11 o'clock – fire!'

I shouted to my gun-layer: 'Feuer!' and our round grazed the top of the Cromwell's cupola and flew past it . . . The enemy disappeared behind the hedge; then we came under fire from the other side. 'To the left!' I shouted, and the PzKpfw IV heaved round with a jolt. The shape of the enemy tank grew larger in the gunsight. The recoil jarred the tank backwards as the round flew towards the thicket. It sounded like a direct hit. Smoke rose up into the sky. Nothing further moved. Evidently they must have been as surprised as we were, and had got out of the tank on impact and thus escaped being killed . . .

With the help of the crew from the damaged tank we managed to fix a tow. At that very moment, a soldier with both arms torn off by a shell appeared in front of me, moaning incomprehensibly in all the din that was going on. We hauled him up on to our tank to get him away to safety and then made our first attempt at towing the other panzer away. Slowly but surely we moved a few metres while the cable tautened. The fire from the British tanks positioned in the little wood was getting more drastic by the minute; we had to get a move on. It was one of those moments when, with no hope of success, there was nothing else to do except get on with it. A young radio operator lent a hand. Shell bursts were hitting the hedge next to us. It seemed unbelievable that it did not occur to the enemy opposite to aim higher, but I expect it must all have taken place in the space of a few seconds. Inside of me a voice was saying: 'It's not going to work,' but I somehow managed to keep cool and was more concerned at the time with getting the tank to move exactly right – to the nearest millimetre – than with how lucky I was . . .

That last journey from Lingèvres is something I shall never forget . . . On top of the tank, sitting or crouching down, were wounded men, most of whom had been badly burned, and as we picked up speed to get away from the artillery they were crying out with pain because of the heat from our exhausts. We were sent to a field hospital which had been set up in a fine chateau and ended up in a gothic hall lit by a few flickering candles. On the wall, I remember, was a portrait of a Renaissance lady. Outside the war rumbled on but here everything was absolutely still. Most of the wounded had been given injections and were lying there quietly. The doctors and nurses talked softly but I was close enough to overhear what they were saying about the wounded man beside me: 'I can't inject him; his skin is completely burnt.' They were talking about a tank man called Schmielewski who lay motionless and silent – and who died that night.

The view from the opposing side:

Driver R.S. Bullen, Hertfordshire Yeomanry

My regiment, the Herts Yeomanry, was a three-battery, self-propelled, 25-pounder field gun unit. Each battery consisted of eight Sextons (25-pounder gun mounted on Sherman chassis) and four Shermans with main armament removed and substituted by a dummy gun barrel, this to enable the gun turret to contain a plotting table and various other items for pin-point bombardment. In addition to these vehicles there were various Bren carriers, armoured cars and, of course, numerous trucks – the idea being that Bren carriers would go forward with the infantry and bring down artillery support where needed and the Shermans would do likewise with armoured units. In our case, our main armament was the No. 19 wireless set and, but for the insistence of the wireless operator to carry a 'walkie talkie', Lingèvres might have taken a little longer to eliminate.

At dusk on June 13, our Commander, Major Kenneth Swann, gathered the crew of 'X' tank and told us that we were to join a squadron of 4/7 Dragoon Guards immediately. We moved off and before complete darkness fell had met up with our 'big boy friends' . . . a term used largely when units were in company with armour.

While the skipper was away at Commanders' briefing, we prepared a cold meal. Fires were not allowed but the cans of self-heating soup were a blessing, as they proved to be on several occasions. While we ate our meal, the skipper gave us crew briefing. Although every detail was covered, it simply meant that at first light several flights of rocket-firing Typhoons would loosen up the enemy, who were holding Lingèvres. While the Typhoons were attacking the armour would advance, giving close support to the Somerset Light Infantry, to capture and hold the village.

The main road at Lingèvres was of secondary standard only, both in terms of width and surface. The village square is bisected by the main road and again by a single track road leading from Longraye to Verrières. Another, even smaller track, led off the Longraye road to Juaye Mondaye, scene of a vicious infantry engagement two or three days previously.

'Stand to' at first light on the 14th was no different from previous ones. It was possible to discern black from grey but not men from shrubs and trees and the tanks in 'league' could have been mistaken for buildings. As the sky lightened and turned to sunrise, it was apparent that the previous day's hot and sunny weather was to continue.

Breakfast, maintenance, checking of guns, ammunition, the wireless nets and dozens of other personal and tank daily checks were done almost in silence. Probably everyone shared the same thought: 'I wonder if . . .'

Around 8 o'clock we heard the RAF arrive and minutes later the familiar sound of rockets came to us. 'Mount . . . start up . . . driver advance . . .' and we were off. We went up a slight rise in the ground, through a hedge and had our first sight of Lingèvres. From the angle we were at, it appeared to be a fairly large village, complete with a church and a few outlying farms, situated about half-way up a small hill. One or two small fires were burning but it wasn't possible to say where as we were still about 2000 yards away. We did, however, have a good view of the Typhoons going in. My own thought was that we would only have the sweeping up to do.

We were now advancing across a large field of corn in company with eight other Shermans in a rough line abreast, with each tank well separated from the next one. As a driver I was getting many changes of direction, unnecessarily I thought, until I realized we were advancing through our own infantry who were invisible to me through my periscope. The corn was almost eye level!

About 500 yards from the village I saw a Dragoon tank hit way over to our right. Suddenly one to our left stopped and the crew baled out. That, too, was hit. Then, quite suddenly, all hell let loose. Small-arms and machine-gun fire was exchanged across the cornfield. The main armament of

tanks fired at targets I couldn't see and the wireless sets
which I could hear in the background were constantly
receiving and sending messages. I can remember one in
particular: 'Mike target . . . Mike target . . . Mike target
. . .' followed by a map reference. This was from my own
Commander and seconds later a barrage of shellfire burst
upon the village. It seemed to go on for an hour or more. In
reality it was only a few minutes. We were now at the end of
the cornfield facing a typical Norman hedge. My instructions
came over the intercom: 'Go through and turn left.' This was
unusual. We had seen tanks defeated by such rows of hedges
before and, of course, the thin armour of the belly of the tank
was exposed. I engaged low gear and went through, made a
left turn and continued ahead. I can remember seeing a car,
motorcycle and machine-gun crew all knocked out. We were
in a very narrow road and about a hundred yards ahead was
the church where some infantry chaps of ours were digging
in.

As we got closer I could see more infantry setting up
machine-gun positions. Then I turned into the village square
and found far more destruction. The church, houses and
shops had obviously been caught in the Typhoon raid. A few
dead German and British soldiers were scattered about. A
Sherman was positioned by the entrance to the church and,
on the other side of what I call a square but was in fact just a
road junction, a Firefly stood with its gun pointing up the
road to Juaye Mondaye.

I was told to stop by a Sherman and wait, engine running.
The Commander called a greeting and waved. In answer to
a request from our skipper he pointed to the Firefly. Our
Commander ran across the road, climbed on the Firefly and
pointed to something out of my vision. I didn't have a chance
to wonder what he was pointing at. Our own wireless
operator shouted into the intercom: 'Driver reverse, right-
hand down and go like —!' I didn't hear the last word – I
was already going!

The tank lurched, a building to our right collapsed, followed by a loud explosion and pieces of flaked enamel came flying around inside the driving compartment of the tank. For a minute I couldn't gather my thoughts. I remember saying to the co-driver: 'Christ!' His reply was something to the effect that his wireless had gone 'diss'.

When the Major rejoined us he gave me directions and guided us across a small field behind the church. We broke through a low hedge and parked in the corner of a field. We found a stream running down one side of the hedge with a culvert about three feet deep in the corner. Taking cover there were about a dozen of the Somersets, most of them wounded. We gathered what might have been useful – grenades, Stens, a Browning, first-aid box and a No. 18 wireless, which the operator extracted from the bowels of a Sherman – and joined the infantry. From our new position we had a good view of the cross-roads and saw that our friendly Sherman had been knocked out. We couldn't see the Firefly. Apart from spasmodic small-arms fire and the occasional thump of a tank gun, it was reasonably quiet.

We learned from the skipper that he had seen an SP gun that required the attention of the Firefly's 17-pounder. While he was directing the fire he spotted a Panther up the Tilly road bringing its gun to bear in our direction. He shouted to our operator to 'move'. The shell, an HE, took us on the right-hand side while we were in reverse. It ricocheted off and exploded in the shop we were going behind for cover. When we examined the damage sustained outwardly there was not too much to see. The shell had left some score marks about a foot long and about an inch deep. The side of the tank was slightly concave for about two feet. Inwardly, the front set was out of commission, as was the forward Browning. Flakes of white enamel covered the driving compartment.

The infantry officer and our own quickly exchanged views on the situation, which wasn't very comforting. Our tanks

had come up against a strong armoured force of panzergre-
nadiers and several of the 4/7 Dragoon Shermans had been
knocked out. Our own infantry had lost a great many men
and those remaining were engaged in house-to-house fighting. About half-a-dozen tanks on the enemy side were
knocked out, along with some SPs, but two or three were
still roaming about. This was particularly disturbing as we
had previously seen shots from the Shermans bouncing off
the enemy armour.

After about half an hour in the one position, our officer
took the No. 18 set and went off to the village to see what was
happening. The ground was higher there. Judging by the
artillery barrage that arrived shortly after, he must have
found things a little sticky as he was bringing shellfire down
on or very close to his own map reference. He arrived back
shortly afterwards and said he had seen a Panther arriving
down the Juaye Mondaye road in our direction. A few
minutes later it arrived and stopped about twenty yards
from our position. Only a hedge separated us. We were
relieved when it moved off again but our relief was short
lived. It stopped at the cross-roads and started traversing its
gun in our direction. Whether it was going to fire at us with
its co-ax or finish off our Sherman we didn't know. Fortunately a Firefly of the 4/7 Dragoons, which looked as if it had
been following the Panther, stopped where the German tank
had originally halted. It fired two quick shots of AP at three
hundred yards. The Panther had no chance with two 17-
pounders up its stern!

Battle Report: 8e BDE, 15 June

The Panther caught fire and the effect was better than could
have been anticipated. The destruction of the tank acted like
a ferret bolting rabbits from a rabbit hole. With a space of
two minutes three other Panthers set off down the road
towards Lingèvres and, as they passed the Sherman at point

C, they were well and truly shot up. The first tank caught
fire. The second one, bypassing the blazing tank, was hit but
continued on out of sight. The third was hit, and exploded.
When the smoke had cleared, the second Panther was seen to
be stationary near the church with a sprocket blown off. Its
crew had bailed out.

*

Donald S. Vaughan, 79th Armoured Division
Normandy
The overwhelming feeling about death, mind, was 'Thank
God it wasn't me!' That's not a very nice thing to say, but
very often that's how we felt.

*

After depositing the men and materials for D-Day and pounding
the German defences with its guns, the Allied Navy did not simply
disappear. Aside from maintaining the steady cargo traffic across
the Channel, the big naval guns were used to bombard German
positions inland until well into the campaign. In the conspicuous
absence of the German Navy the main threats came from mines
and night attacks by the dwindled Luftwaffe. Gradually, though,
the naval side of Overlord settled into routine and even boredom.

Lieutenant A.J. Holladay, RA
Diary, 8 June [at Mulberry Harbour, Arromanches]
Thursday D+2. As soon as fighter cover disappears – at
midnight – the fun begins. Enemy a/c [aircraft] over beaches
and terrific Bofors barrage goes up. Red chains of floating
light cover the sky for miles like a Brock's benefit display. We
open on a FW [Fokker Wolf] and an Me [Messerschmitt]
which comes our way and score a hit on FW. Other guns
then open on it too, and it finally crashes.

Alfred Leonard, Merchant Navy
In the Merchant Navy we weren't told much about the military campaign, but from the ship we could tell things were going OK. Within a week the gunfire was far away.

G.G. Townsend, Combined Operations
We made an attack up the mouth of the River Orne, a location which compelled us to go in one at a time to blast the enemy force, an affair which epitomized the craziness of it all and the spirit in which war is often fought. The lead craft had made her run, suffering damage from enemy fire both fore and aft in completing her solo effort, and as she passed us her captain shouted over the loud hailer 'Tally ho, old chap, your turn next, we've woken them up for you, good hunting.' With these words ringing in our ears we galloped into the hornets' nest, feeling somewhat like the cavalry in 'The Charge of the Light Brigade', only pulling out at the last moment as we came perilously close to being stranded on the shoreline, where we would have been a sitting target. It must have all looked pretty spectacular because when we eventually returned, the crew of the cruiser HMS *Belfast*, gave us three hearty cheers, and subsequently our Captain, our midshipman and the coxswain were mentioned in despatches for this action.

Marine Stanley Blacker, RM
They decided to hold a conference on the beach to find out who was missing, and what everybody was doing. A lot of our landing craft were beached while this was going on, and suddenly at the back of the high ground at the beach behind Asnelles and Ver-sur-Mer a single German fighter-bomber appeared. It came on and on towards us. Nobody fired a shot. I thought to myself, 'What's happening? Why isn't somebody firing at it?' It came on and on. You could see it clearly, a single bomb under the aircraft – and he dropped it spot on. You could see it come floating down and it pitched

right where my commanding officer and a group of other officers had gathered. It killed him and about six others. Pitched right on top of them. I was only about 50 yards away, and I flung myself down. You could see it coming on and on. It was bound to hit somebody. His batman cried like a baby on the beach. Cried like a baby.

William Seymour, RN
On the boat, you'd get off to sleep then the alarm would go, and you'd be off to action stations. Climbing the ladder all you could see were these red stars coming at you. You'd stand still, but not for long because the other sailors behind you were trying to push their way up the ladder. But it gave you such a shock from being asleep to see these things coming at you that you stared at it.

Seaman C.J. Wells, Merchant Navy
If you think you're going to get it, you get it. It's no good getting terrified on a ship because there's nowhere to run to.

. . . .

On the trips across the Channel after D-Day we used to go straight across to Cherbourg, and then along the coast. This used to take us over a minefield of acoustic mines, and we used to go over them real slow, about four or five knots, so as not to fetch them up from the bottom. What used to tickle me was that the minesweepers would be coming the other way, towards us, setting the mines off. There'd be explosions all over the place.

Lieutenant-Commander R.C. Macnab, RN, aboard HMS *Glasgow*
After the first day our function slowly diminished until we are now hardly firing a shot! We have bombarded Vierville,

Isigny, Carentan, St Vaast in the Cherbourg peninsula and various 'targets of opportunity', as they call them. But the waits in between are deadly and an anti-climax to what our idea of the invasion of Europe would be . . . Here we lie off the sunny coast of France (St Vaast) doing next to *nothing*. Most of the villages look practically undamaged; it is green, wooded, undulating and very pretty – much the same I suppose as four years ago. Somehow one had expected it to be grey, forbidding and cowed under the wicked Hun; I think Winston Churchill was responsible for that picture. Apart from spasmodic explosions ashore, gay and sparkling lights (anti-aircraft fire) and the occasional destruction of mines being swept by day, one really wouldn't know that the grim hand of war had stretched here at all.

At times, Normandy threatened to become for the ordinary soldier – the 'dog-face', the 'Tommy', the *'fussoldaten'* – an almost unbearable test of endurance, a constant round of close combat, lack of sleep, shelling, and capricious elements (torrential rain, blazing sun), punctuated by moments of bravery, camaraderie and strangely intense experiences. The German soldier, on top of everything else, had to face apocalyptic levels of bombing on occasion. For most of its three months, the battle was fought over a hundred-mile front for little geographical gain by upwards of two million soldiers. It was a hard slog.

Sergeant G.E. Hughes, 1st Battalion, Royal Hampshire Regiment
Diary
June 7. Still going. Dug in at 02:00 hrs. Away again at 05.30. NO FOOD. Writing few notes before we go into another village. CO out of action, adjutant killed. P Sgt lost. I do P Sgt['s job]. More later.

June 8. 07.30, fire coming from village. Village cleared. Prisoners taken. Night quite good but German snipers lurking in wood. Had 2 hrs' sleep. Second rest since the 6th.

June 9. 06.30 hrs went on wood clearing. Germans had flown. Only one killed for our morning's work. We are now about 8 to 10 miles inland. Promoted to Sgt.

June 10. Joan darling, I have not had you out of my thoughts. T[hank] God I have come so far. We have lost some good men. Our brigade was only one to gain objectives on D-Day.

The French people give us a good welcome. Had wine.

June 11. Contact with enemy. Lost three of my platoon. Very lucky T[hank] God. Only had 5 hours sleep in 3 days.

June 12. This day undescrible [sic] mortar fire and wood fighting. Many casualties. T[hank] God I survived another day.

June 13. Just had my first meal since Monday morning. Up all night. Everyone in a terrible state. I keep thinking of u.

June 14. Counter-attack by Jerry from woods. Mortar fire. 13 of my platoon killed or missing. After heavy fighting yesterday CSM also wounded, also Joe. O[fficer] C[ommanding] killed. I am one mass of scratches. Advanced under creeping barrage for 3 miles. Drove Jerry back. It is hell. 3 Tiger tanks came here, up to lines during night.

June 16. [resting] Received letter from home. Wrote to Joan and Mum.

June 17. [resting]

June 18. Day of Hell. Counter-attack.

June 19. Day of Hell. Counter-attack.

June 20. Day of Hell. Advanced. Counter-attacked.

June 21. Quiet day. We have been fighting near Tilley [Tilly]. Bayonet charge. Shelled all day. Letters from home.

June 22. Out on patrol. Got within 35 yards of Tiger before spotting it. Got back safely T[hank] God. Shelled to blazes. Feeling tired out.

June 23. No sleep last night. Exchanged fire, out on patrols

all day, went on OP for 4 hours. Stand-to all night.
Casualties.

Just about had enough.

June 24. Had to go back to CCS [Casualty Clearing
Station]. Malaria.

Sergeant Hughes was hospitalized with malaria for most of the rest
of the Normandy campaign. Malaria was a surprisingly common
problem.

Trooper W. Hewison, 1st Royal Tank Regiment
Diary

July 22. Mosquitoes another pest . . . Am bumps all over face
and head and arms with the blighters. Bloody annoying.

July 23. No, want to get home pretty quickly. Most of the
chaps shell-happy now – 'specially the old 8th army wallahs.
They can see the end of the war in sight and want to make
the last lap.

July 26. Yesterday was a very black day for the regiment.
Went into action again and had a proper balls-up . . . all
regiment going slap-happy if nothing is done. We've had
about enough. No RAF over. 88s and SPs ringed the ridge
and the squadron hadn't had much of a chance.

August 6. Got a prisoner yesterday. Luckily Vick could
speak German fairly fluently. Was 42, an Austrian from
Vienna, married with two children (photo of youngest girl –
3 years – was really beautiful). Glad to get out of the war –
had umpteen small-arms wounds in thighs. Wasn't surprised
that we treated him well . . . a decent chap – made me think
really hard – this war's so bloody futile. There's ordinary
blokes on each side with no desire to kill each other, yet here
we are.

August 9. The days seem an eternity, and with being
cooped up in the turret all day – we have to sleep in the
tank because of shelling. I think I've tried every position

under the sun on that gunner's seat – still can't get comfortable.

W. Emlyn 'Taffy' Jones, 1st Special Service Brigade
Of course, one of our biggest enemies in Normandy wasn't the Germans, it was the mosquitoes. Those mossies used to come down in the evening while you had to stand-to in your slit trench, and they used to take blood out of you right, left and centre. You used to come out in all sorts of bumps and bruises and God knows what. I once went back to Lovat's HQ, and I saw this chap coming up towards me and I thought, 'My God, it's the Invisible Man.' He had bandages all over his face and head – with just little slits for his eyes, his mouth and nose – and hands. It turned out to be Corporal so-and-so who thought he'd be a clever bugger and had found a bicycle pump somewhere and used it to flit his whole trench with petrol to get rid of the mossies. So it came to stand-to and he'd jumped into his trench, thought he'd have a cigarette, lit a match – and had blown himself right out of the ruddy trench! A proper Charlie Chaplin.

Trooper Peter Davies, 1st East Riding Yeomanry
We were pestered by a lot of mosquitoes – we used to get bitten unmercifully by mosquitoes. And of course there were so many dead animals around – well, humans as well as animals. Loads of dead cows, dead horses. The Germans used a lot of horse transport, and there was a lot of dead horses always. We spent a whole afternoon trying to bury a huge bloated carthorse. We tried to set fire to it but couldn't, we tried to get rid of it in all sorts of ways because it stank to high heaven. We fired shots at it, but they didn't penetrate and bounced off. So an officer had a bright idea that if we all took a shovel and stood round it we could dig enough soil to cover it in and stop the stink. We did. We sweated for about three hours, about thirty men, shovelling away as hard as we

could to try and cover the damned horse which was there with its legs in the air. We covered it up and everybody shouted 'hooray'. Two minutes later a German artillery shell landed on it and everybody had a share in the damned horse. They spread it all over the place.

Driver John Osborne, RASC

We were shelled every day for weeks, at first from inland, then later by a big coastal gun from Le Havre. The huge shells sounded like an express train as they came through the air and exploded with a tremendous crash. But after a few days we more or less ignored them – unless they dropped fairly near, then we would swear a bit.

Captain Borthwick, British Second Army

This place we found was the high-water mark of the airborne advance. The whole story was there on the ground – the little handcarts full of ammunition and stores, hidden in a hedge; the German armoured car brewed up, with its dead around it; the sixty corpses, German and British, in the corn between the hedge where the fight began [and] the outskirts of the village where it ended. There was a pond near the hedge. One airborne man had dragged his helpless comrade there for shelter and, fearing he would drown, had tied him by the arms to a tree which grew on the bank, so that he lay half in the water and half out of it. Then he himself had been killed, barely a yard away. They lay there still. We went out that night and buried them. It was not quite dark when we went in and waded waist-deep through the corn, following the white tape (this marked a passage through a minefield): and every now and then there was a bold patch in the corn, perfectly symmetrical, with the flattened stalks radiating precisely from the centre where a mortar bomb had fallen. The standing corn hid the dead, but the smell of death lay in little pools along the way . . . Some trees were blown in half.

Others were split down the centre. It was now dark and muddy and we were heavily laden. We went slithering along the track, not knowing where we were but following the muddy tape, until it brought us to a sea of mud, and trenches and sandbags, and corrugated iron. The 2nd Battalion was suspiciously glad to see us . . .

It was a nagging sort of warfare. There was nothing big or decisive about it, but every night their patrols were prodding at our defences and every day they shelled us . . . Our own defences were in a tight square in country where the fields were so small and the trees and hedgerows so numerous that it was almost a continuous wood. Visibility, except westwards out into the plain, was nowhere more than 50 yards . . . We came to know the 858th Regiment [Wehrmacht] quite well. Deserters used to drop in to see us nearly every morning. Before long we knew almost as much about the German positions as we did our own. These men who came in were all Poles or Russians, each protesting that he was in the Wehrmacht against his will, and anxious to prove his good faith by giving his friends away down to the last detail.

War reporter, SS Leitheft
Thousands of aircraft, rolling barrages of the batteries, massed tank attacks hammered them in with bombs and shells. The earth heaved thunderously. An inferno was unleashed. But faith was the strongest support of courage. Smeared with blood, covered with dust, gasping and fighting, doggedly dug into the earth, these youths brought the Anglo-Americans to a halt.

Private Zimmer, 12th SS Panzer Division
Diary, 10 July [at Hill 112]
From 6.30 to 8.00 a.m., again heavy machine-gun fire. Then Tommy attacks with great masses of infantry and many tanks. We fight as long as possible but we realize we are in a

losing position. By the time the survivors try to pull back, we realize that we are surrounded.

General Fritz Bayerlain, Panzer Lehr

Back and forth the bomb carpets were laid, artillery positions were wiped out, tanks overturned and buried, infantry positions flattened and all roads and tracks destroyed. By midday the area resembled a moonscape, with the bomb craters touching rim to rim . . . All signal communications had been cut and no command was possible. The shock effect on the troops was indescribable. Several of my men went mad and rushed around in the open until they were cut down by splinters. Simultaneously with the storm from the air, innumerable guns of the American artilley poured drumfire into field positions.

Alan Hart, RCS

Diary, July 8
The following night, however, the boot was very definitely on the other foot and after the evening's entertainment was over everyone's morale was high, to say the least. I was again on duty in the signal office at about 21.15 hours when the RAF heavy bombers started to go over in the direction of Caen. Over Caen they met heavy flak but it did not seem to have any effect . . . we stood and watched the planes streaming towards Caen, towards the mass of shellbursts which were markedly decreasing. For over an hour the sky was full of huge, four-engined bombers. Never have I been so much stirred. It was a sight which cannot easily be forgotten.

That stream never seemed to end, each plane pushing inevitably towards its target . . . to the French it was 'bon travail' or 'Caen finit'. It did us the world of good, and everyone agreed there could have been no better tonic for the victims of the 'flying bombs' back in England. Caen is approximately ten miles from Hermanville, and half an hour after the attack finished there was a cloud of dust over the village – it was no smoke screen.

Wehrmacht *Army Newssheet*
12 July 1944

Tanks forward! So this is it. Now the real magic starts. Three machine guns are hammering in front of us. A German anti-tank gun, and another one, whips its bullets over towards the attackers. American tanks answer. Hand grenades. Machine guns. A spectacle of Hell, drowned again and again by artillery fire.

Gefreiter Werner Kortenhaus, 21st Panzer Division

I can paint you a strange picture which stays with me still. On 28 June we mounted an attack west of Caen and succeeded in getting through the British line. The battle lasted a very long time, from 10 in the morning until 5 in the afternoon, but around midday there was a lull in the battle. Suddenly the battleground was filled with dance music. Some infantrymen had gone and played with an English radio set, and dance music had come on, filling the air. It was a little unusual.

. . . .

One day, right at the beginning of the invasion, we were standing around our tanks quietly smoking cigarettes, with no sound of battle at all, when out of the blue a light English tank came shooting out from our right, out of some woods, came towards us, went between some tanks and crashed into a tree. Nobody had fired because we were taken completely by surprise. Two English soldiers got out of the tank, they were wounded and gave themselves up. I imagine they had panicked because they had somehow lost their way and suddenly found themselves in the middle of so many tanks and then made a bad reaction. So of course we were interested to have a look inside an English tank, and inside I found a large thermos flask. My crew were very pleased because it was full of delicious hot coffee.

A few days later this thermos flask slipped out of my hands and broke – and I was really sworn at by the crew. The wireless operator always had to look after the provisions, and the thermos flask was a real prize. When I broke it I was much told off.

Sergeant H.M. Kellar, Devonshire Regiment

We must have suffered a lot of casualties, because instead of being in charge of a section (ten men) I found myself acting as a platoon commander (thirty men). Promotion was very rapid in action, but you seldom lasted long enough to get paid for it.

Private Robert Macduff, Wiltshire Regiment

A 'Moaning Minnie' was heard coming over, so we ran across the gap in the hedge and crouched down to avoid it. Unfortunately one dropped quite close to us, killing one and blowing the rest of us off our feet. We got up and moved as fast as we could, but the rake of the mortars followed us, and we were constantly being blown over. At the end of the lane we reached the assembly point. We were badly shaken and began to cry constantly. In the 1914–18 war it would have been called shell shock. We were all sent back to B echelon to be checked. After a few hours though, after a bath, a change of clothes and a good feeding, we were sent back.

Lance-Bombardier Stanley Morgan, RA

They'd opened up a road through a field of wheat. This wheat was a lovely crop of wheat – being a farmer I noticed it. And we went right through it.

Alan Melville, RAF war correspondent

Normandy, before we overran it, was a green and pleasant land. There is nothing luxuriant about it: it is nice, ordinary country with dour, down-to-earth countryfolk living on it. I drove hundreds of miles daily along the same appalling roads and in and out of the same seemingly endless convoys, and I suppose Hermione contributed to a surprisingly large extent – considering her size – to the fact that the Allies changed the colour of this corner of France. Though only a few very brave men with special duties saw them, I am sure that the trees and the fields on the evening before D-Day were really green; twenty-four hours later they had lost their freshness and were coated with the dust which D-Day had raised. The coating got thicker with every hour and every vehicle that passed, until the trees and the gardens and the houses – at any rate those near a road – became faded and war-weary. Dust was the one really outstanding feature of our life: we swore at it and swallowed it wholesale. It was stupid to drive without goggles, and a blue battle-dress was turned in a few miles to a pale shade of grey – a fact which on at least two occasions proved slightly embarrassing, and necessitated long explanations before I could convince people that I was friend and not foe. When even a Jeep accelerated, it sent up a great swirling cloud of thick dust behind it and the man in the vehicle following it choked and cursed. Three-tonners raised really prodigious clouds, and the peak was reached when our aircraft arrived in Normandy. They had only to touch down or take off, or merely start revving up, for the whole neighbourhood to be engulfed in dense grey-brown dust. It got into everything: one's mouth and ears and eyes and food and clothes, and especially one's hair. I had lost my hat in the cavortings on the beach on the afternoon of D plus 2, and the amount of foreign matter that got into my hair in the course of half an hour's drive was unbelievable. It was impossible to tug a comb through the matted entanglement, and whenever I washed my hair I had to take care to do so when there was nobody about, for I was much too ashamed to let anyone see the state of the water after one's ablutions. The dust even defeated our aircraft, and many of them had to be sent back to England in relays to be fitted with a filter device to keep the engines free. And pilots who had served under Broadhurst in the Middle East and were now with him in Normandy said that they would rather have the sand any day.

Sadi Schneid, Waffen SS

We had been spared by the felt lice but their brothers, the lovely white ones, defeated us. As if the Allied invasion was not enough! I escaped from them only when I became an American prisoner six months later. I could never understand why the Germans with all their excellent chemists could not find something effective against this plague. The only thing available was Lysol, which had no effect, and cleaning our clothes in steam baths. The result was that we had permanent lice, and our leather equipment became stiff from steam. Our pullovers were so crawling with lice that we could not bear to put them on. Those Norman civilians who found underwear missing from their cupboards must forgive me for helping myself, but the constant torture of lice was sometimes worse than the fighter-bomber attacks.

Alfred Leonard, Merchant Navy

Even though it was a strained time, there was a light air about it as well. Being young the crew looked out for my safety, and gave me a bright orange hat to wear – so that if the ship was hit and we were in the water it would be visible. The troops coming down from the troopships used to see this hat and call me 'Marigold'.

Sergeant William B. Smith, Intelligence Corps

Only on one occasion did we ourselves come under fire. One night a single gun started firing over the house. We lay on the floor in our room, as we normally did to sleep, and I counted exactly fifty shells – typical German preciseness! In the silence after the fiftieth round one of us said he wanted a Jimmy-riddle. We told him to do it out of the window. While he was thus engaged, somebody gave a perfect impression of the sound of an approaching shell. He leapt back with such alacrity that he fell among all our cooking utensils and other equipment, making more noise than the whole bombardment.

Lieutenant A.J. Holladay, RA
Diary 19 June D + 13

Woke to really dirty day and the heaviest sea I have seen. The ship is moving very considerably on the bottom – shifting and swinging – which is very unpleasant. Our decks are completely engulfed and the waves are terrific. At least this should get rid of the filthy oil that has been on our decks for two weeks. All the small craft rush to our shelter, but lengthen their hawsers and lie discreetly off when they see how we are shifting. Our stern is bashing against bows of 308 and plates on both ships are buckled. We drift quite a way apart from next ship towards Bob, and the bridge is shattered . . . At low tide we tie hawsers to neighbouring ships to try and hold us steady in the night. Wind still blowing gale force in evening. What a bloody life! As tide rises again in evening storm grows in ferocity . . . water comes lashing up round bridge. Nasty moments . . . only three ropes holding us forward now and terrific strain coming on them in snatches with the waves. Turn in at midnight.

20 June (D + 14)

. . . Storm continues, if anything, worse than before. Only one rope holding now . . . water halfway up main superstructure. Tide comes up very high indeed and enters my cabin. Wireless operators climb on top of wireless cabin and are half drowned and buffeted there. We get on top of bridge. Power of sea simply terrific – slowly smashing the boat to pieces. Send SOS to 324 and barge picks up men from focsle. Wireless ops can't be rescued and they spend a bloody night soaked to skin and in considerable danger of being swept away.

21 June (D + 15)

Tide goes down eventually at about 3.30 a.m. Find wireless ops soaked through and all sleeping in one bed at back of cabin. Rest of cabin completely wrecked, including wireless sets . . . position becoming serious. When will this ruddy gale die down!?

22 June (D + 15)

Storm subsided. Sea still choppy but sun and blue sky.

Commendation for the award of the Military Medal: Lewis Edward Richards, British 231 Infantry Brigade Signal Section

At approx. 22.30 hrs 12 JUN in the TRUNGY area South of BAYEUX, after heavy fighting during the day, enemy tks [tanks] in strength started to infiltrate through the posns [positions] occupied by 2 DEVON. This constituted a serious threat to the whole of the Div front, and consequently comn [communication] between Bde [Brigade] HQ and 2 Devon became vital. The line was severed, and the wireless link was subject to heavy local interference, making comn difficult, and, at times, impossible.

In an endeavour to restore comns, Cpl RICHARDS went well fwd in a wireless-fitted Jeep, and acted as a relay station.

Despite the fact that the posn he had taken up was made extremely dangerous by enemy fire, he remained at his post alone until relieved at 04.00 hrs 13 Jun, when the threat had diminished.

During this period the courage, skill and devotion to duty displayed by this NCO was instrumental in restoring comn between Bn [Battalion] and Bde HQs, which resulted in the effective direction of the sp arms.

Marine Stanley Blacker, RM

There was no toilet or anything like that on the LCM. It was over the side or nothing. There was no shelter either, so you had to sleep on it in the open. It was bad weather, so we were wet through for days and nights on end. Later on, when the beach was cleared, we slept there and used a large tarpaulin we found. We spread it out, laid on it and pulled the other half up over us.

Private Robert Macduff, Wiltshire Regiment

I well remember the awful fatigue that overtook us after a few days of constant movement, fear and hunger and lack of sleep. I remember once stopping by the roadside, sat down and immediately fell asleep in seconds, only to be roused after five minutes. My mouth tasted foul because of the lack of fresh food.

Captain Douglas G. Aitken, Medical Officer, 24th Lancers

We are all tired and it is getting dark. Suddenly a shot rings out and a fellow comes running: 'I think Corporal — is dead.' I go over to the tank; the men stand at the front looking sheepish; down the side of the tank, near the back, the body of this wretched fellow is squatting and next to him is the cooker still burning. His hands are in his pockets and he is very dead. On examination it's obvious that the accidental discharge of one round of machine-gun fire from the neighbouring tank killed him straight out. I tell Pip – acting squadron leader – and he suddenly flares up: 'He's dead! He's dead and all bloody day long from bloody dawn he fights and sits up there against the Boche. All bloody day and the poor bugger comes in and gets shot while brewing up his first cup of tea of the day!' 'OK, sorry Doc,' he adds.

The hardship of the Battle of Normandy was also inflicted on French civilians caught between the warring armies.

Odette Lelanoy, Vire

One morning we woke up to find the fields around the house full of Germans, tanks, lorries and munitions etc. My father said, 'Right, I think it's time to pack our things, because we're going to be bombed' – the Germans made such a target. And so it was. The English planes came during the day and it was all machine guns and bullets. As soon as things calmed down, we set out down a small path across the fields . . . After a while we were joined by others, refugees, caught in the pincer of the American movement and the English front which was moving down. The Germans were in amongst us too, being pushed back. At the outset there weren't many of us, but gradually the numbers grew, because of all the people, all the peasants retreating from the front. Horses, carts, peasants, cars, bicycles, Germans, lorries, tanks, were all mixed together. We kept getting caught in bursts of fire and bombing by the planes. We lived in fields in the rain all through June and July. We lived in trenches, in farm buildings, in hayricks. We washed in a stream or a well, we dug up vegetables from gardens and ate dead cows killed in the bombings and by the machine-gun fire. All the pigeons which had been killed we ate. Our clothes became rags. We had nothing.

After many days on the march the large group we had been began to break up, and went their different ways. Our family was now completely on its own. Eventually we arrived at Magny, which was deserted. We were exhausted and couldn't go any further. So we looked for somewhere to shelter. I spotted a large house which had been ransacked, doors open, everything taken. I went in and saw that it had two bedrooms which were empty. As I pushed open the door to the third bedroom I awoke a German officer who was sleeping on a bed. He jumped to his feet, pointed his revolver at me and said, 'What do you want?' I explained that all I wanted was a place for my family to sleep, that we had had enough, that we had now been on the march for two months solid, and wanted to stop here. He said, 'Okay, you can take this house. I'm giving it to you.' Well, as I was then 20 years of age, I would answer back a bit and didn't stand for him addressing me in familiar terms – he'd used 'Du' [the familiar form of 'you'] with me. So I said, 'Why are you being so familiar? You don't speak to young girls like that.' Well, he was obviously taken aback, laughed and said, 'I beg your pardon, miss,' made an exaggeratedly low bow and then left. My parents, my brother and I moved in and waited for the Americans to arrive.

*

Sub-Lieutenant Alun Williams, RNVR
Normandy
Then suddenly – within only a few days of D-Day – the English coastline became virtually deserted, the contrast in such a short time being quite unbelievable and unreal. Even more so was getting back to Dartmouth with orders to close down the Base, only to find that security restrictions on the beaches had been lifted. I found myself having to make my way through families with children holding buckets and spades where days before there had been barbed wire.

*

Perhaps the most telling measure of the bloodiness of Normandy was the fact that the Everett Tables used by the British to forecast battle casualties had to be extended in mid-campaign to include a new category of fighting: 'Double Intense'. It became pitifully obvious to those in the infantry units at the sharp end of battle that their chances of not being wounded or killed were slim. In June and July there were 100,000 American casualties alone. Field hospitals and evacuation hospitals overflowed. Corpses littered fields and ruins. Every evening, company commanders in front-line units wrote letters to bereaved wives and mothers. And every day in homes across the Allied countries and Germany the long-dreaded telegram arrived at the door.

Major F.D. Goode, Gloucestershire Regiment

I now went out to help the wounded man. There was some firing from the snipers but I was lucky. He had been hit by a shell fragment under the right armpit and the lung was exposed. I put a field dressing on it but it was inadequate and I managed to fill the syringe and gave him a shot of morphia. I found out later that he had died. The MO told me that if I had simply plastered the wound with a cow pat it might have saved him as it would have restored the vacuum in his lungs.

Bombardier Harry Hartill, RA

A sight which held my attention was an American glider which had come down, having perhaps lost its bearings, into the British sector. It had caught overhead wires, causing it to nose-dive into the ground at terrific force. Inside one man sat at the wheel of his Jeep ready to drive out. The Jeep had shot forward with such force it had doubled up, trapping the driver between the driving wheel and the back of the vehicle.

Inside the glider were still all the crew, dead without firing a shot. What brought a lump to my throat was the huge white letters on each side of the glider saying 'HOME VIA

BERLIN' and 'DON'T WORRY MOM, WE'LL BE BACK.'

. . . .

In another location was what remained of a small cottage with a few fruit trees at the rear. Scattered around were the remnants of a fighter plane, the pilot's torso was caught in the branches of one apple tree and on the ground was a flying boot among the debris with part of a leg inside. Everywhere we went there was carnage and havoc, hardly anything to resemble a former building, everywhere flattened with RAF bombings.

Post Office Telegram
From PTY-CC OHMS

TO MRS J H BEADLE, 146 HAMILTON RD, SOUTH MNT VERNON, GLW E2

REPORT RECEIVED FROM WESTERN EUROPE THAT LIET AGI SMART ROYAL ARMOURED CORPS WAS WOUNDED ON 21ST JUNE 1944. THE ARMY COUNCIL EXPRESSES SYMPATHY. LETTER FOLLOWS SHORTLY.

UNDER SECY OF STATE FOR WAR.

Captain Douglas G. Aitken, Medical Officer, 24th Lancers

[Yesterday], quietly, in the middle of a field we buried Ted Webb; the grave had been dug to the size and shape of a man but the blanketed remains were just a shapeless mass. He was burnt in his tank. Everyone was very subdued and we all thought of poor Winifred. They were such a very devoted couple. Odd, these burials; the padre tells us, and at the appointed hour a few wander from all directions and stand around in a group; the padre looks very wan and I fully sympathize with him in his horrid task of scraping remains out of tanks. We took a three-tonner into St Pierre to get Ted and managed to blow it up on a mine, but was OK. The sun

is shining, the sky is blue and the grass waves lightly in the
breeze. The padre says his sentences between the bangs of
our own guns, then he sprinkles a little earth, and it is all
over. We fall away very quietly and without speaking, and
by the time Ian and I have reached the hedge it seems silly
not to have spoken and I say, 'It's a lovely day,' and Ian says
'Yes' and he adds 'Poor Winnie' and we are silent again.

.   .   .   .

I hope to God what I am going to write is not true. We are
sitting at L'H — d'A and Basil has returned with the news
that Ian is dead. I can't really think. I feel that there must be
some hope. As yet, I don't know the circumstances. Everyone
here is terribly hit by the news for was there ever a more
popular officer? I personally feel through my tears a great
hate for the whole bloody business and a sense of impotency
to reap from the Germans the penalty for the death of one of
the most loved of all officers.

Private Robert Macduff, Wiltshire Regiment

A tank went too far up the hill and was observed from the
[German-held] hillock opposite, and we were raked with
mortar fire. There was no chance to dig in, so a Sergeant-
Major, another soldier and I got down behind a very
large tree. The explosions were terrific, terrifying. A
soldier had crawled under a stationary tank and a mortar
dropped by the tank, blowing his foot off. Several more
dropped by the side of the tree, killing the Sergeant-Major
and the soldier beside me. My arm was stuck out – I felt a
pain, which became numb. There was blood everywhere.
A Canadian officer appeared and applied my field dressing and a tourniquet. He led me down to the base of the
hill, but I couldn't find any of my men so I insisted on
going back to blow up the radio set, as per instructions,
believing we were being overrun. Subsequently I was put
on a tracked vehicle and carried with other wounded –

there seemed to be a lot of us. The numbness was beginning to go, and I passed out.

Corporal Peter Roach, 1st Royal Tank Regiment

I lay marvelling at my infinite luxury as I smoked a last pipe. Putting pipe, tobacco and matches into my boot for safe keeping, I drifted off, as contented a man as ever there was. I awoke to loud bangs and a thump in the back. I pulled my blankets closer and buried my head. Was it a piece of mud thrown up by a bomb? There were aircraft overhead. As I dozed again amid the bedlam of ack-ack fire and bomb bursts safe in the warmth of my blankets, a warm trickle ran down my back, paused, and then raced down the hollow of my spine. I passed a hand along and found a wet patch on my shoulder, then a hole the size of the end of my finger; no pain.

I told Chalky that I was going to a dressing station, and made my way from guarded light to guarded light until I found a three-ton truck being used to treat casualties. A man was brought in with severe cordite burns to his hands, and I stood humbly aside, imagining his agony. The orderly patched me up with a dressing and I made my way back to the tanks. We made some tea on a petrol stove and passed the rest of the night dozing and smoking.

I arrived at the control point before the day had shown its face, and was met by two operators sheltering in a trench covered with a very perforated ground sheet, glumly facing a ruined wireless set.

The day came but there was still no communication and I sat waiting to announce the reaching of a crucial point whereupon the tanks could begin their task. The sun came up and what I took to be the brigade major sat in his van reading *Esquire* and drinking tea.

Slowly messages began to come back – the usual hold-ups, counter-attacks. But now things were moving and my map had a scrawl of coloured chinagraph lines on it. Intelligence officers coming in from other units, seeing me, were asking and receiving a briefing on the position. I was too tired and stiff by now to care, and I was pretty sure that I had as much information as anyone else.

The tanks made their way forward and there was jubilant report of successes. I was happy; they certainly deserved the successes. Then the German Tigers joined in and there were swift reports of tanks brewing and calls for the doctor. Frustration set in. With the guns we had, it was almost impossible to winkle out the heavily armoured and magnificently gunned German tanks.

Rocket-firing Typhoons were our only recourse and this was not the best thing for the morale of the tank crews. Smoke shells were fired to identify the German positions and they, with great presence of mind, fired them back at our positions, giving the impartial Typhoon a field day. The Canadians were aggrieved at one of their tanks being knocked out and I had a tedious tangle to untie, especially as no one wanted to listen.

By three-thirty I had had enough. The attack had bogged down, minds were numb and I was feeling actively sick. I took my small pack, said goodbye to my crew and Chalky, and made my way back to a forward dressing station. From there it was a line of stations, M and B tablets and tetanus jabs.

In the early evening a van load of us arrived at a field hospital, gentle in the green Normandy fields. They made us welcome and we lay in the evening sun smoking and drinking tea. Their kindness and gentleness almost reduced me to tears. A lethargy stole over me. For the moment I could do nothing, was expected to do nothing, and even my inner mind was prepared to let me rest. There was nothing here for me to learn, nothing to test my courage.

Lying in a real bed in a great tented ward, the lights very dim, the air warm and muggy, I slept leadenly but not deeply. Quiet figures were working among the innumerable beds, turning back the covers, looking, probing gently, making notes, unceasingly kind and gentle. I hardly woke as they looked at my shoulder. By ambulance to the beachhead, a DUKW amphibious truck out to a hospital ship and the magic was gone, only the staleness and pent-up feelings remained.

This was part of Britain and I preferred the army. By ambulance train, stark white and simple but kind, to hospital and real beds and stuffy air and routine, but a bath. Two days and then dressed and back in the train. Where to? To Falkirk! All wounded would be treated as near home as possible, but I suppose that as walking wounded we could reasonably go further afield. I slept on the floor of the train. Early in the morning we left the train and were met by a women's organization giving out smiles and packets of cigarettes. Anger welled inside me and yet I was ashamed not to be able to thank them for their cold comfortless efforts to bring some humanity to us. To a long immaculate ward, an immaculate bed and a dragon of a sister.

Captain Edward W. McGregor, US 1st Infantry Division

There was to be a major attack on the American front at St Lo. It was to be called Operation Cobra. The attack began on 25 July, preceded by a strategic bombing by the American 8th Air Force – Flying Fortresses, B17s – and, well, some of these bombs fell short – on top of our 9th Infantry Division and, I believe, our 3rd Infantry Division. I know the 9th was hit and I think it was the 3rd. Anyway, we were in reserve and were then ordered to advance through the decimated front lines of these divisions and attack. Which we did and it was really something. There were these huge craters from the bombs, all over the place. We had a whole battalion of tanks attached to my battalion, the 1st Battalion of the 18th Infantry, and we couldn't use them, the ground was so torn up. And the Germans *still* had pockets of resistance that fought us all day long.

Well, in the mid-afternoon I told the Battalion Commander – we had just had a new Battalion Commander – that I'd better go up. He didn't want me to move up with the troops, but with the old Battalion Commander we always used to move up with the advance echelon. So I went up and kicked tail – or kicked ass, to use that expression – with A Company and C Company. And then some sergeant comes running up: 'Captain McGregor, the Battalion Commander has been killed and also Captain Cameron' – who was our Heavy Weapons Company Commander.

Well, I rushed back to the rear with him and the Battalion Commander was very badly wounded – but not dead – but there was my buddy, Captain Archie Cameron, deader than a mackerel. I cried like a baby. Then comes along some war correspondent, demanding to know what the situation was. A large man with a stick. Well, there were bullets flying all over the place and I was heartbroken, so I told him to get the hell out of there or I'd shoot him. At the time I didn't give a damn who it was, it could have been the Holy Ghost. Somebody said, 'Jeez Captain, that's Ernest Hemingway.' And I'm not certain, but I think it was Hemingway.

Bombardier Richard 'Dickie' Thomas, RA

One morning, looking over the edge of Mulberry Harbour – the sea was down about five or six feet – and there were twenty or thirty dead bodies floating in the water. Most unfortunately, two or three days of terribly hot sunshine came. I didn't know how a dead body floated, but I soon discovered that they floated face down, and it was a terrible sight to see: all the backs and backs of their legs became burnt by the terribly hot sun. They were burnt black like niggers. Eventually the navy came and sorted it out. It was a horrible sight.

Miss C.S.M. Petrie, 601(M) HAA Battery, RA
Diary, 9 June [Gosport]

More hospital work – lots of blood. I am sorry for the men, all shot away and encased in plaster and so willing to tease and laugh at an AT who is trying to help, but not doing much else! Spoke to one man who looked rather blank and was gleefully informed that he was a Jerry by the next inmate. Leapt sky high – and so did he – and the ward, weak as it was, laughed and nearly cried with laughing. I nearly cried at their good fellowship and happiness and me so helpless to do anything further at all.

Captain Joseph T. Dawson, US 1st Infantry Division

That afternoon my wound on my leg, my knee, had swelled up to the point where I had to be evacuated that afternoon, 7 June, when I was sent back to Malvern [England]. As soon as I was able to get the bullet fragment removed, and the fluid released – the wound even to this day bothers me – I made my way to Weymouth, where I caught a boat to Omaha and caught up with my unit. I was out of combat there for about ten days.

Telegram, Ottawa Ont July 28 1015A 1944
TO: MRS A R WILKINSON

17769 MINISTER OF DEFENCE REGRETS TO INFORM YOU C97125 PRIVATE ARTHUR CAMPBELL WILKINSON HAS BEEN OFFICIALLY REPORTED KILLED IN ACTION EIGHTEEN JULY 1944 STOP WHEN FURTHER INFORMATION BECOMES AVAILABLE IT WILL BE FORWARDED AS SOON AS RECEIVED

DIRECTOR OF RECORDS

Letter, 6 Airborne Div, BWEF, 30 June 1944

Dear Mrs Blower,
It is difficult for me to put into words my heartfelt sympathy
for you in the loss of your gallant son [Lieutenant John
Blower, RA] in action.

To a commander like myself these losses are hard to bear:
and yet for you it must be so much worse.

You know, however, that you have our deepest sympathy
and that your son gave his life for a great enterprise and a
great cause.

Yours sincerely
Richard N. Gale
Major-General

Letter, Buckingham Palace

The Queen and I offer you our heartfelt sympathy in your
great sorrow. We pray that your country's gratitude for a life
so nobly given in its service may bring you some measure of
consolation.

George R.

Sergeant H.M. Kellar, Devonshire Regiment

While trying to look through the long grass on top of the
bank to try and find something to shoot at, I suddenly
realized I couldn't bend my right knee, also that the
handgrip on the stock of my rifle was splintered – so I
suppose the bullet would have hit me in the chest had it
not been deflected into my knee. Also, the velocity was
greatly reduced, so that the bullet merely clipped a small
piece of bone off my kneecap and then lodged in the joint.
After that earlier clash with a Spandau [machine gun], when
I found my Sten gun useless, I had changed to a rifle, a fact
which probably saved my life.

I slid back down the bank and made my way back where I met the platoon officer coming forward with his radio operator. I apologized and said I would have to go back, and he said 'Oh, bad luck!' Bad luck! It was the best bit of luck I've ever had to get away from that hell.

Ernie Pyle, war correspondent

After breakfast that first morning we had to round up about fifty dead Germans and Americans in the series of orchards where we were camping, and carry them to a central spot in a pasture and bury them.

I helped carry one corpse across a couple of fields. I did it partly because the group needed an extra man, and partly because I was forcing myself to get used to it, for you can't hide from death when you're in a war.

This German was just a kid, surely not over fifteen. His face had already turned black, but you could sense his youth through the death-distorted features.

The boys spread a blanket on the ground beside him. Then we lifted him over onto it. One soldier and I each took hold of a foot, and two others took his arms. One of the two soldiers in front was hesitant about touching the corpse. Whereupon the other soldier said to him:

'Go on, take hold of him, dammit. You might as well get used to it now, for you'll be carrying plenty of dead ones from now on. Hell, you may even be carrying me one of these days.'

So we carried him across two fields, each of us holding a corner of the blanket. Our burden got pretty heavy, and we rested a couple of times. The boys made wisecracks along the way to cover up their distaste for the job.

When we got to the field we weren't sure just where the lieutenant wanted the cemetery started. So we put our man down on the ground and went back for instructions. And as we walked away the funny guy of the group turned and shook a finger at the dead German and said: 'Now don't you run away while we're gone.'

Many thousands of soldiers left Normandy not as casualties but as prisoners of war. In the confused fighting and constantly shifting front line it was all too easy to walk into the hands of the enemy. In general, POWs were treated reasonably by both sides, even if taken in the heat of the moment of battle when feelings were highest. This is not to say that POW crimes did not take place; they did.

Corporal Ted Morris, 6th Airborne Division

Jimmy Warkup, a sergeant-major, came down with some German prisoners and left me with these Germans and a Sten gun. I said to him that the Sten was no good to me, I was a non-combatant. He said it didn't matter because it had a bullet jammed in it and it didn't fire in any case. I had some lovely souvenirs off these Germans: I had a lovely belt with 'Gott Mitts Uns' on, and some stamps with Hitler's head on. I thought, 'Oh, I'm all right here!' Anyway, Warkup came back with a lance-sergeant, called Eddie Walker, on a stretcher, who had been shot in the stomach – I think by one of his own officers by mistake. He had internal bleeding.

Warkup said, 'We'll take this bloke back. Have four German POWs to carry the stretcher.' I had a lance-corporal – Wilkinson was his name – with me from the Paras, with a Sten gun pointing at the Germans. They picked up the stretcher and away we went, with me walking in front. I got so far and I found some Paras holding the perimeter and they had a Bren. I said, 'Is that the road back?' – there was a sort of sunken road in front. They said, 'Yes, you go on through there, you'll be all right.' Well, just then we got mortared, but they were only ranging on the village and after a few shells it went. A couple of medical orderlies from another battalion appeared with a badly wounded chap on a stretcher, his arm was all bloody and that. I said that I couldn't take another stretcher, but the chap got off the stretcher and said he could walk, and sure enough he bloody walked. With that we set off down the sunken road, and we'd only got a few hundred yards from the Bren gun lads and all of a sudden there was a little Jerry in front of me with a Schmeisser. It was typical, what you see in the movies: 'Hande hoch.' There were Germans everywhere, coming out of the sunken road. They didn't shoot because they were looking for prisoners, to see who we were. So that's how I was captured.

T. Tateson, Green Howards

Sergeant Potterton told us he didn't know where the hell Major Sparks had got to. He told us to stay put under cover of a ditch while he went off to arrange for more ammunition. He did not return and it soon became obvious to us that under cover of darkness the Germans had put in a heavy counter-attack, and that in fact we had walked into a carefully planted trap. They were all round us, tanks on the road to our rear and German voices shouting in the woods nearby. There was heavy and constant firing all around, but mostly from our rear, and we realized that we had been completely cut off. Ted Russell, now being the senior NCO, told us to ditch our equipment, including the wireless set, and this we did. The intention was that we should try to filter back through the enemy . . . However, matters were decided for us when, with Germans approaching our scanty cover, Ted leaped up and surrendered . . .

The psychological effect of being taken prisoner is an almost complete numbing of the senses. We were lined up with our hands on our heads by men with Schmeisser automatics and it went through my head that they might shoot us out of hand. The dulling effect of anti-climax, however, meant that the thought simply left me with a detached feeling almost of curiosity rather than fear. From prolonged intense excitement leading to near exhaustion we now experienced a complete lowering of the senses, even that of self-preservation. When dumping my kit I had recovered a leather writing wallet containing a photograph of Olive and her letters to me, and simply slipped them inside my battle-dress blouse. Now, with my hands on my head, the wallet slipped down and fell to the floor. I stooped down and picked it up, in so doing risking an instant burst of fire and a quick death.

Private Zimmer, 12th SS Panzer Division
Diary, 10 July

By the time the survivors try to pull back, we realize that we are surrounded. In our sector, we had driven back the British infantry attack, but they had bypassed us to left and right. I moved back as fast as I could under the continuous firing. Others who tried to do the same failed. When the small-arms fire stopped our own guns got going. I lay there in the midst of it all. I still cannot understand how I escaped, with shelling falling two or three metres away, splinters tearing around my ears. By now I had worked my way to within 200 metres of our own lines. It was hard work, always on my stomach, only occasionally up on hands and knees. The small-arms fire began again, and the English infantry renewed their attack. My hopes dwindled. The advancing Tommies passed five or six paces away without noticing me in the high corn. I was almost at the end of my tether, my feet and elbows in agony, my throat parched. Suddenly the cover thinned out and I had to cross an open field. In the midst of this, wounded Englishmen passed within ten metres without seeing me. Now I had to hurry. There were only ten metres to go to the next belt of corn. Suddenly three Tommies appeared and took me prisoner. Immediately I was given a drink and a cigarette. At the concentration point for prisoners I met my *unterscharführer* and other comrades of my company . . .

Marine Stanley Blacker, RM

As we moved along a narrow winding tarmac road we heard the sound of a horse approaching and as we waited tensely ready to open fire what should come around the bend but a Mongolian riding bareback a huge shire horse and dressed in German uniform. He was unarmed, arms raised and smiling happily. Glad to be out of it, I suppose, so we just stood aside and sent him on his way to the rear.

The first German prisoners I saw came down through the village of Ver-sur-Mer to the beach. There were about 300 of them. Feelings were very bitter, and a lot of people would have shot them if they could have got away with it. I felt very bitter about them too because if it wasn't for them we wouldn't have been there.

Private Robert Macduff, Wiltshire Regiment

I had a line break but everyone else had been designated other jobs, so I went out on the line repair on my own. Really this was forbidden but, anyway, I followed the line, head down, and came to a log where the line ran alongside – and noticed a pair of jack boots and the grey uniform of a German soldier. As I raised my eyes there was a German officer sitting on the log. My heart dropped, and I was waiting for the bullet . . . it never came. When I spoke to him he told me that he had been instructed to wait there for the Royal Engineers to come and collect him. He was a POW. He looked to me as if he had had enough.

. . . .

In the early hours of the morning there was a noise above the signal trench. Looking out I saw a German soldier crawling over the top. 'Schiessen mich nicht. Frau und zwei kinde in Deutschland,' he said. We got him into the trench and he said he hadn't eaten anything for two or three days, so I gave him half my biscuits and water. A superior officer came over to see what was going on and was enraged at my sharing my rations with a POW. I was put on a charge.

Alfred Leonard, Merchant Navy

The German prisoners used to come out in launches and over our deck up into the troop carriers. There was a terrific amount of bartering going on for war mementos. Cigarettes for medals, and so on. The nasty ones, the SS, used to come out too. You could tell they were nasty, even though we couldn't speak German, and they couldn't speak English. It was their attitude, they were still very arrogant. They weren't bartering. The average German soldier, though, looked glad to be out of it.

Anonymous, Wehrmacht 352nd Infantry Division

To be honest it annoyed me that the 'Amis' always thought that we were going to shoot them [when captured]. There were occasions when feelings ran high, after the death of friends. I can only think of one time when it happened in my platoon, when someone lost their head and shot an American prisoner. But no, it was not usual. At least with the Wehrmacht, and I can only speak for the Wehrmacht. We were professional soldiers. Indeed, when were retreating down the Cotentin we let Americans go, return to their side. That's strange, isn't it? But they would have been an encumbrance, so we let them go.

The SS were a completely different case, of course. As everyone now well knows they frequently killed prisoners. This is a matter of war crimes history. The SS, though, were nothing to do with us. We were a professional army.

Anonymous British infantryman

A comrade heard loud moaning and investigated. I went down to find two German soldiers in a dug-out. One looked mortally wounded and the other, who was wounded, was trying to help him out. We got them out into the open air and reported to a passing officer who told us to shoot them. This we refused to do. Three riflemen nearby also refused to shoot them. So he pulled out his revolver and shot the two Germans dead. A few days later it was reported to me that this officer, who I think was a Lieutenant S—, was shot in the back by his own men, several firing at once. Apparently he had a reputation of shooting all prisoners he came across. The platoon he commanded was afraid that if they had been captured and the enemy had heard of this officer's actions they would be dealt with in the same way.

Away from the immediacy of combat the preoccupations of soldiers in Normandy were remarkably constant: a desire to get clean, well fed (particularly if they were British) and write – and especially receive – mail.

Sergeant H.M. Kellar, Devonshire Regiment

At some point we were told that we were being withdrawn from the front in small groups and sent into Bayeaux for a shower. This duly took place and we were taken to the public bath house in the middle of the town. This was very enjoyable and badly needed as we were all filthy. And of course there was the possibility of fleas and lice.

Letters to his wife from Colonel G. Tilly, 5th Dorsets

France 24 June

Dear Dorothy

. . . there is a stream near here and when I have written this letter I am off for a quick scrub down, and I am waiting my turn as only a few of us can go away at a time.

Had a glass of milk this morning – 5 francs: not bad really
and straight from a cow.

France 29 June

Dear Dorothy

Had a drop of 'Homemade French Champagne Brandy' last
night – whoosh nearly lifted my head off.

We have got a cow – poor dear mooing its head off full of
milk and shrapnel – and then it gets milked about every half-
hour – still, makes the good old cup of tea taste good.

Do you remember Jack Atherton? He and his wife had
dinner with us in the Fleur de Lis in Sandwich about two
years ago . . . he was a bit unlucky the night before last and
was killed.

I am very well Dot so there is no need for you to worry at
all – only thing is I really would like a good bath.

Sergeant William B. Smith, Intelligence Corps
In one field there was a live cow and eventually an 18-year-
old farmer's daughter appeared on the scene with a bucket to
milk the cow. Needless to say, her arrival started a veritable
chorus of wolf whistles.

**General Matt B. Ridgway, US 82nd Airborne
Division**
I woke with the first light, sore and stiff but refreshed, filled
my helmet with hot water, and started to shave, with one of
these little injector razors with a rotating head that a
paratrooper likes because it is small, all in one piece, and
takes up not much more room than a pencil. I had gotten a
leather-cased field telephone in by this time, and when I was
about half through shaving, it rang – a battalion down by

the river reporting on the night's activities. When I put down my phone and reached for my razor again, it was gone. Some SOB had stolen it.

Lance-Bombardier Stanley Morgan, RA
When leave started everybody had to be dusted with DDT dust. They had to open their trousers and up under their arms because they didn't want typhoid coming to this country [Britain].

.   .   .   .

We were living off iron rations, and when bread came across it was snow white. It was a relief after the iron biscuit things. They were terrible.

Trooper Peter Davies, 1st East Riding Yeomanry
Although there's little space inside a tank I once kept chickens in there, in a wire-mesh box we had made. They gave us eggs – and chicken in the end.

Anonymous, Highland Division
Egg hunting was the only possible sport in Ste Honaire, and it was pursued so diligently by the garrison that some claimed eggs were snatched before they even touched the straw. All the hens certainly had a harassed look.

Bombardier Harry Hartill, RA
We had been living on biscuits for quite a while and one morning while running across an open space to the breakfast dishing-out place we were shelled as usual. But the day was special – we were to receive a whole round each of white bread, which we had forgotten ever existed. So we kept on running.

William Seymour, RN

The way we used to get our joy was finding American emergency kits floating in the water, from landing craft which had sunk, and we'd hook them on board, and they were full of sweets and cigarettes and the like – that was our sort of perk.

Marine Stanley Blacker, RM

The Yanks were better fed than us. They had a ship offshore baking bread 24 hours after D-Day. The smell used to drive us frantic. We just used to have biscuits that would make your gums bleed.

G.E. Dale, ROC, seconded to US liberty ship off Omaha

Diary, 7 June

Up at 7.00 . . . for breakfast at 7.30. Fruit or glass of fruit or tomato juice, cereal if required, two fried eggs with huge slices of ham, hot cakes spread with butter and maple syrup, toast, marmalade and coffee. The fare provided on the *J.D. Ross* was a revelation to a ration-ridden Englishman.

Trooper Ken Tout, 1st Northamptonshire Yeomanry

14 June

Morning finds us slowly nosing out to sea. The huge 'Landing Ship (Tank)', with its collapsible bows, is a ponderous and slow craft. It turns with a kind of arthritic limping and skewing. Its path is complicated by the mass of shipping which lies like the tufts of a continuous carpet from Southampton out past the Isle of Wight and into the Channel.

Ships are detaching themselves from the mass and heading in the same general direction towards the mists of the sea horizon. The departing ships ease out into a formation reminiscent of hounds and huntsmen. Somewhere out on the flanks, naval destroyers, minesweepers and patrol boats ride flank on our main procession. For a while the incredible multitude of ships fascinates us, and we search for words: shoals, armadas, swarms, swaths, hordes – clustered upon the grey-green sea like blackfly on a leaf.

Then we turn to conversation with the American sailors. In 1944 Yanks are still strange creatures to most British people except in southern towns invaded by their new armies. From childhood I have seen Texans bidding for bulls in the market at Hereford, but Yanks in general are still a novelty, a mixture of Edward G. Robinson, Gary Cooper and Bing Crosby. Obviously to them we are an equal novelty – our rough clothes, our primitive armaments, our meagre rations, our pale faces, our stilted speech.

The Stuart is an American-built tank, as is also the Sherman, but it is obviously unknown to the sailors, who clamber over it with interest. One sailor fingers my Sten gun superciliously. 'What's this, son? A toy for your little brother back home?' I too am not impressed by the Sten, which, they say, is patched together in back street garages. It is liable to jam and, when actually firing, sprays its bullets wildly, depending on profusion of bullets rather than accuracy of aim.

'Are you aiming to fight Germans with this, son?' persists the sailor, waving the fragile-looking Sten. 'Aw, don't give me that. Here, come and look at some real guns.'

We go up to the seamen's quarters. My friend pulls out an old blue kitbag. Opens it. Extracts a tommy-gun. The style of the old gangster films. Solid, compact, sinister. 'Accurate!' says my Yank. 'Reliable. That's a real gun. Take it, son. You'll be fighting Fritzies. We won't be meeting any Fritzies in this baked bean tin of a ship. Take it and shoot a few for me and my friends from Tacoma, Washington.'

'You can't mean it,' I say. 'Don't you have to sign for it?'

Or return it to stores? Or lay it out for kit inspections?'

'Sign for it? Stores? Kit inspections? Where do you think you are? Bucking-Ham Palace? Take it, son. There's plenty more where that came from.'

Sid is also in the seamen's quarters, squatting on a bunk and laying out our forty-eight hours ration pack for the Yanks to see. We have a small cake of soup powder looking like a solidified version of the scum one finds at the sea's edge. We have tea powder, incorporating coarse tea, lumpy dehydrated milk and grey sugar. We have porridge powder looking similar to, but even more anaemic than, the soup. We have hard biscuit. We have all the luxuries of the Café Royal. Someone has described our powdered soup as 'dehydrated tablecloth'.

One of the seamen snorts in disgust. 'If the Germans don't bump you off, that chow will. You can't go ashore with nothing to eat. Hey, Barney, fetch the Quartermaster. These boys can't starve on those beaches.'

The Quartermaster has an even thicker jungle of stripes than our guide of yesterday. He picks over our pocket-sized rations for forty-eight hours. Looks sad. 'Bloody graveyard food,' he says. 'Wouldn't feed a hundred-year-old corpse. This a joke of that thin beanpole Montgomery? We must do something about this. Follow me, boys.'

We descend a number of iron ladders into a large store-room. Rows and rows of cardboard boxes stand piled around the iron walls. 'Help yourselves, boys. Take what you want. Nothing to pay. A birthday present from your Uncle Sam. Bloody beanpole Montgomery! Take what you want. One thing: don't leave any half-empty boxes. If you open a box, empty it and throw the box over the side. And give the Fritzies hell.'

We tear a box out of the nearest pile. Rip open the cover. Tinned 'Chicken', carol the labels. We reach for another pile. 'Tomato Juice', the labels laugh. We stagger to the other end of the room. 'Corned Beef Hash', the labels chant.

And across the room, 'Yellow Cling Peaches', the labels whisper. This is Paradise, Aladdin's Cave and Fortnum & Mason's all in one. Glory, glory, Hallelujah. Hip! Hip! for Uncle Sam! AND his Quartermaster!

Sid, Johnny and I fill two cartons with assorted goods. Lug them up ladders, along gangways past grinning Americans, down into our cavern. Load up the American tank with American luxuries. I see the Sherman behind us, not one of our Regiment, tossing out 75-mm shells. Laying the shells on the engine covers. Loading on more American goods.

'What are you going to do with those shells?' I ask the driver of the Sherman. 75-mm shells are massive contraptions. Made in one piece, bright brass case and black iron shot joined together, the finished product is about as long as my arm and about as broad as my lower thigh. They take up a lot of room in the turret and in the storage spaces in the hull called 'sponsons'.

'Bugger me if we're going to carry all that lot ashore when we can stock up with Yankee food,' says the driver. 'We'll toss the shells into the sea once it gets dark.'

'They'll get shot at dawn,' says Bernard. 'We're not going to do that are we, Ken?' My disciplined body shudders at the thought. 'If I'm going to get shot,' I reply, 'I leave it to some Jerry at a thousand yards and not a dozen blokes in a firing squad at ten paces, thank you!' But we discard a spare can of water, and Sid throws out an old case from in his compartment, and we grow more like Lipton's without specifically infringing any regimental ordinances.

Tally-Ho: The Goathland News Bulletin
No. 24. 14 July 1944
Ships News: To-day for the first time the ship has run a liberty – the restrictions and the difficulties are many and the landing place is not 'Gay Paree' of popular imagination – nevertheless it is a sign of the success of the invasion. Reports

from those who went ashore are interesting. A football match between a Highland Division and the 51st Division was in progress. The French had a parade this morning and laid flowers on the graves of Canadian soldiers who fell in the initial attack. Many civilians have returned to their homes in the coastal villages.

Poem:

> Shylock had his Ducats
> Henry had his Wives
> Cruso had his Friday
> A cat has got Nine Lives
> Charwomen have their Buckets
> Bill Posters have a Pail
> So why the Hell can't Goathland
> Get some Ruddy Mail.

Captain Edward McGregor, US 1st Infantry Division

The mail started coming in and I received a package from my little Wren [member of Womens' Royal Naval Service]. It was a tin, a fair-sized one, maybe about a foot in length. I opened it up and there was a loaf of bread in there. I thought, 'My God, what's she sending me a loaf of bread for?' But inside the loaf of bread was a bottle of scotch. The British are terrific. Ingenious.

John Hall, Winnipeg Rifles

Every letter written by the troops had to be censored by an officer. This meant that I had to read about fifty letters a day when we were not in action. I soon acquired the knack of skimming through them without involving myself in the personal content. It was certainly a revelation to me to read some of them. I had one gunner who wrote exactly the same letter to his wife and to six other young ladies. I could not imagine what sort of life he had led at home. Another man, who was a real moaner and full of grumbles, wrote to a friend called Jack giving him all sorts of prohibited information. I tore the letter up and gave it back to him, and he then told me that Jack was a member of Parliament and his personal friend. This cut no ice with me and he had a further short and sharp lecture. However, the troops as a bunch were marvellous and we all got on famously together.

Letter, Canadian Soldier 10 July
Dear Mother

I feel like a heel for not writing regularly to you and I know how anxious I would feel if I didn't hear from you. Please never stop writing dear.

I cannot tell you much about what is going on over here, as we haven't been very far inland and cannot tell about the people or the country either. I can say this though: it is a gigantic business and we are fighting a tough enemy.

Mother, before I close for a while, I am a bit mixed up about things but am straight on this: Dad and you are my ideal couple. If I can be half the man Dad is and have the outlook you have on life, I won't ever have to worry. I have been scared and I guess there will be plenty of times in the future when I will be scared, but as long as I don't let you, Dad, Dot, Rich and David down, I shall be happy, no matter the outcome of this do, in so far as it affects my personal future behaviour. Will say cheerio for now, sweetheart.

All best love,
Art

The fighting in Normandy was but the tip of a vast Allied supply effort. All who set foot on the beaches of Normandy that year were amazed by the flow of goods coming ashore, ferried by the

ubiquitous DUKW, while behind the scenes men laboured away
to keep the war machine running.

Richard Dimbleby, BBC war correspondent
11 June 1944
I saw the shining, blue sea. Not an empty sea, but a sea
crowded, infested with craft of every kind: little ships, fast
and impatient, scurrying like water-beetles to and fro, and
leaving a glistening wake behind them; bigger ships in
stately, slow procession with the sweepers in front and the
escort vessels on the flank – it was a brave, oh, an inspiring
sight. We are supplying the beaches all right – no doubt of
that. We flew on south-west, and I could see France and
Britain, and I realized how very near to you all at home in
England is this great battle in Normandy. It's a stone's throw
across the gleaming water.

I saw it all as a mighty panorama, clear and etched in its
detail. There were the supply ships, the destroyers, the
torpedo boats, the assault craft, leaving England. Half
way over was another flotilla, and near it a huge,
rounded, ugly, capital ship, broadside on to France. There
in the distance was the Cherbourg peninsula, Cherbourg
itself revealed in the sun. And there, right ahead now, as we
reset course, were the beaches. Dozens, scores, hundreds of
craft lying close inshore, pontoons and jetties being lined up
to make a new harbour where, six days ago, there was an
empty stretch of shore.

Alexandre Reynaud, Mayor of Ste Mere Eglise
On a beautiful day in mid-June I was finally invited by a
Canadian officer, Captain Tanner, of Civil Affairs, an active
and cheerful person and an excellent soldier, to accompany
him in his Jeep to visit the big new landing ports. This was a
huge favor, since access to the beaches was strictly off-limits
to civilians. But already I was beginning to get the impres-

sion that 'off-limits' doesn't mean exactly the same thing to Americans as the word 'verboten' to Germans.

So we took off via Sainte-Marie-du-Mont, along the back roads bordered with hedges, and which groups of boy scouts were working to widen. Soon, at a turn, we came upon the dunes bordering the ocean.

Hundreds of balloons which looked exactly like monstrous fish were suspended in the sky above us and inland as far as the eye could see. Some were only a few yards above the dunes, others were a little higher, and still others were swaying gently, several hundred metres up. Some of them were lying on the ground, partly deflated. The cables that kept them tied to earth looked like giant seaweed.

Our Jeep, like a poor little spider lost in the midst of these monsters, raced over the metal trackways on the beach.

Like woodlouse whose dimensions were in keeping with those of the landscape, the ten-metre long amphibious 'ducks', which had wheels and propellers, climbed up the dunes, deposited their loads, then disappeared once again behind them at fifty kilometres an hour.

Here and there were huge piles of crates that trucks were carrying off toward the roads. All sorts of debris were piled up between the dunes; smashed 'ducks', trucks, tanks, boats, metal, as though they had been washed up in some gigantic shipwreck.

Not a single tree remained standing after the great air raids of June; there was nothing but sand and cement blocks torn from the German blockhouses, from which long iron rods were sticking up.

During a long time, it seemed to us, very tiny insects, that we were gliding in the depths of a vast sea spangled with wrecks, filled with a huge flora and a prehistoric fauna.

Suddenly, the Jeep took a different track and turned off between two dunes. The wheels were no longer squeaking: we were on the beach and the sand was hard.

From Foucarville to Vey's Bay, hundreds of ships had run aground or were still floating. There were little barges, rowboats, tankers, and massive cargoes. All had flat bottoms and stood perfectly upright on the sand. The hull of the cargoes had been opened like closet doors, and from them had emerged Jeeps, trucks, tanks and cannons. Cars zigzagged along the beach between the huge carcasses. At high tide, the latter closed their trap-doors and quickly sped off to England.

'Ducks' were constantly arriving from the dunes, coming down to the ocean and entering the water; their propellers beat the waves, and they took up positions alongside the rails of the large floating ships that had remained in the water. Immobile, they allowed themselves to be filled with all sorts of light cargo: men, food, clothing, munitions.

Thus, without wasting time, each cargo would be ready when came the time of day when the tide would allow it to open up and empty its hold.

Heavier equipment and crates were unloaded onto barges that had been sunk end-to-end to form a metal bridge, and trucks and trailers loaded up alongside this new type of wharf.

Above each ship, one of the monstrous fish on the end of a cable kept watch.

Leonard Miles, 168 General Transport Company

DUKWs were not popular in the company, mostly because driving a DUKW on the sea was a monotonous job. The engine was noisy and ran very hot, and the trip from ship to shore to a transhipment area, off loading, and then back through DUKW control to sea went on time after time. But the DUKW was an excellent vehicle for the job, the making of the landings. You could inflate the tyres to the pressure you wanted from the driver's panel. It was possible to deflate the tyre pressures when entering the sandy beaches or inflate them on a normal road. In the event of getting stuck in very loose sand, the DUKW had a winch which could be anchored to some firm object. It was American, the DUKW, and all their vehicles and equipment were out of this world compared to ours. Without the American equipment we wouldn't have won.

Alan Melville, RAF war correspondent

Down on the beaches things were becoming hourly more organized. One-way traffic systems were put into force, and very nearly drove us mental. It was quite a normal procedure, if you wanted to go fifty yards from Point A to Point B, to be sent round a four-mile circuit and – just as you were reaching your objective – to be told by an unbending MP that there was no left turn to the spot you wanted to reach. It was all like a game of Snakes and Ladders, with very long and tenuous snakes and very short and unreliable ladders. Beating the service policemen by dodging illegally down a one-way road against the traffic became a popular pastime. A DUKW backed into Hermione on one such trip and very nearly squashed the life out of her. When a DUKW decides to do that sort of thing, there is nothing you can do about it except toot madly: the wretched things are so high off the ground that they simply ride roughshod over such puny objects as Jeeps. Eventually, the corporal at the wheel or helm (I never quite knew with these amphibious affairs) realized that all was not well in the neighbourhood of his stern or rear bumper. Both he and I got out; we were hot and white with dust and short of temper, and I hurled abuse at the man, ending by asking him what the hell he meant by reversing without making sure that there was nothing behind him. He shrieked back at me, 'I've been four times round this bloody circuit and I'm so bloody browned off I don't care what I bloody well back into' and then added a quite redundant 'sir' and hoisted himself back into his DUKW. There was no answer to that one except to retire with as much dignity as possible and extricate Hermione from the entanglement. The Pioneer Corps were already at work widening the first lateral road and filling in the bunkers on it. There was a track along one side of the road on which some form of tram had run from Ouistreham to Luc-sur-Mer, and great gangs of men were engaged on hauling this up by its roots. The road was really only wide enough to take one line of traffic, and as you frequently had to negotiate your way past the heaviest types of tanks which had just come off the beaches, the number of Pioneers who risked the opposite of decapitation by sticking their behinds out into the roadway must have been very great. In spite of the shelling, we had an enormous quantity of material ashore.

Citation for Croix de Guerre, awarded to Lance-Corporal Reginald Jenkins, RASC

Placed in charge of a section of vehicles with the task of supplying smoke equipment for the purpose of covering the Eastern Sector of the beachhead, this NCO showed outstanding qualities of leadership and initiative. Although unable to reach his position on D-Day, he arrived with his vehicles as soon as a way could be cleared, and from D + 2 until the whole detachment was relieved on D + 51 he was continually in charge of this section. He himself was a driver of a vehicle, he carried out major and other repairs to the vehicles in his section and by his unusual mechanical ability prevented any vehicle from being unserviceable for more than 2 hours. Despite damage by shell blast, fire, and rough country, the vehicles under his control were kept in good condition by his supervision and prompt action – sometimes unorthodox but always effective. He and the drivers under his command were daily under enemy fire and the encouragement which he gave; by act and word, to his men undoubtedly contributed in large measure to the high and sustained morale and efficiency of his section. Despite the fact that a smoke screen had sometimes to be maintained all

day for days on end, and also on moonlight nights, the supply
of generators never failed at any time and this satisfactory
performance was due in very great measure to the initiative
and leadership displayed by Lance-Corporal Jenkins.

They sang rude songs about their leaders ('Hitler only had one ball
/ Goring had two, but very small / Himmler had something similar
/ But poor old Goebbels had no balls at all') and called them
'Krauts' and 'Jerries', but the insouciant attitude of the Allied
soldier towards his German counterpart hid a wide range of
feelings.

Sergeant William B. Smith, Intelligence Corps

That morning I had my first actual work. A batch of
something like a hundred prisoners was brought in, among
them an officer who was shouting out to the men that if they
were interrogated they must not disclose any military
information. He was quickly removed from the scene in
accordance with standard drill, that officers must be removed immediately from the men in case they should try to
organize any resistance. The mentality of the Germans was
most interesting, though. Our most important job was to
identify the German units and the number of prisoners from
them. I got the Germans to do my job for me. When a
substantial number arrived, I would line them up and call
for the senior NCO. Somebody, usually a sergeant, would
step forward and I would tell him to sort the men into
groups, one group for each company. Invariably they would
conscientiously carry out my orders, anxious to demonstrate
to us how efficient they were. They did not seem to realize
that they were, in fact, helping the enemy.

. . . .

I decided that I wanted a slit trench dug for myself in case of
air attack or shelling, and gave two young prisoners spades

and set them to work. They worked marvellously, quite oblivious that I was the enemy. They were interested in talking to me, asking if I was an 'Aktiver' (professional soldier). When the trench was deep enough, they set about camouflaging it from the air, by covering the dug-up soil with grass. The Germans had laid a lot of mines in these fields, and to show which fields had mines in had twisted the wire of the fence in a certain way. The grass in the next field, quite close to my trench, was much better than that in our field, and they had a discussion as to whether they should go into that field to gather some. They decided that no mines would have been laid within a few feet of the fence, and went over to collect enough to finish my shelter for me.

Ernie Pyle, war correspondent
Another high-ranking [German] officer was brought in and the first thing he asked was the whereabouts of his personal orderly. When told that his orderly was deader than a mackerel, he flew off the handle and accused us of depriving him of his personal comfort.

'Who's going to dig my foxhole for me?' he demanded.

Captain Edward W. McGregor, US 1st Infantry Division
Having lived through the nightmare years of the thirties in high school and college I regarded the Nazis with absolute hatred for the things they had perpetrated in Germany. However, as a professional soldier myself, I had a high respect for their infantry, who fought very tenaciously. They were crackerjack troops.

Seaman C.J. Wells, Merchant Navy
We'd had a lot of propaganda about the Germans, so we'd got to the point where we hated them. But the Germans had a bit of guts, whatever you say about them.

Leonard Miles, 168 General Transport Company

They weren't bad [people], most of the Germans were only there because of the say so of a dictator. In fairness, they were a very difficult force to reckon with, they were very good soldiers. I had great respect for them really. Once they had had enough they hoisted a white flag, and there were no dirty tricks, no throwing of hand grenades after they surrendered. I had had experience of Rommel in the days in the desert beforehand and he had impressed me there.

Anonymous British soldier

We caught two SS men – well, boys really. They were only about 15 or 16. Arrogant like you'd never believe! So we thought we'd take them down a peg or two and made them lie on the ground, and measured them out – like we were digging graves for them. Then we made them dig these 'graves' and get in. I think we even lined up like we were going to shoot them – I'm not proud of this by the way, it was a terrible thing to do – and do you know what? We couldn't break them. It ended up scaring us more than it scared them. They wouldn't break.

Donald S. Vaughan, 79th Armoured Division

They were there and we had to go through them. We were trained to shoot at them, and that was it.

Captain Albert H. Smith, US 1st Infantry Division

The German soldiers were very professional, good soldiers – the ones we met. We hadn't met the SS yet, we hadn't met the people who committed the atrocities yet. We were just fighting one professional division against another, German, professional division. I must say we were giving them, from the standpoint of artillery and airstrikes, ten times what we were taking. And they were sitting there – they were holding their positions. As you know the British were unable to take Caen for a month and a half, and taking terrible casualties every time they mounted one of their operations. This is until about the end of the first week in August. Then, when the Germans knew they had been defeated, when they knew they had to get back to the Siegfried Line, when they knew they had to get back to Germany – then you ran into a different kind of German. You ran into one who was willing to surrender if he was back of you, and get out of your way if he was in front of you. From the landing in June, though, until the end of July we were fighting the toughest kind of German they could put in the line. Very professional, and made it very tough for us.

Lt. Elliott Johnson, US 4th Infantry Division

The fifth night we were there, we were in dug-in fox holes, in a very checkered position. There were Germans ahead of us and Germans in the back of us. Americans over there ahead of these Germans. The infantry and the artillery were side by side. There was no infantry out in front. When the infantry moved, we moved. There was no straight front line. It was a mess.

We were surrounded by hedgerow fences. One corner would be cut down so cattle could go and drink. In one such corner, there was a sniper. He was shooting at us. Every time I'd stick my head out of the fox hole, I'd get shot at. I called two very dear friends on the telephone. We fanned out, each of us with a grenade. At a given point, we pitched our grenades and accomplished what we had to do.

I avoid using words like 'kill a man' because I like to divorce myself from that. We recognized that we were in a war, but we recognized that they came from families like we came from families and that they had loved ones and they were good guys and they were bad guys. We were called on by our government, that our country was in jeopardy.

Therefore we had to fight for it. Personally, I had no malice at any time toward the Germans.

There were only one or two times we ever had face-to-face confrontations with storm troopers. The SS. They were the elite. They were so brainwashed they were impossible to reason with. Those people made me angry.

The ordinary Germans, the boys we took prisoner, were so glad to be out of it. We'd take their shoes and they'd walk down the road. The last thing they'd do is come back and either shake hands with us or embrace us.

There is a myth about Normandy, which runs to the effect that the French were unanimously overjoyed to be liberated by the Allies (who in turn were always courteous to the *Normandais*) from the tutelage of the Germans. In fact, the reality was infinitely more complex.

Richard McMillan, war correspondent

I entered Bayeux with the first troops. It was a scene of rejoicing as the people went wild. The streets were blocked with cheering men and women and children. The Tricolor and Union Jacks were hung in the windows. Cafés threw open their doors and pianists began to play British and French patriotic tunes. Crowds danced and shouted, 'Vive Tommy', 'Vive l'Amerique.'

It was a scene of mingled war and peace through which I passed as I drove a Jeep into the interior along part of the front line. After a dusty dreary morning, the sun burst through and the skies cleared. It was a perfect summer day. Driving through the coastal defense belt, I saw the havoc wrought by the Allied naval and air bombardment which had wrecked some roads and many hamlets which the Germans had used as headquarters . . .

In the fields peasants tended their sheep and cattle as if this day were no different from any other. The Allied war machine rolled past along the dusty highways, but the only sign the stolid peasants gave was a wave of the hand. It was the townspeople, like those of Bayeux, who really showed their appreciation, repeating again and again, '*C'est le jour de la liberation.*'

Marine Stanley Blacker, RM

In the chateau next to the churchyard at Ste Cambes, I always gave a bar of chocolate to a little French boy who came up to the gates. He never knew me and I never knew him, and I shall never know him. He used to take the chocolate and run indoors.

Trooper Peter Davies, 1st East Riding Yeomanry

We met quite a lot of resentment, not a little abuse in the first few weeks. The Germans had left that part of Normandy fairly free, they hadn't bothered the people to a great extent apart from building the Atlantic Wall. We arrived with tanks, shells and everything, tanks cutting through corn-fields, through crops, not doing them a lot of good. They were all given chits by officers to claim compensation at a later date, but there was resentment. I can understand that. A squadron of tanks going through somebody's cornfield makes a hell of a mess.

Rex North, *Sunday Pictorial* war correspondent

I met Jeanne rushing down a village street, hair awry, her coat torn on barbed wire. She was clutching at the arm of a German prisoner who was being marched to the coast.

She was not alone. Seven other women were doing the same to seven other German prisoners. Presumably for the same reasons as Jeanne.

The war? There was no war in Normandy when we marched in.

Private Robert Macduff, Wiltshire Regiment
During the clearance a sniper from a church tower fired on,
and killed, several of our soldiers. It turned out to be a
woman collaborator.

W.C. Weightman, RCS
Diary, 8 June
German prisoners being led out and French women kissing
them.

Alan Melville, RAF war correspondent
When the newspapers began to come through, I read some
amazing stories of the hysterical welcome which the local
population had given our troops. This may have happened
over on the centre and right flanks; I certainly saw no sign of
it on our own sector. The single example of true Gallic
emotion which I saw displayed was when a poodle dog was
snatched from almost under the wheels of a three-ton lorry in
Douvres. Then there was a great to-do of arms being flung in
the air, and general handshaking all round, and kissing and
embracing while the poodle was returned to the bosom of its
owner. But in my own experience rose-throwing, which to
judge from some reports seemed to be the main occupation of
the people of Normandy, was conspicuous by its absence. I
had only one rose thrown at me during the first ten days I
was in France; that was on D plus 3, and I don't mind
admitting that I ducked. The people of Normandy are not,
in any case, your typically emotional type of Frenchman.
They are honest-to-God, slightly dour peasant stock – the
sort of folk you meet on cold, wind-swept farms up in
Buchan. Folk who take quite a while to sum you up and
then, if you prove yourself to their satisfaction, show their
friendship in a quiet, sober way. In the early days in
Normandy no civilian ever spoke to you first. If you said
'Bonjour' they answered politely enough, but they never

opened a conversation. They stood in the doorways of their damaged homes, and watched us rumble past in tanks and lorries – with their arms folded and on their faces no hint of what they were thinking. Or, more probably, they went on with their work in the fields, completely unconcerned that a new colour of uniform had appeared all round them. And, after all, who could blame them for not going berserk with delight at our arrival? They had had years of German occupation, and on the whole they had been well treated. Normandy is a rich agricultural district, and Germany had decided to save it and not spoil it. Though wine and sugar and soap and certain other things were rationed, there was no real shortage – certainly nothing approaching the line of starvation. I found an old woman in one village who consented to do my laundry for me, and whenever I went to her house around a meal-time there was a mountain of fresh butter – I should think about four pounds – on her table. It made me think sadly of the ridiculous two-ounce pat I used to collect from my grocer in Soho. The fields and gardens were stacked with produce, and I saw no signs of anyone being hungry.

Anne de Vigneral, Ver-sur-Mer

Diary 12 June
In the village the enthusiasm diminishes, as the [Canadian] soldiers pillage, break everything and go everywhere under the pretext of looking for Germans. A soldier who went up into my bedroom while we were lunching searched our rooms, and we later found my father's wedding ring and chevaliere stolen – my gold watch also. The doors of my cupboard were axed, the locks broken, my linen chests emptied, contents thrown on the floor, towels stolen.

And all the time in our home we give drinks to the officers – delighted with our calvados and champagne, which they had not tasted since the war began.

9 July
Some officers take me to Bayeaux . . . Then I go to the official office to reclaim all the objects and jewels which have been stolen from us.

Private Islwyn Edmunds, South Wales Borderers
On finding that the enemy had left Bayeux, we were ordered to withdraw and take up positions guarding a road. We dug trenches outside a house, and the lady of the house invited us in to share a meal with them. They had so little to give us, but we were given a soup with a little meat. We were enjoying this meal when we observed a small boy crying in the corner, and in our best French enquired why the boy was crying. We were told that we were eating his rabbit.

Anonymous GI
18 June

Dear Mom,
We get milk and cider off these French people. It looks like they are very glad to see us yanks. They should be these dirty Germans tried to make slaves out of them. I met a little boy I used to go to school with on the boat crossing the channell [sic].

There is lots of things I would like to tell you but maybe later I will be able to.

I still have my little prayer book and I have used it. I am sure it has done me lots of good, you know what I mean . . . Take care of yourself,

love,
Son.

Lieutenant A.J. Holladay, RA

Diary, 14 July

Le Quatorze Juillet. Fine day at last. Sadly bitten by mosquitoes in night – lip and eye. Hang French and English flags and cross of Lorraine over gateway at farm and chalk 'Vive La France' on all the trucks. Pilotless aircraft cross over at 08.15. Range-tables for 88 mm arrive. Half-day to celebrate. Stroll with corporal down to Hermanville and go into the church and the curé, then on to the estaminet and find all the villagers there, having been to mass in their Sunday best. Drink a couple of glasses of white wine and give a toast of le quatorze juillet to the company . . . Back for a magnificent lunch cooked by madame – roast chicken, new potatoes and cauliflower . . . back to Hermanville and meet the curé who comes out to thank the men for their gift to the children. The whole troop volunteered their sweet rations for them. Men are paraded and he thanks them, then his speech is interpreted to them. We learn from madame that he was an ardent collaborationist with the Boche. In the evening we drink wine and talk with the French people of the house, and afterwards down to the village green to see the dancing. The Germans burnt the dancing floor because the French wouldn't dance with them. Incipient romance between Marcelle and the airborne sergeant who was the first British soldier they saw. Back to the farm and Gibb plays music, finishing with hearty rendering of Marseillaise. Monsieur is very drunk by now. Heavy air activity at night. Ken (here for the court martial) sleeps in barn with us. Russians take Pinsk.

Captain Joseph T. Dawson, US 1st Infantry Division

At Mayenne we had considerable battle with the Germans withdrawing through the Falaise gap and we were greeted with a number of Resistance members there, in Mayenne, and a little contingent of them – twelve of them – joined me and stayed with me throughout the battle through France and into Germany. There they had to be removed from the combat area because the situation did not allow for volunteers. But they were very effective in going through France and we enjoyed having them with us.

Trooper W. Hewison, 1st Royal Tank Regiment
Diary, 18 August
From the reverse Jerry seems to be falling back all along the line. I believe that the hard fighting is over for the time being . . . people really glad to see us, waving and smiling and throwing stuff on the tank.

War diary, Algonquin Regiment
18 August, Dives
It is the first time that the battalion received the first-hand acclaim of the newly liberated populace. Their greeting and generosity was unexcelled.

Captain Albert H. Smith, US 1st Infantry Division
As we broke out of the lodgement and took a turn for Paris, we were always seeing the Resistance, and the French people threw flowers at us, and apples. Now, apples are alright if you're walking but if you're in a lorry, as we were sometimes, and you've got your helmet off and an apple comes through the air and hits you at 30 m.p.h. – it makes a crack.

For the German Army the Battle of Normandy, after the failure to drive back the Allies in the first few days of the invasion, was a desperate exercise in holding back an ever greater tide. Throughout June, July and August columns of men and supplies wound their way to the Normandy front, but were critically hampered by Allied fighter-bomber attacks. And back in Germany itself the industrial workshop was simply not providing enough goods of war. The German Army in Normandy – as elsewhere – was critically short of fuel, armour, ammunition – and just about everything else. The German soldier himself was a mixture of hope and hopelessness, buoyed by a belief in himself as the consummate professional soldier.

Staff Officer, 17th SS Panzer Grenadier Division

On 7 June our division received orders to leave the marshalling area in Thouars and to move to the invasion front in Normandy. Everyone was in a good and eager mood to see action again – happy that the pre-invasion spell of uncertainty and waiting was snapped at last.

Our motorized columns were coiling along the road towards the invasion beaches. Then something happened that left us in a daze. Spurts of fire flicked along the column and splashes of dust staccatoed the road. Everyone was piling out of the vehicles and scuttling for the neighbouring fields. Several vehicles were already in flames. This attack ceased as suddenly as it had crashed upon us fifteen minutes before. The men started drifting back to the column again, pale and shaky and wondering how they had survived this fiery rain of bullets. This had been our first experience with the *Jabos* [fighter-bombers]. The march column was now completely disrupted and every man was on his own, to pull out of this blazing column as best he could. And it was none too soon, because an hour later the whole thing started all over again, only much worse this time. When this attack was over, the length of the road was strewn with splintered anti-tank guns (the pride of our division), flaming motors and charred implements of war.

The march was called off and all vehicles that were left were hidden in the dense bushes or in barns. No one dared show himself out in the open any more. Now the men started looking at each other. This was different from what we

thought it would be like. It had been our first experience
with our new foe – the American.

During the next few days we found out how seriously he
was going about his business. Although now we only
travelled at nights and along secondary roads rimmed with
hedges and bushes, we encountered innumerable wrecks
giving toothless testimony that some motorists had not
benefited from the bitter experience we had had.

Letters to his wife, Field Marshal Erwin Rommel
10 June 1944

Dearest Lu,
. . . It is a hard fight that the army is having to withstand. I
was up at the front yesterday and am going again to-day.
The enemy's air superiority has a very grave effect on our
movements. There's simply no answer to it. It's quite likely
to start at other places soon. However, we do what we can.

. . . .

14 June 1944
Very heavy fighting. The enemy's great superiority in aircraft, naval artillery, men and material is beginning to tell.
Whether the gravity of the situation is realized up above, and
the proper conclusions drawn, seems to me doubtful. Supplies are getting tight everywhere. How are you both? Still
no news has arrived.

. . . .

18 June 1944
There's a chance of sending you a quick letter to-day by one
of the men. I saw the Fuehrer yesterday, who is at present in
the west. I gave him a detailed report and clarified everything. If the OKW at first had the idea that the troops at the
front were not fighting well, this idea has now been revised.
Our opponents themselves have provided my army with the
best of all possible testimonials. Of course large forces of ours

were overwhelmed by the immense weight of the enemy
bombing and naval barrage, but every man still living
fought like the devil. If people had listened to me we would
have counter-attacked with three divisions on the first
evening, and would probably have beaten off the attack.
Frightful delays were caused by the panzer divisions having
to travel between 250 and 400 miles to the front and in many
places the battle was going badly. Much of this has now
sorted itself out and I am looking forward to the future with
less anxiety than I did a week ago. The long-range action has
brought us a lot of relief. A number of generals fell in the first
few days of battle, among them Falley, who was killed on the
first night – the 5–6th June.

. . . A quick enemy break-through to Paris is now hardly a
possibility. We've got a lot of stuff coming up. The Fuehrer
was very cordial and in a good humour. He realizes the
gravity of the situation.

.   .   .   .

23 June 1944
Militarily things aren't at all good. The enemy air force is
dealing extremely heavily with our supplies and at the
moment is completely strangling them. If a decisive battle
develops, we'll be without ammunition. You can imagine
how worried I am. Even Cherbourg will not be able to hold
out for long in these circumstances. We must be prepared for
grave events.

War diary, Panzer Lehr Division
9 June 1944
12.30. As a result of the frequent air attacks, the troops'
baggage trains have been considerably held up or have been
misrouted. Because of this provisions for the fighting troops
have begun to dwindle.

19.00. Message from Ia. 2-cm and 8.8-cm anti-aircraft
ammunition urgently needed. Special measures necessary to

secure this. 8000 rounds of 8.8-cm and 60,000 rounds of 2-cm munition requested from Q Corps.

Conversation with Q Corps about whole question of provisions. The Quartermaster gives his support, however, Q Corps has no tonnage available. Tank ammunition cannot be obtained. Difficulties are caused by the petrol supply. New petrol supplies cannot be expected for at least 48 hours.

Corporal Ted Morris, 6th Airborne Division

Not long after I was captured, I started talking to the German corporal who was in charge of us – his name was Herman. To my amazement, he said to me: 'You – the Allies – should give up, you know.' He really meant it. To him it was fact. The other thing was, he was absolutely convinced of Hitler's secret weapons. 'It's going to be bad for you,' he'd say, and shake his head.

H. Schluter, 716th Infantry Division

You know, I was not in an 'elite' division. I was in the division which was crushed by the bombardment and invasion, the 716th. Mostly old men and young boys. But even to us – those of us who were left – the Allied soldier seemed very naive. Why did we keep going? What else could we do? We were soldiers.

Gefreiter Werner Kortenhaus, 21st Panzer Division

Hitler should have ended the war on 9 June at the latest because, after all, he had said that if we weren't successful in pushing back the Allied landing, we would have lost the war. We had three fronts – Poland, Italy and the West. It would have been impossible to win.

Captain Hartdegen, Panzer Lehr

Unless a man has been through these fighter-bomber attacks he cannot know what the invasion meant. You lie there, helpless, in a roadside ditch, in a furrow on a field, or under a hedge, pressed into the ground, your face in the dirt – and there it comes towards you, roaring. There it is. Diving at you. Now you hear the whine of the bullets. Now you are for it.

You feel like crawling under the ground. Then the bird has gone. But it comes back. Twice. Three times. Not till they think they've wiped out everything do they leave. Until then you are helpless. Like a man facing a firing-squad. Even if you survive it's no more than a temporary reprieve. Ten such attacks in succession are a real foretaste of hell.

Our staff car was a gutted heap of metal on the road; it was smouldering and smoking. Corporal Kartheus lay dead in the ditch. As if by a miracle General Bayerlein got away with a few cuts and shrapnel wounds. As for me, I was saved by the culvert.

After seven and a half weeks in Normandy the Allies had drawn the bulk of German armour and men to the eastern end of the front, in and around Caen. On 26 July the Americans, at the western end of the line, began to drive south, finding little in front of them except two Panzer divisions, and one division of Panzer grenadiers. Generals Patton – whose forces were in the lead – Bradley, and Montgomery began to encircle large numbers of the German Army at Falaise. Hitler unwittingly helped the Allies by ordering a counter-attack westwards towards Mortain, pushing more troops into the 'pocket' the Allies were about to close. General Crerar's 1st Canadian attacked from the north towards Falaise, reaching it on 16 August. The Canadians in the north and the Americans in the south were then only fifteen miles apart. The gap between Falaise and Argentan was closed on 20 August. Fifty thousand German troops were trapped in the Falaise pocket. A few remnants of the German Army escaped, but had to leave their equipment behind. The Allies had not only broken the siege but captured their besiegers. The Battle of Normandy was over – and with it any chance that Germany could win the war. There would still be fighting ahead – Arnhem, the Ardennes – but the defeat in Normandy spelt the end for Nazi Germany. It was now only a question of when.

Captain Albert H. Smith, US 1st Infantry Division

Operation Cobra was preceded on 25 and 26 July by heavy bombing by thousands of planes, and it was done also in front of the other US divisions and in front of the British divisions. Then we attacked, broke out of the beachhead, broke out of the lodgement area as some people called it – that was a very, very wonderful operation. Not that it proceeded without casualties, but once we broke through the German crust we started to move by miles rather than yards. And before we knew it we were in the small city of Mayenne. There we stopped heading south and we headed for Paris – all this took place in the last couple of days of July, and the first week of August. I still recall the drive for Paris – it was wonderful, it was exhilarating. The troops loved it. We took some casualties but at the same time we knew things were going our way.

Wing Commander 'Johnnie' Johnson, RAF

When the Spitfires arrived at Falaise, over the small triangle of Normandy bordered by Falaise, Trun and Chambois, the Typhoons were already hard at work. One of their favourite tactics against the long streams of enemy vehicles was to seal off the front and rear of the column by accurately dropping a few bombs. This technique imprisoned the desperate enemy on a narrow stretch of dusty lane, and since the transports were sometimes jammed together four abreast, it made the subsequent rocket and cannon attack a comparatively easy business against the stationary targets. Some of the armoured cars and tanks attempted to escape their fate by making detours across the fields and wooded country, but these were soon spotted by the Typhoon pilots and were accorded the same treatment as their comrades on the highways and lanes.

Immediately the Typhoons withdrew from the killing ground the Spitfires raced into the attack . . . [back at base] ground crews worked flat out in the hot sunshine to rearm and refuel the aircraft.

The Times war correspondent, in the Falaise pocket

Nearly every yard of ground must have been pin-pointed by batteries of all calibres: coming down from Trun there is hardly a yard of the road, along which sporadic fighting was still going on yesterday, that does not tell its grim tale. The ditches are lined with destroyed enemy vehicles of every description, the green verges have turned blue-grey with German uniforms and equipment, and up on the banks or at the fringes of cornfields the dead lie as they fell in a blind attempt to get away.

For four days the rain of death poured down, and with the road blocked with blazing tanks and trucks little can have escaped it. Nothing can describe the horror of the sight in the village of St Lambert sur Dives, an enemy graveyard over which his troops were struggling yesterday in an effort to break through the cordon hedging them off from the seeming escape lanes to the Seine. Within an area of about a square mile hundreds of tanks and armoured cars, great trucks and guns and horse-drawn wagons, lie burned and splintered in hideous disarray.

This was no organized formation but a collection of oddments from several divisions which had been mad enough to pack themselves tightly into what they thought were hidden lanes and orchards. They must have been spotted from the air, for before dark the guns caught them with merciless accuracy. The lanes were jammed with vehicles, crammed with loot from French villages, nosing their way towards the exit; horses and wagons had crashed down into a narrow stream, and when the Canadians came in this morning the hospital on the hill and the few undamaged houses were full of bewildered German wounded, many of them no more than boys, who asked only to be taken away from the place.

On the Chambois road to-day, Canadian troops, dog-tired from days and nights of fighting, lay asleep in the sun; the hills and valleys were silent save for the rare splutter of a fanatic's machine gun, and all manner of enemy vehicles that had escaped destruction were being driven back to our own lines under white flags or hastily designed white stars. Everywhere one felt the reaction that comes after battle, the sudden loosening of taut nerves. A group of American soldiers were mounted, with the air of Texas rangers, on sleek German horses round whose necks were tied vivid strips of crimson cloth, probably used by the enemy as air recognition signals.

Untersturmfuhrer Herbert Walther, 12th SS Panzer Division, in the Falaise pocket

My driver was burning. I had a bullet through the arm. I jumped on to a railway track and ran. They were firing down the embankment and I was hit in the leg. I made 100 m, then it was as if I was hit in the back of the neck with a big hammer. A bullet had gone in beneath the ear and come out through the cheek. I was choking on blood. There were two Americans looking down at me and two French soldiers, who wanted to finish me off.

The Americans took pity on Walther and carried him to a casualty station. Thirteen bullets were removed from Walther's leg. He was one of the handful of the 12th SS to survive Normandy. The Division had fought itself to annihilation.

Letter home, Wehrmacht Soldier
[Late August, 1944]
I was in the Argentan-Falaise pocket and I still don't know
how I got out of it. We were running in wild fiery circles with
artillery and aerial bombs dropping around us. After I got
out of there I had to fight partisans and our own soldiers to
get on the ferry across the Seine.

War diary, Algonquin Regiment
18 August, Trun
Nos 1 and 2 Squadrons took over forty prisoners and had a
wonderful time searching through the captured vehicles.
Captain Greenleaf captured a coupe and a motorcycle in
running order . . . Everyone captured some trophy or
another. A huge, red flag with a black swastika on a circular
white background was taken with the intention of hanging it
in the armoury in Montreal.

Aftermath

Ernie Pyle, war correspondent

Dispatch, Summer 1944

I took a walk along the historic coast of Normandy in the country of France.

It was a lovely day for strolling along the seashore. Men were sleeping on the sand, some of them sleeping forever. Men were floating in the water, but they didn't know they were in the water, for they were dead.

The water was full of squishy little jellyfish about the size of your hand. Millions of them. In the center each of them had a green design exactly like a four-leaf clover. The good-luck emblem. Sure. Hell yes.

I walked for a mile and a half along the water's edge of our many-miled invasion beach. You wanted to walk slowly, for the detail on that beach was infinite.

The wreckage was vast and startling. The awful waste and destruction of war, even aside from the loss of human life, has always been one of its outstanding features to those who are in it. Anything and everything is expendable. And we did expend on our beachhead in Normandy during those first few hours.

For a mile out from the beach there were scores of tanks and trucks and boats that you could no longer see, for they were at the bottom of the water – swamped by overloading, or hit by shells, or sunk by mines. Most of their crews were lost.

You could see trucks tipped half over and swamped. You could see partly sunken barges, and the angled-up corners of Jeeps, and small landing craft half submerged. And at low tide you could still see those vicious six-pronged iron snares that helped snag and wreck them.

On the beach itself, high and dry, were all kinds of wrecked vehicles. There were tanks that had only just made the beach before being knocked out. There were Jeeps that had burned to a dull gray. There were big derricks on caterpillar treads that didn't quite make it. There were half-tracks carrying office equipment that had been made into a shambles by a single shell hit, their interiors still holding their useless equipage of smashed typewriters, telephones, office files.

There were LCTs turned completely upside down, and lying on their backs, and how they got that way I don't know. There were boats stacked on top of each other, their sides caved in, their suspension doors knocked off.

In this shoreline museum of carnage there were abandoned rolls of barbed wire and smashed bulldozers and big stacks of thrown-away lifebelts and piles of shells still waiting to be moved.

In the water floated empty life rafts and soldiers' packs and ration boxes, and mysterious oranges.

On the beach lay snarled rolls of telephone wire and big rolls of steel matting and stacks of broken, rusting rifles.

On the beach lay, expended, sufficient men and mechanism for a small war. They were gone forever now. And yet we could afford it.

We could afford it because we were on, we had our toehold, and behind us there were such enormous replacements for this wreckage on the beach that you could hardly conceive of their sum total. Men and equipment were flowing from England in such a gigantic stream that it made the waste on the beachhead seem like nothing at all, really nothing at all.

A few hundred yards back on the beach is a high bluff. Up there we had a tent hospital, and a barbed-wire enclosure for prisoners of war. From up there you could see far up and down the beach, in a spectacular crows-nest view, and far out to sea.

And standing out there on the water beyond all this wreckage was the greatest armada man has ever seen. You simply could not believe the gigantic collection of ships that lay out there waiting to unload.

Looking from the bluff, it lay thick and clear to the far horizon of the sea and on beyond, and it spread out to the sides and was miles wide. Its utter enormity would move the hardest man.

As I stood up there I noticed a group of freshly taken German prisoners standing nearby. They had not yet been put in the prison cage. They were just standing there, a couple of doughboys leisurely guarding them with tommy guns.

The prisoners too were looking out to sea – the same bit of sea that for months and years had been so safely empty before their gaze. Now they stood staring almost as if in a trance.

They didn't say a word to each other. They didn't need to. The expression on their faces was something forever unforgettable. In it was the final horrified acceptance of their doom.

If only all Germans could have had the rich experience of standing on the bluff and looking out across the water and seeing what their compatriots saw.

Alexandre Reynaud, Mayor of Ste Mere Eglise

Before returning to Ste Mere Eglise, the captain stopped along the coast, near the former village of La Madelaine, in the commune of Sainte-Marie-du-Mont. A few years earlier, this little Normandy village was living a peaceful existence. It included several comfortable properties, half farm, half vacation home. A few hundred metres to the back, in the cemetery where no one had been buried for years, stood a very old chapel. It had a small openwork belfry in which a bell slept as though in a cage. It was surrounded by large trees: yews, oaks and elms, which almost hid it from view. It was an old, unused sanctuary which seemed to have retired there like an old woman behind her windowpanes.

Now, nothing remained of the village, not even ruins. The ground had been turned up, and the few stones that hadn't been pulverized by shells and bombs, had been used first by the Germans, then by the Americans, to pave the roads. The chapel was still standing, but it had been hit in several places and the belfry was awry.

In front of the village, on the dunes overlooking the sea, which were fairly high in this area, the Germans had built a blockhouse. It had been hit by navy shells. We could still see the threatening mouths of the cannons sticking out of the loopholes facing the sea. Inside the enormous mass of reinforced concrete were several compartments separated by armored doors. A metal ladder was embedded into the wall, to enable the lookout to climb to the top from inside and see the horizon with a minimum of danger.

Odette Lelanoy, Vire

Ruins. You might say that Normandy had been ravaged. The country houses, the hamlets hadn't been touched, but we had been caught in the shell fire, the gun fire from the planes, the bombs. As soon as lorries grouped around a farm to find water or provisions, like hens, they took the horses to pull their lorries which had run out of petrol. There were houses and barns on fire. The towns had been damaged, all those which had been in the battleground during those long weeks while the Germans were holding out. All those villages, such as Tinges Bre, Condé sur Noireau, Falaise, had been destroyed. We returned home to find our house hadn't been touched. It had been taken over. Only a small part of the building had been destroyed. But it had been used as a command post and when we returned to the house there was nothing left inside. We found bits and pieces in the dining room and the cellar which indicated that our house had been taken and used as a command post. Anyway, they'd driven us out by saying 'You must leave. If we find you here tomorrow we'll shoot you.' That's what they said all the way through the war. They slipped into our midst in order to be able to retreat. But the house was untouched.

Friedrich Gadecke, Wehrmacht
Letter, France, 27 August 1944

Dear Parents,
A time of uncertainty, apprehension and fear is now beginning for you as well. I pray sincerely that God gives you courage each day, and that you don't sink into worry but hold onto the certainty that your prayers will be heard. Rest assured and be happy! That is my wish and my plea to you. Don't be afraid, even during the days when you hear nothing and can know nothing about how things are for me. Everything that I experience and am permitted to live through in these times reassures me that I will be kept safe for you, for God does nothing by halves. I shall come through these dangers. God granted me life through you. For that I am always grateful to you.

Your son,
Friedrich
[Died 13 September 1944]

Trooper Peter Davies, 1st East Riding Yeomanry

I hated Hitler and what he stood for, and I felt that we were there to free the French people – which we were. It was a just war.

. . . .

It's still terribly difficult when I visit my friends' graves. It's still hard to think back. It still brings a lump to my throat. I'm lucky, I'm here. It was worthwhile because if we hadn't stopped Hitler and the Nazis doing what they did we wouldn't be able to live the life we live today, wouldn't have the freedom we have today. If we contributed only one little bit to the freedom of the world in 1944 it was worthwhile.

. . . .

You shove the bits you want to forget into the back of your mind. If you can. You can't always do it. Try and push them out of the way. You remember the fun, the comradeship that you had, the men that you lived with – they were like brothers, closer than brothers some of them, closer than your own family because you relied for your life on them, and they relied on you.

Leonard Miles, 168 General Transport Company

When I got home at the end of the war I found it very difficult adjusting. I felt terrible. As a matter of fact it took me a very long time – two or three years, really – because it was so different from the war. And we'd left so many behind, and I couldn't get that out of my system. I was forever thinking about them.

Captain Edward W. McGregor, US 1st Infantry Division

Hell, what the English went through in the war. Nothing like it happened in America of course and that permeated my thinking. Incidentally I had an American girlfriend and had written her and said that I had met this very nice English girl. Well, she didn't accept that I guess but I couldn't disassociate myself from the war and everything. It was so different in America. I even kind of resented coming back to the States. I went through a terrible period – a psychological period – that started as soon as the war ended, by which time we were in Czechoslovakia. I was a Major then, the S3, plans and operations officer. Suddenly I received the order on the telephone from Division on 7 May: the order was 'Cease all further forward movement.' The effect, no guns any more . . . well there wasn't a great feeling of elation to tell you the truth. We had been at it so long, those of us who had come all the way through. It was a very selfish thing in a way, but I realized that a mode of life had changed. It was the end of an era. I didn't know what the future held in store. I wasn't a regular officer then, I was a reserve officer – a lot of us were – on extended active duty. I didn't know what to expect when I got home.

Marine Stanley Blacker, RM
I felt very, very proud of my country, and I felt proud of serving. I still do. We felt we were liberating Europe. There were hundreds who did more than I did, far more. But we all felt we were on a mission to liberate Europe from an age of darkness.

William Seymour, RN
We wouldn't be free today. There's a feeling of satisfaction to have been involved.

John G. Coleman
A little while later we heard reports that all the Americans based at the Penllwyn Pontllanfraith were killed on the Omaha beach landing.

Our hearts were sad for we knew those guys over the months they were camped at the Penllwyn, and now they were gone. I shall not forget them.

Captain Joseph T. Dawson, US 1st Infantry Division

My whole life since has been one of readjusting my feelings, because I had a very intense bitterness towards the Germans. I felt that they were an enemy that had to be destroyed, and I looked on them in that light rather than any human light, because I was not accustomed to taking human life. I was never a professional soldier. I was a civilian that was granted the opportunity to defend my country. My feelings had been developed over the years, a feeling that the Germans under Hitler were a menace to humanity. I volunteered as a private and ended up a colonel at the end of the war. I could see the war clouds in 1935 when we were shipping steel to Japan; it was obvious that the axis of Germany and Japan was hell-bent on America's destruction and the dominance of the world. My personal feeling deepened when I was in England, when I came into contact with the English. My admiration for them is boundless. I couldn't help but feel that they provided the front line of defence for the world.

· · · ·

I have come to realize, very deeply, that that moment of D-Day marked a turning point of the twentieth century – it was perhaps *the* most dramatic moment of the twentieth century, because it enabled the freedom of the world. There's something sacred about it.

· · · ·

I was offered a full commission in the regular army if I retained my position, if I stayed in the army.

I will say with a great deal of pride that all my friends that served with me on Omaha beach retired as Major-Generals and Lieutenant-Generals and have made notable careers in

the service. However, I was not a professional soldier – I was
in the oil business before the war and thought I could serve
my country in some other capacity than the army. But I
didn't know how I could adjust, having had so much of it,
the war, in me for four and a half years, and in active combat
for three years of that. So I had a real emotional and mental
problem to resolve; fortunately the men that I was associated
with prior to the war had saved a position for me with their
company and I was able to adjust, through their help and a
resolution on my part to make a life of service as a civilian.
Mostly though I was able to adjust because I met the girl I
would marry, who would become my wife. I think that was
the thing which stabilized my life.

. . . .

To be effective as an infantryman and to be able to
subordinate your feelings to the reality that you're destroying the enemy . . . well, that's about as 180 degrees from
civilian life as you can get. In war, you condition your mind
to the reality of leaving all emotion out of your personal
feelings and direct yourself to being effective in destroying
the enemy. You can't take that into civilian life, where if you
have conflicts you don't settle them in a mortal way. That
was the main difficulty I had, getting the army and the war
out of my system. It took a number of years to do that, but I
was able to do it largely because of the wonderful relation-
ship I have had with my family. War is ugly, it's deadly, it's
dirty. A man has to almost reduce himself to an animal to be
effective, because he's got to lose all degree of emotion to be
effective.

. . . .

It's taken years to overcome my bitterness towards the
Germans, but at the same time I can't ever completely
erase my feelings. Near the termination of the war I had
the unfortunate experience of being at Dachau [Nazi death
camp] when we opened it up. It was something that has

stayed with me so vividly throughout my life. At the time I was there I couldn't have food on my stomach for a week, it unnerved me so much . . . I guess that's the reason I've had such a deep bitterness towards the German people: they couldn't have helped but know the things that were going on. There's no way in God's green earth that they didn't know. There's a certain strain in there that is evil – I can't think of any other way of saying it. I know we all become bestial in combat, but combat is one thing and destruction of humanity in that way is disgusting, obscene. I'll never get over it.

War is not a noble thing. You have to realize that in doing your duty you've got to do things which are bestial . . . but I guess you've got to go through the muck to get to the shining hour. It had to be done. You only had to visit one concentration camp to realize the nadir the German people had reached.

. . . .

It is awesome, even now, to me to see how we could possibly have survived, because the terrain there [Omaha] is remarkable in that it has the high ridge overlooking the beach itself, in such a dramatic way. When I go back with members of my company today, we marvel how we ever got off there in the first place because they commanded such a tremendous advantage over us. It was only just the luck of God that allowed me to find a little opening which permitted us to get off of the beach. I've always felt a degree of humility as well as thanking God for having had the opportunity for making a break which allowed us to proceed off of Omaha.

Private Robert Macduff, Wiltshire Regiment

It seems to me sometimes that Nature's way of overcoming the conscience factor and the traumas one goes through is to put them right at the back of the mind. If ever recalled, it becomes very painful.

Flight Lieutenant J.G. Hayden, RAF

At the time I left the RAF there was a cry for teachers. So I took the course, which was a new thing altogether, a new challenge which helped me adjust to civilian life reasonably well.

W. Emlyn 'Taffy' Jones, 1st Special Service Brigade

It was peculiar, you know, going back home afterwards. You didn't know what to find, what reception you'd have. I saw a film once – oh, what was it called? About the Vietnam war and a Pole. *The Deerhunter*, that's it – and it had one thing which stuck out in my mind, that moved me. It was when the character came back from Vietnam to his home town and he hid behind a telegraph pole or a tree wondering whether to go in or not. I had that same sort of feeling. It took me a couple of years to get myself sorted out. It was a sort of cooling down, I suppose . . . They – the war years – were happy days for me. I was among men. In a way I miss those days.

Nevin F. Price, USAAF 39th Bomb Group

If we hadn't invaded Normandy, we'd all be speaking German now.

Alfred Leonard, Merchant Navy

Cordite. I can remember vividly the smell of cordite. It stays with you, and when you get a smell which is near it it can sort of trigger off the memories. It's a very difficult smell to describe . . . I've smelt it a little bit with electrics, if you get a short and there's a metallic smell. That smells more or less like it.

It was a very short time in my life, a very hectic time, and I was trying to take it all in.

Sergeant Richard W. Herklotz, US 29th Division

It was not an heroic operation. I don't think of it as heroic. There was a cause that the nation wanted us to do, and we did it. And those who survived can thank their lucky stars that they did.

Gravestone epitaphs from British Commonwealth Cemeteries, Ryes and Bayeux:

Private A. Richards, Hampshire Regiment
I wonder why you had to die without a chance to say goodbye. Eileen and family.

Private F.A. Kelly, Devonshire Regiment
Beloved / Your Duty Bravely Done / Rest in Peace / Mum.

Trooper A.J. Cole, 61st Regiment, Recce Corps, RAC
The Dearest daddy and Husband in the World. We will love you for Ever, Darling.

APPENDIX 1

Order of the Day

The Supreme Commander issued an order of the day to the troops under his command on 5 June:

Soldiers, sailors and airmen of the Allied Expeditionary Force. You are about to embark on a great crusade, toward which we have striven these many months. The hopes and prayers of liberty-loving people everywhere go with you. In company with our brave Allies and brothers in arms on other fronts you will bring about the destruction of the German war machine, elimination of Nazi tyranny over the oppressed peoples of Europe, and security for ourselves in a free world.

Your task will not be an easy one. Your enemy is well trained, well equipped and battle-hardened. He will fight, fight savagely. But in this year of 1944 much has happened since the Nazi triumphs of 1940 and 1941.

The United Nations have inflicted upon the Germans great defeats in open battle, man to man. Our air offensive has seriously reduced their strength in the air, and their capacity to wage war on the ground.

Our home fronts have given us an overwhelming superiority in weapons and munitions of war, and have placed at our disposal great reserves of trained fighting men.

The tide has turned. The free men of the world are marching together to victory. I have full confidence in your courage, devotion to duty and skill in battle. We will accept nothing less than full victory.

Good luck and let us all beseech the blessing of Almighty God upon this great and noble undertaking.

This order was distributed to assault elements. It was read by appropriate commands to all other troops in the Allied Expeditionary Force.

APPENDIX 2

Allied Order of Battle and Map

SUPREME HEADQUARTERS ALLIED EXPEDITIONARY FORCE

Supreme Allied Commander
General Dwight D. Eisenhower

Chief of Staff
General Walter Bedell Smith

TWENTY-FIRST ARMY GROUP
General Sir Bernard L. Montgomery
Commander-in-Chief
Major-General Sir Francis W. de Guingand
Chief of Staff

GHQ AND ARMY TROOPS

79th Armoured Division
Major-General Sir Percy C.S. Hobart

30th Armoured Brigade
22nd Dragoons
1st Lothians and Border Horse
2nd County of London
  Yeomanry, (Westminster
  Dragoons)
141st Regiment RAC

1st Tank Brigade
11th, 42nd and 49th Battalions
  RTR

1st Assault Brigade RE
5th, 6th and 42nd Assault
  Regiments RE

79th Armoured Divisional Signals
1st Canadian Armoured Personnel Carrier Regiment

INDEPENDENT BRIGADES

4th Armoured Brigade
The Royal Scots Greys
3rd County of London
  Yeomanry (Sharpshooters)
  (to 28.7.44)
3rd/4th County of London
  Yeomanry (Sharpshooters)
  (from 29.7.44)
44th Battalion RTR
2nd Battalion the King's
  Royal Rifle Corps (Motor)

6th Guards Tank Brigade
4th Tank Battalion Grenadier
  Guards
4th Tank Battalion
  Coldstream Guards
3rd Tank Battalion Scots
  Guards

27th Armoured Brigade
(to 29.7.44)
13th/18th Royal Hussars
1st East Riding Yeomanry
The Staffordshire Yeomanry

8th Armoured Brigade
4th/7th Royal Dragoon
  Guards
24th Lancers (to 29.7.44)
The Nottinghamshire
  Yeomanry
13th/18th Royal Hussars (from
  29.7.44)
12th Battalion the King's
  Royal Rifle Corps (Motor)

33rd Armoured Brigade
1st Northamptonshire
  Yeomanry
144th Regiment RAC (to
  22.8.44)
148th Regiment RAC (to
  16.8.44)
1st East Riding Yeomanry
  (from 16.8.44)

31st Tank Brigade
7th Battalion RTR (to 17.8.44)
9th Battalion RTR (to 31.8.44)
144th Regiment RAC
   (23–31.8.44)

34th Tank Brigade
107th and 147th Regiments
   RAC
153rd Regiment RAC (to
   24.8.44)

2nd Canadian Armoured Brigade
6th Armoured Regiment (1st
   Hussars)
10th Armoured Regiment (the
   Fort Garry Horse)
27th Armoured Regiment (the
   Sherbrooke Fusiliers
   Regiment)

HQ Anti-Aircraft Brigades
74th, 76th, 80th, 100th, 101st, 105th, 106th and 107th

Heavy Anti-Aircraft Regiments
60th, 86th, 90th, 99th, 103rd, 105th, 107th, 108th, 109th, 112th,
113th, 115th, 116th, 121st, 146th, 165th and 174th; 2nd Canadian

Light Anti-Aircraft Regiments
20th, 27th, 32nd, 54th, 71st, 73rd, 93rd, 109th, 112th, 113th, 114th,
120th, 121st, 123rd, 124th, 125th, 126th, 127th, 133rd, 139th and
149th

Searchlight Regiments
41st

[*56th Infantry Brigade*]
(Became integral part of the
   49th Division from 20.8.44)
2nd Battalion the South Wales
   Borderers
2nd Battalion the
   Gloucestershire Regiment
2nd Battalion the Essex
   Regiment

1st Special Service Brigade
Nos. 3, 4 and 6 Commandos
No. 45 (Royal Marine)
   Commando

47th Special Service Brigade
Nos. 41, 46, 47 and 48 (Royal
   Marine) Commandos

OTHER FORMATIONS AND UNITS

Armoured
GHQ Liaison Regiment RAC
  ('Phantom')
2nd Armoured Replacement
  Group
2nd Armoured Delivery
  Regiment
25th Canadian Armoured
  Delivery Regiment (The
  Elgin Regiment)

Artillery
HQ Army Groups Royal Artillery:
  3rd, 4th, 5th, 8th and 9th;
  2nd Canadian

  Heavy Regiments: 1st, 51st,
  52nd, 53rd and 59th

  Medium Regiments: 7th, 9th,
  10th, 11th, 13th, 15th, 53rd,
  59th, 61st, 63rd, 64th, 65th,
  67th, 68th, 72nd, 77th, 79th,
  84th, 107th, 121st and 146th;
  3rd, 4th and 7th Canadian

  Field Regiments: 4th RHA,
  6th, 25th, 86th, 147th, 150th
  and 191st; 19th Canadian

Engineer
*HQ Army Groups Royal
  Engineers:* 10th, 11th, 12th,
  13th and 14th; 1st Canadian

  GHQ Troops Engineers: 4th,
  7th, 8th, 13th, 15th, 18th,
  48th and 59th

  Airfield Construction Groups:
  13th, 16th, 23rd, 24th and
  25th

  Army Troops Engineers: 2nd, 6th
  and 7th; 1st and 2nd
  Canadian
  2nd and 3rd Battalions Royal
  Canadian Engineers

Signal
Twenty-First Army Group
  Headquarters Signals
Second Army Headquarters
  Signals

Infantry
4th Battalion the Royal
  Northumberland Fusiliers
  (Machine Gun)
First Canadian Army

First Canadian Army
  Headquarters Signals
Air Formation Signals, Nos.
  11, 12, 13, 16, 17 and 18
1st Special Wireless Group

Headquarters Defence
Battalion (Royal Montreal
Regiment)

Royal Marine
Armoured Support Group: 1st
  and 2nd Royal Marine
  Armoured Support
  Regiments

Army Air Corps
Glider Pilot Regiment: 1st and
  2nd Glider Pilot Wings

Special Air Service
1st and 2nd Special Air
  Service Regiments
3rd and 4th French Parachute
  Battalions

European Allies
1st Belgian Infantry Brigade
Royal Netherlands Brigade
  (Princess Irene's)

ARMIES, CORPS AND DIVISIONS

Second Army
Lieutenant-General Sir Miles C. Dempsey
General Officer Commanding-in-Chief
Brigadier M.S. Chilton
Chief of Staff

First Canadian Army
Lieutenant-General H.D.G. Crerar
General Officer Commanding-in-Chief
Brigadier C.C. Mann
Chief of Staff

I Corps
Lieutenant-General J.T. Crocker
The Inns of Court Regiment RAC (Armoured Car)
62nd Anti-Tank, 102nd Light Anti-Aircraft, 9th Survey
Regiments RA
1 Corps Troops Engineers   I Corps Signals

VIII Corps
Lieutenant-General Sir Richard N. O'Connor
2nd Household Cavalry Regiment (Armoured Car)
91st Anti-Tank, 121st Light Anti-Aircraft, 10th Survey
Regiments RA
VIII Corps Troops Engineers   VIII Corps Signals

XII Corps
Lieutenant-General N.M. Ritchie
1st the Royal Dragoons (Armoured Car)
86th Anti-Tank, 112th Light Anti-Aircraft, 7th Survey
Regiments RA
XII Corps Troops Engineers   XII Corps Signals

XXX Corps
Lieutenant-General G.C. Bucknall (to 3.8.44)
Lieutenant-General B.G. Horrocks (from 4.8.44)
11th Hussars (Armoured Car)
73rd Anti-Tank, 27th Light Anti-Aircraft, 4th Survey
Regiments RA

XXX Corps Troops Engineers   XXX Corps Signals

II Canadian Corps
Lieutenant-General G.G. Simonds
18th Armoured Car Regiment (12th Manitoba Dragoons)
6th Anti-Tank, 6th Light Anti-Aircraft, 2nd Survey
Regiments RCA
II Canadian Corps Troops Engineers   II Canadian Corps Signals

Guards Armoured Division
Major-General A.H.S. Adair

5th Guards Armoured Brigade   *32nd Guards Brigade*
2nd (Armoured) Battalion   5th Battalion Coldstream
Grenadier Guards   Guards

1st (Armoured) Battalion
  Coldstream Guards
2nd (Armoured) Battalion
  Irish Guards
1st (Motor) Battalion
  Grenadier Guards

3rd Battalion Irish Guards
1st Battalion Welsh Guards

Divisional Troops

2nd Armoured
  Reconnaissance Battalion
  Welsh Guards
Guards Armoured Divisional
  Engineers

55th and 153rd Field, 21st
  Anti-Tank and 94th Light
  Anti-Aircraft Regiments RA
Guards Armoured Divisional
  Signals

7th Armoured Division
Major-General G.W.E.J. Erskine (to 3.8.44)
Major-General G.L. Verney (from 4.8.44)

22nd Armoured Brigade
4th County of London
  Yeomanry (Sharpshooters)
  (to 29.7.44)
1st and 5th Battalions RTR
5th Royal Inniskilling
  Dragoon Guards (from
  29.7.44)
1st Battalion the Rifle Brigade
  (Motor)

131st Infantry Brigade
1/5th, 1/6th and 1/7th
  Battalions the Queen's
  Royal Regiment

Divisional Troops
8th King's Royal Irish
  Hussars
7th Armoured Divisional
  Engineers
7th Armoured Divisional
  Signals

3rd and 5th Regiments RHA;
  6th Anti-Tank and 15th
  Light Anti-Aircraft
  Regiments RA

11th Armoured Division
Major-General G.P.B. Roberts

29th Armoured Brigade
23rd Hussars
2nd Fife and Forfar Yeomanry
3rd Battalion RTR
8th Battalion the Rifle Brigade
(Motor)

[*159th Infantry Brigade*]
3rd Battalion the
Monmouthshire Regiment
4th Battalion the King's
Shropshire Light Infantry
1st Battalion the Herefordshire
Regiment

Divisional Troops

2nd Northamptonshire
Yeomanry (to 17.8.44)
15th/19th the King's Royal
Hussars (from 17.8.44)
11th Armoured Divisional
Engineers

13th Regiment RHA; 151st
Field, 75th Anti-Tank and
58th Light Anti-Aircraft
Regiments RA
11th Armoured Divisional
Signals

3rd Division
Major-General T.G. Rennie (to 13.6.44)
Brigadier E.E.E. Cass (acting)
Major-General L.G. Whistler (from 23.6.44)

8th Brigade
1st Battalion the Suffolk
Regiment
2nd Battalion the East
Yorkshire Regiment
1st Battalion the South
Lancashire Regiment

9th Brigade
2nd Battalion the Lincolnshire
Regiment
1st Battalion the King's Own
Scottish Borderers
2nd Battalion the Royal
Ulster Rifles

185th Brigade
2nd Battalion the Royal Warwickshire Regiment
1st Battalion the Royal Norfolk Regiment
2nd Battalion the King's Shropshire Light Infantry

Divisional Troops

3rd Reconnaissance Regiment RAC

3rd Divisional Engineers

3rd Divisional Signals

7th, 33rd and 76th Field, 20th Anti-Tank and 92nd Light Anti-Aircraft Regiments RA

2nd Battalion the Middlesex Regiment (Machine Gun)

6th Airborne Division
Major-General R.N. Gale

3rd Parachute Brigade

8th and 9th Battalions the Parachute Regiment

1st Canadian Parachute Battalion

[*5th Parachute Brigade*]

7th, 12th and 13th Battalions the Parachute Regiment

6th Airlanding Brigade

12th Battalion the Devonshire Regiment

[2nd Battalion the Oxfordshire and Buckinghamshire Light] Infantry

1st Battalion the Royal Ulster Rifles

Divisional Troops

6th Airborne Armoured Reconnaissance Regiment RAC

6th Airborne Divisional Engineers

53rd Airlanding Light Regiment RA

6th Airborne Divisional Signals

15th (Scottish) Division
Major-General G.H.A. MacMillan (to 2.8.44)
Major-General C.M. Barber (from 3.8.44)

44th (Lowland) Brigade

8th Battalion the Royal Scots

6th Battalion the Royal Scots Fusiliers

46th (Highland) Brigade

9th Battalion the Cameronians

2nd Battalion the Glasgow Highlanders

6th Battalion the King's Own Scottish Borderers

7th Battalion the Seaforth Highlanders

227th (Highland) Brigade
10th Battalion the Highland Light Infantry
2nd Battalion the Gordon Highlanders
2nd Battalion the Argyll and Sutherland Highlanders

Divisional Troops

15th Reconnaissance Regiment RAC
15th Divisional Engineers
15th Divisional Signals

131st, 181st and 190th Field, 97th Anti-Tank and 119th Light Anti-Aircraft Regiments RA
1st Battalion the Middlesex Regiment (Machine Gun)

43rd (Wessex) Division
Major-General G.I. Thomas

129th Brigade
4th Battalion the Somerset Light Infantry
4th and 5th Battalions the Wiltshire Regiment

130th Brigade
7th Battalion the Hampshire Regiment
4th and 5th Battalions the Dorsetshire Regiment

214th Brigade
7th Battalion the Somerset Light Infantry
1st Battalion the Worcestershire Regiment
5th Battalion the Duke of Cornwall's Light Infantry

Divisional Troops

43rd Reconnaissance Regiment RAC
43rd Divisional Engineers
43rd Divisional Signals

94th, 112th and 179th Field, 59th Anti-Tank and 110th Light Anti-Aircraft Regiments RA
8th Battalion the Middlesex Regiment (Machine Gun)

49th (West Riding) Division
Major-General E.H. Barker

70th Brigade (to 20.8.44)
10th and 11th Battalions the Durham Light Infantry
1st Battalion the Tyneside Scottish

146th Brigade
4th Battalion the Lincolnshire Regiment
1/4th Battalion the King's Own Yorkshire Light Infantry
Hallamshire Battalion the York and Lancaster Regiment

147th Brigade
11th Battalion the Royal Scots Fusiliers
6th Battalion the Duke of Wellington's Regiment (to 6.7.44)
7th Battalion the Duke of Wellington's Regiment
1st Battalion the Leicestershire Regiment (from 6.7.44)

56th Brigade (from 20.8.44)
See under GHQ

Divisional Troops

49th Reconnaissance Regiment RAC
49th Divisional Engineers
49th Divisional Signals

69th, 143rd and 185th Field, 55th Anti-Tank and 89th Light Anti-Aircraft Regiments RA
2nd Princess Louise's Kensington Regiment (Machine Gun)

50th (Northumbrian) Division
Major-General D.A.H. Graham

69th Brigade
5th Battalion the East
   Yorkshire Regiment
6th and 7th Battalions the
   Green Howards

151st Brigade
6th, 8th and 9th Battalions
   the Durham Light Infantry

231st Brigade
2nd Battalion the Devonshire Regiment
1st Battalion the Hampshire Regiment
1st Battalion the Dorsetshire Regiment

Divisional Troops

61st Reconnaissance Regiment
   RAC
50th Divisional Engineers
50th Divisional Signals

74th, 90th and 124th Field,
   102nd Anti-Tank and 25th
   Light Anti-Aircraft
   Regiments RA
2nd Battalion the Cheshire
   Regiment (Machine Gun)

51st (Highland) Division
Major-General D.C. Bullen-Smith (to 26.7.44)
Major-General T.G. Rennie (from 27.7.44)

152nd Brigade
2nd and 5th Battalions the
   Seaforth Highlanders
5th Battalion the Queen's
   Own Cameron Highlanders

153rd Brigade
5th Battalion the Black Watch
1st and 5th/7th Battalions the
   Gordon Highlanders

154th Brigade
1st and 7th Battalions the Black Watch
7th Battalion the Argyll and Sutherland Highlanders

Divisional Troops

2nd Derbyshire Yeomanry
   RAC

126th, 127th and 128th Field,
   61st Anti-Tank and 40th

51st Divisional Engineers
51st Divisional Signals

Light Anti-Aircraft
Regiments RA
1/7th Battalion the Middlesex
Regiment (Machine Gun)

53rd (Welsh) Division
Major-General R.K. Ross

71st Brigade

1st Battalion the East
Lancashire Regiment (to
3.8.44)
1st Battalion the Oxfordshire
and Buckinghamshire Light
Infantry
1st Battalion the Highland
Light Infantry
4th Battalion the Royal Welch
Fusiliers (from 5.8.44)

158th Brigade

4th and 6th Battalions the
Royal Welch Fusiliers (to
3.8.44)
7th Battalion the Royal Welch
Fusiliers
1st Battalion the East
Lancashire Regiment (from
4.8.44)
1/5th Battalion the Welch
Regiment (from 4.8.44)

160th Brigade

2nd Battalion the Monmouthshire Regiment
4th Battalion the Welch Regiment
1/5th Battalion the Welch Regiment (to 3.8.44)
6th Battalion the Royal Welch Fusiliers (from 4.8.44)

Divisional Troops

53rd Reconnaissance
Regiment RAC
53rd Divisional Engineers
53rd Divisional Signals

81st, 83rd and 133rd Field, 71st
Anti-Tank and 116th Light
Anti-Aircraft Regiments RA
1st Battalion the Manchester
Regiment (Machine Gun)

59th (Staffordshire) Division
Major-General L.O. Lyne

176th Brigade (to 26.8.44)
7th Battalion the Royal
  Norfolk Regiment
7th Battalion the South
  Staffordshire Regiment
6th Battalion the North
  Staffordshire Regiment

177th Brigade (to 26.8.44)
5th, 1/6th and 2/6th Battalions
  the South Staffordshire
  Regiment

197th Brigade (to 26.8.44)
1/7th Battalion the Royal Warwickshire Regiment
2/5th Battalion the Lancashire Fusiliers
5th Battalion the East Lancashire Regiment

Divisional Troops

59th Reconnaissance
  Regiment RAC
  (to 31.8.44)
59th Divisional Engineers
59th Divisional Signals

61st, 110th and 116th Field (to
  31.8.44), 68th Anti-Tank (to
  26.8.44) and 68th Light
  Anti-Aircraft (to 22.8.44)
  Regiments RA
7th Battalion the Royal
  Northumberland Fusiliers
  (Machine Gun) (to 24.8.44)

4th Canadian Armoured Division
Major-General G. Kitching (to 21.8.44)
Major-General H.W. Foster (from 22.8.44)

4th Armoured Brigade
21st Armoured Regiment (the
  Governor General's Foot
  Guards)
22nd Armoured Regiment (the
  Canadian Grenadier Guards)
28th Armoured Regiment (the
  British Columbia Regiment)
The Lake Superior Regiment
  (Motor)

10th Infantry Brigade
The Lincoln and Welland
  Regiment
The Algonquin Regiment
The Argyll and Sutherland
  Highlanders of Canada
  (Princess Louise's)

Divisional Troops

29th Reconnaissance Regiment (the South Alberta Regiment)
4th Canadian Armoured Divisional Engineers

15th and 23rd Field, 5th Anti-Tank and 8th Light Anti-Aircraft Regiments RCA
4th Canadian Armoured Divisional Signals

2nd Canadian Division
Major-General C. Foulkes

4th Brigade
The Royal Regiment of Canada
The Royal Hamilton Light Infantry
The Essex Scottish Regiment

5th Brigade
The Black Watch (Royal Highland Regiment) of Canada
Le Régiment de Maisonneuve
The Calgary Highlanders

6th Brigade
Les Fusiliers Mont-Royal
The Queen's Own Cameron Highlanders of Canada
The South Saskatchewan Regiment

Divisional Troops

8th Reconnaissance Regiment (14th Canadian Hussars)
2nd Canadian Divisional Engineers
2nd Canadian Divisional Signals

4th, 5th and 6th Field, 2nd Anti-Tank and 3rd Light Anti-Aircraft Regiments RCA
The Toronto Scottish Regiment (Machine Gun)

3rd Canadian Division
Major-General R.F.L. Keller (to 8.8.44)
Major-General D.C. Spry (from 18.8.44)

7th Brigade
The Royal Winnipeg Rifles
The Regina Rifle Regiment
1st Battalion the Canadian
  Scottish Regiment

8th Brigade
The Queen's Own Rifles of
  Canada
Le Régiment de la Chaudière
The North Shore (New
  Brunswick) Regiment

9th Brigade
The Highland Light Infantry of Canada
The Stormont, Dundas and Glengarry Highlanders
The North Nova Scotia Highlanders

Divisional Troops

7th Reconnaissance Regiment
  (17th Duke of York's Royal
  Canadian Hussars)
3rd Canadian Divisional
  Engineers
3rd Canadian Divisional
  Signals

12th, 13th, and 14th Field, 3rd
  Anti-Tank and 4th Light
  Anti-Aircraft Regiments
  RCA
The Cameron Highlanders of
  Ottawa (Machine Gun)

1st Polish Armoured Division
Major-General S. Maczek

10th Polish Armoured Brigade
1st Polish Armoured Regiment
2nd Polish Armoured
  Regiment
24th Polish Armoured
  (Lancer) Regiment
10th Polish Motor Battalion

3rd Polish Infantry Brigade
1st Polish (Highland)
  Battalion
8th Polish Battalion
9th Polish Battalion

Divisional Troops

10th Polish Mounted Rifle
  Regiment
1st Polish Armoured Divisional
  Engineers

1st and 2nd Polish Field, 1st
   Polish Anti-Tank and 1st
   Polish Light Anti-Aircraft
   Regiments
1st Polish Armoured Divisional
   Signals

LINES OF COMMUNICATION AND REAR MAINTENANCE AREA

*Headquarters Lines of
   Communication*
Major-General R.F.B. Naylor
Nos. 11 and 12 Lines of
   Communication Areas
Nos. 4, 5 and 6 Lines of
   Communication Sub-Areas
Nos. 7 and 8 Base Sub-Areas
Nos. 101, 102 and 104 Beach
   Sub-Areas
Nos. 10 and 11 Garrison

Engineers
Nos. 2, 3, 5 and 6 Railway
   Construction and
   Maintenance Groups
No. 3 Railway Operating
   Group
No. 1 Canadian Railway
   Operating Group
No. 1 Railway Workshop
   Group
Nos. 2, 6, 8, 9, 10 and 11 Port
   Operating Groups
Nos. 1, 2, 4 and 5 Port
   Construction and Repair
   Groups
Nos. 3 and 4 Inland Water
   Transport Groups
No. 2 Mechanical Equipment
   (Transportation) Unit

Signals
Nos. 2 and 12 Lines of
   Communication
   Headquarters Signals
No. 1 Canadian Lines of
   Communication
   Headquarters Signals

Infantry
5th and 8th Battalions the
   King's Regiment
7th Battalion the East
   Yorkshire Regiment
2nd Battalion the
   Hertfordshire Regiment

6th Battalion the Border
Regiment
1st Buckinghamshire Battalion
the Oxfordshire and
Buckinghamshire Light
Infantry
5th Battalion the Royal
Berkshire Regiment
18th Battalion the Durham
Light Infantry

UNITED STATES TWELFTH ARMY GROUP

Lieutenant-General Omar N. Bradley
Commanding General
Major-General Leven C. Allen
Chief of Staff

First Army

Lieutenant-General Courtney
H. Hodges
Commanding General
(Succeeded General Bradley
from 1.8.44)
Major-General William B.
Keen
Chief of Staff

Third Army

Lieutenant-General George S.
Patton, Jr
Commanding General
Major-General Hugh J.
Gaffey
Chief of Staff

Corps

V. Major-General Leonard T.
Gerow
VII. Major-General J.
Lawton Collins
VIII. Major-General Troy H.
Middleton
XII. Major-General Gilbert
R. Cook (to 18.8.44)

Divisions

Armored: 2nd, 3rd, 4th, 5th,
6th and 7th; 2nd French
Infantry: 1st, 2nd, 4th, 5th,
8th, 9th, 28th, 29th, 30th,
35th, 79th, 80th, 83rd and
90th
Airborne: 82nd and 101st

Major-General Manton S.
Eddy (from 19.8.44)
XV. Major-General Wade H.
Haislip
XIX. Major-General Charles
H. Corlett
XX. Major-General Walton H. Walker

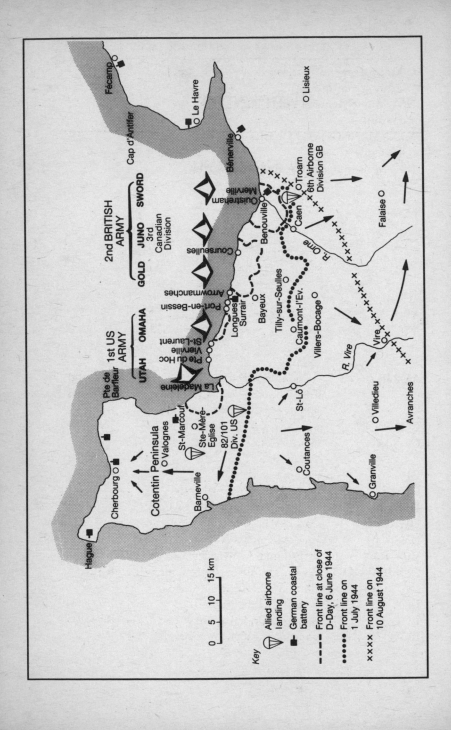

Key

- Allied airborne landing
- German coastal battery
- --- Front line at close of D-Day, 6 June 1944
- ⋯⋯ Front line on 1 July 1944
- ××× Front line on 10 August 1944

0 5 10 15 km

Hague

Cherbourg ○

Cotentin Peninsula

Barneville ○

Valognes ○
St-Marcouf

Ste-Mère-Eglise ○

82/101 Div. US

Pte de Barfleur

1st US ARMY

UTAH OMAHA

La Madeleine

St-Laurent
Vieville
Pte du Hoc

Longues Surrain

Port-en-Bessin

GOLD Arromanches

2nd BRITISH ARMY

JUNO SWORD
3rd Canadian Division

Courseulles ○

Merville
Ouistreham

Bénerville

Cap d'Antifer

Fécamp ○

Le Havre ■

Lisieux ○

Benouville

Caen ○

Troarn ○

6th Airborne Division GB

Falaise ○

R. Orne

Bayeux ○

Tilly-sur-Seulles ○

Caumont-l'Ev. ○

Villers-Bocage ○

Vire ○

R. Vire

St-Lô ○

Coutances ○

Villedieu ○

Granville ○

Avranches

APPENDIX 3

Glossary

Ack-Ack [AA]	Anti-aircraft fire
AP	Armour-piercing shells
AT (ATS)	Auxiliary Territorial, in full: the Auxiliary Territorial Service, now the Women's Royal Army Corps
AVRE	Armoured Vehicle Royal Engineers – a modified Churchill Tank mounted with a Petard short-range mortar
COBRA	American offensive, 25–9 July
COSSAC	Chief of Staff to the Supreme Allied Commander
CP	Command Post
CSM	Company Sergeant-Major
DD	Duplex-Drive amphibious tank
DUKW	Duplex-Drive amphibious truck
ENSA	Entertainments National Services Association
EPSOM	British 2nd Army offensive, 26 June
GOODWOOD	British assault on Bourgebus ridge, 18 July
Ia	Chief Staff Officer
LCA	Landing Craft Assault
LCI	Landing Craft Infantry
LCM	Landing Craft Motor Launch

LCT	Landing Craft Tank
LCVP	Landing Craft Vehicle and Personnel
LMG	Light Machine Gun
LST	Landing Ship Tank
ML	Motor Launch
NAAFI	Navy, Army and Air Force Institutes
NEPTUNE	Naval phase of Allied invasion of Normandy
ODs	Olive Drabs – American infantry combat clothing
OP	Observation Post
PIAT	British hand-held anti-tank gun
RAC	Royal Armoured Corps
RASC	Royal Army Service Corps
RE	Royal Engineers
SHAEF	Supreme Headquarters Allied Expeditionary Force
SP	Self-propelled gun
TOTALIZE	Canadian attack towards Falaise, 8–11 August

APPENDIX 4

Sources and Acknowledgements

Aitken, D.G.	Letters, 1944 (Imperial War Museum)
Anon., Berkshire	Quoted in *Over Here* by Juliet Gardner
Arnold, James	Quoted in *D-Day* by Warren Tute
Baxter, K.P.	Quoted in *D-Day* by Warren Tute
Bellows, J.H.	Normandy Veterans Associations newspaper
Blacker, Stanley	Interview with author, 1993
Bloemertz, Gunther	*Heaven Next Stop*
Bone, H.T.	Letter, 1944 (Imperial War Museum)
Bradley, Omar	*A Soldier's Story*, 1954
Bullen, R.S.	Quoted in *Normandy: Then and Now*
Burgett, Donald	*Screaming Eagles*, 1962
Burkinshaw, Philip	*Alarms and Excursions*, 1992
Butcher, H.C.	*My Three Years with Eisenhower*, 1962
Burton, J.E.	Memoir in *D-Day Chronicles* by Rupert Curtis (unpub.)
Byrom, James	*Unfinished Man*
Coleman, John G.	Letter to author, 1993
Collard, G.	Letter to author, 1993
Coney, Ken	Quoted in Alan Hart (q.v.), diary, 1944
Cooling, J.H.	Letter, 1944 (Imperial War Museum)
Dale, G.E.	Diary, 1944 (Imperial War Museum)

Davies, Peter	Interview with author, 1993
Dawson, Joseph T.	Interview with author, 1993
Edmunds, Islwyn	Letter to author, 1993
Gale, Richard	*With the 6th Airborne Division in Normandy*
Gariepy, Leo	Quoted in *D-Day* by Warren Tute
Gillies, H.S.	Letter, 1944 (Imperial War Museum)
Goode, F.D.	Unpublished memoir (Imperial War Museum)
Hall, John	*A Soldier of World War II*
Hart, Alan	Diary, 1944
Hartill, Harry	Letter to author, 1993
Hayden, J.G.	Interview, 1993
Hayn, Friederich	Quoted in *Defeat in the West* by M. Shulman
Hemingway, Ernest	*By-Line*
Herklotz, Richard	Interview with author, 1993
Hewison, W.	Unpublished memoir (Imperial War Museum)
Hodenfield, H.	*Stars and Stripes*, 1944
Holladay, A.J.	Diary, 1944 (Imperial War Museum)
Houston, R.J.	*D-Day to Bastogne*, 1991
Hughes, G.E.	Diary, 1944 (Imperial War Museum)
Johnson, Elliott	Quoted in *The Good War* by Studs Terkel
Johnson, Johnson	*Wing Leader*
Jones, Gordon	Interview, 1993
Jones, W. Emlyn	Unpublished narrative and interview with author, 1993
Keegan, John	Six Armies in Normandy
Kellar, H.M.	Unpublished memoir
Kiefer, Philippe	*Beret Vert*, 1982
Kortenhaus, W.	Interview, 1993
Lelanoy, Odette	Interview, 1993
Leonard, Alfred	Interview with author, 1993
Leveel, M.	Interview, 1993
Macduff, Robert	Taped memoir, 1993

McGregor, Edward W.   Interview, 1993
Macnab, R.C.   Letter, 1944 (Imperial War Museum)
Melville, Alan   *First Tide*
Meyer, Kurt   *Panzermeyer*, 1971
Miles, Leonard   Interview, 1993
Moorehead, Alan   *Eclipse*
Morgan, Frederick   *Overture to Overlord*
Morgan, Stanley   Interview, 1993
Morris, Ted   Interview, 1993
Osborne, J.V.   Letter to author, 1993
Petrie, Miss   Diary, 1944 (Imperial War Museum)
Poppel, Martin   *Heaven & Hell*
Price, Nevin F.   Letter to author, 1993
Prior, Peter   Quoted in *Hereford Times*, 1974
Pritchard, P.H.B.   Unpublished memoir (Imperial War Museum)
Pyle, Ernie   *The G.I.'s War*, 1974
Rehm, Mike   Quoted in *D-Day*, ITN Granada, 1984
Reynaud, A   *Ste Mere Qglise*
Richards, Lewis   Memoir 1944, and official citation
Ridgway, Matt B.   *Soldier*, 1958
Roach, P.   *8.15 to War*, 1969
Rommel, Erwin   *The Rommel Papers*, edited by Basil Liddell-Hart.
Seymour, William   Interview, 1993
Smith, Albert H.   Interview, 1993
Smith, William B.   Letter to author, 1993
Staff Officer, 17
SS Panzer Grenadiers   Quoted in *Defeat in the West* by M. Shulman
Stover, Russell   Memoir published in *Twenty-Niner Newsletter*, the journal of the 29th Division Association
Tateson, T.   Unpublished narrative (Imperial War Museum)
Thomas, Donald   Interview, 1993

Thomas, Richard	Interview, 1993
Thomas, Mary	Interview, 1993
Tilly, G.	Letters, 1944 (Imperial War Museum)
Tout, Ken	*Tanks, Advance*
Townsend, G.G.	Unpublished memoir
Vaughan, Donald	Interview, 1993
de Vigneral, Anne	Diary, 1944 (Imperial War Museum)
Weightman, W.C.	Diary, 1944 (Imperial War Museum)
Wells, C.J.	Interview, 1993
Williams, Alun	Letter to author, 1993
Wright, Ken	Letter, 1944, in *D-Day Chronicles* by R. Curtis (unpub.)
Young, Peter	*Storm from the Sea*, 1974
Zimmer, Private	Unpublished diary (Library of Congress)

The author has made every effort to trace the holders of any rights to copyrighted material which appears in this volume, and trusts that his apologies will be accepted for any omissions. Any queries regarding any such rights should be addressed to the author c/o the publisher. The author thanks the following publishers and others for permission to reprint extensively from copyrighted material: Henry Holt for extracts from *A Soldier's Story* by Omar Bradley; by H.C. Butcher; Bantam Publishers and Century Hutchinson for extracts from *Screaming Eagles* by Donald Burgett; Philip Burkinshaw for extracts from *Alarms and Excursions*; Secker and Warburg Publishers for extracts from *8.15 to War* by P. Roach; the estate of Rupert Curtis for extracts from the *D-Day Chronicles* (unpublished); HarperCollins Publishers for material from *By-Line*, copyright © 1944 Ernest Hemingway; Sidgwick and Jackson for material from *D-Day* by Warren Tute; Spellmont Publishing for extracts from *Heaven & Hell* by Martin Poppel; Hodder and Stoughton for material from *Overture to Overlord* by Frederick Morgan; Chatto and Windus for material from *Unfinished Man* by James Byrom.

Band of Brothers

Richard Winters

Damien Lewis